MEETINGS WITH
REMARKABLE
PEOPLE

OSHO books also published by Watkins Publishing Ltd

When the Shoe Fits
Inner War and Peace
The Buddha Said

About the Author

The Osho teachings defy categorization, covering everything from the individual quest for meaning to the most urgent social and political issues facing society today. His books are not written but are transcribed from audio and video recordings of extemporaneous talks given to international audiences over a period of 35 years. Osho has been described by the *Sunday Times* in London as one of the "1,000 Makers of the 20th Century" and by American author Tom Robbins as "the most dangerous man since Jesus Christ".

About his own work Osho has said that he is helping to create the conditions for the birth of a new kind of human being. He has often characterized this new human being as "Zorba the Buddha" – capable both of enjoying the earthy pleasures of a Zorba the Greek and the silent serenity of a Gautama Buddha. Running like a thread through all aspects of Osho's work is a vision that encompasses both the timeless wisdom of the East and the highest potential of Western science and technology.

Osho is also known for his revolutionary contribution to the science of inner transformation, with an approach to meditation that acknowledges the accelerated pace of contemporary life. His unique "Active Meditations" are designed to first release the accumulated stresses of body and mind, so that it is easier to experience the thought-free and relaxed state of meditation.

MEETINGS WITH REMARKABLE PEOPLE

Bodhidharma · Gautama the Buddha · Chiyono · Chuang Tzu

Dionysius · Kahlil Gibran · Gurdjieff · Heraclitus · Jesus

Krishna · J. Krishnamurti · Lao Tzu · Meera · Nietzsche

Pythagoras · Rabiya al-Adabiya · Rumi · Sanai · Socrates

WATKINS PUBLISHING

LONDON

Distributed in the USA and Canada by Sterling Publishing Co., Inc.
387 Park Avenue South, New York, NY 10016

This edition first published in the UK and USA 2008 by
Watkins Publishing, Sixth Floor, Castle House,
75–76 Wells Street, London W1T 3QH

1 3 5 7 9 10 8 6 4 2

Designed by Jerry Goldie

Typeset by Dorchester Typesetting Group

Printed and bound in Great Britain

Library of Congress Cataloging-in-Publication Data Available

ISBN 13: 978-1-905857-54-8
ISBN 10: 1-905857-54-3

www.watkinspublishing.co.uk

For information about custom editions, special sales, premium and
corporate purchases, please contact Sterling Special Sales
Department at 800-805-5489 or specialsales@sterlingpub.com.

CONTENTS

Preface

Your minds are from the very beginning distorted, channelized towards utilitarian ends. You are taught mathematics, you are taught geography, history. Now history is all bunk, utterly useless. Why go on reading about the ancient idiots? For what purpose? It is better to forget all about them. Why bother about Genghis Khan, Tamburlaine, Nadir Shah, Alexander, Napoleon? For what? What these people have given to human consciousness? They are like poisons; they have stopped in every possible way human progress, human evolution.

And in your history books you will not find the names of Lao Tzu, Chuang Tzu, Lieh Tzu, Ko Hsuan – not even in the footnotes. And these are the people who are the real foundations of human consciousness, these are the people who are the real hope. But you will not find their names even mentioned; on the contrary, historians will always create doubt in you whether Jesus ever existed, whether Krishna is a historical person or just a myth, whether Mahavira was a reality or just a fiction; did Buddha really walk on the earth or has he been a projection of our dreams, of our desires?

Sigmund Freud says that these people are wish-fulfillments. We want there to be people like these, but they have not really existed and even if they have existed they have not existed the way we have described them. That was the cause of the rift between Freud and his disciple Carl Gustav Jung; the rift was of tremendous significance. Freud is very pragmatic; Jung is far more poetic. Jung has tremendous trust in mythology and has no trust in history. And I absolutely agree with Jung about this.

All the mythologies of the world are closer to truth than your so-called histories. But we teach our children history, not mythology. We teach them arithmetic, not poetry. And the way we teach a little bit of poetry – we teach it in such a way that they become so fed up and bored with it that once the student leaves the university he will never read Shakespeare again, he will never look at Milton's works again. The very names of Shakespeare, Milton, Kalidas, will create a kind of nausea in him. The professors have tortured him so much behind these names that he is finished forever. His interest has not been encouraged, he has not become more poetic; he has lost all interest in poetry. He has not been supported to be creative, he has not been helped to learn how to poetize.

The scholars are so clever in destroying all that is beautiful by their commentaries, interpretations, by their so-called learning. They make everything so heavy that even poetry with them becomes non-poetic.

I myself never attended any poetry class in the university. I was called again and again by the head of the department, and he would say, "You attend other classes, why you don't come to the poetry classes?"

I said, "Because I want to keep my interest in poetry alive. I love poetry, that's why. And I know perfectly well that your professors are absolutely unpoetic; they have never known any poetry in their life. I know them perfectly well. The man who teaches poetry in the university goes for a morning walk with me every day. I have never seen him looking at the trees, listening to the birds, seeing the beautiful sunrise."

And in the university where I was, the sunrise and the sunset were something tremendously beautiful. The university was on a hill surrounded by smaller hills all around. I have traveled all over this India; I have never seen more beautiful sunsets and sunrises anywhere. For some unknown mysterious reason Saugar University seems to have a certain situation where clouds become so colorful at the time of sunrise and sunset that even a blind man will become aware that something tremendously beautiful is happening.

But I have never seen the professor who teaches poetry in the university bother to look at the sunset, to stop even for a single moment. And whenever he would see me watching the sunset or the sunrise or the trees or the birds, he would ask me, "Why you are sitting here? You have come for a morning walk – do your exercise!"

I told him, "This is not exercise for me. You are doing exercise; with me it is a love affair."

And when it rained he never came. And whenever it rained I would go and knock at his door and tell him, "Come on!"

He would say, "But it is raining!"

I said, "That's the most beautiful time to go for a walk, because the streets are absolutely empty. And to go for a walk without any umbrella while it is raining is so beautiful, is so poetic!"

He thought I was mad, but a man who has never gone in the rains under the trees cannot understand poetry. I told the head of the department, "This man is not poetic; he destroys everything. He is so scholarly and poetry is such an unscholarly phenomenon that there is no meeting ground between the two."

Universities destroy people's interest and love for poetry. They destroy your whole idea of how a life should be; they make it more and more a commodity. They teach you how to earn more, but they don't teach you how to live deeply, how to live totally. And these are the ways from where you can get glimpses of Tao. These are the ways from where small doors and windows open into the ultimate. You are told the value of money but not the value of a rose flower. You are told the value of being a prime minister or a president but not the value of being a poet, a painter, a singer, a dancer.

But we are very much afraid of losing ourselves, and we keep on feeding our egos in 1,001 ways. We are doing two things in our life: closing all windows and doors to the sun, to the moon, to the stars, to the wind, to the rain, to the birds, to the trees, to love, to beauty, to truth. We are closing all the windows, we are creating a grave around ourselves with no doors and no windows. We are becoming Leibniz monads, windowless capsules. Our life is encapsulated. That is one part that we go on doing. And the second part is to go on making the walls thicker and thicker. That is done by competition, ambition: have more and more; whether you need or not, that is not the point at all.

Do you think the richest people in the world need more money now? They have more than they can use, far more. But the desire for more does not stop, because it is not a question that they need money; the question is to go on making the walls of the ego thicker and thicker. They are continuously in competition with each other. Competition creates conflict. Conflict keeps your ego alive.

History knows only friction, history knows only mischief. History knows only mischief-mongers. History knows only mad people – because history records only when something goes wrong. When everything goes absolutely in tune, it is out of time and out of history also.

History does not report much about Jesus – in fact, nothing. If the Bible was not in existence, there would have been no record about Jesus. And I would like to tell you that many people like Jesus have existed, but we don't have any record about them. History never took any note. They were so meek, they were so silent, they were so in tune, so deep in harmony, that not even a ripple was created around them. They came and they left, and they have not left even a footprint.

History has not been recording the buddhas. That's why when you hear about a Buddha or a Mahavira or a Zarathustra, they look like mythological figures, not historic. It appears that they never existed, or they only existed in the dreams of man, or they existed only in the poetries of a few imaginative, romantic people. They look like wish-fulfillments. They look like how man would like man to be ... but not realities.

They were real. They were so real that no trace has been left behind them.

Bodhidharma

In the long evolution of human consciousness there has never been such an outlandish buddha as Bodhidharma – very rare, very unique, exotic. Only in some small ways George Gurdjieff comes close to him, but not very close – and only in some ways, not in all ways.

There have been many buddhas in the world, but Bodhidharma stands out like an Everest. His way of being, living, and expressing the truth is simply his; it is incomparable. Even his own master, Gautama the Buddha, cannot be compared with Bodhidharma. Even Buddha would have found it difficult to digest this man.

This man Bodhidharma traveled from India to China to spread the message of his master. Although they are separated by 1,000 years, for Bodhidharma and for such men there is no time, no space – for Bodhidharma, Buddha was a contemporary. Superficially there is a thousand-year gap between Buddha and Bodhidharma, but there is not even a single moment's gap in reality, in truth. On the circumference Buddha was already dead for 1,000 years when Bodhidharma arrived on the scene, but at the center he is together with Buddha. He speaks the essence of Buddha – of course he has his own way, his own style. Even Buddha would find it strange.

Buddha was a very cultured man, very sophisticated, very graceful. Bodhidharma is just the opposite in his expression. He is not a man but a lion. He does not speak, he roars. He has not the grace which belonged to Gautama the Buddha; he is rough, raw. He is not polished like a diamond; he is just from the mine, absolutely raw, no polishing. That is his beauty. Buddha has a beauty that is very feminine, very polished, very fragile. Bodhidharma has his own beauty, like that of a rock – strong, masculine, indestructible, a great power.

Buddha also radiates power, but his power is very silent, like a whisper, a cool breeze. Bodhidharma is a storm, thundering and lightning. Buddha comes to your door without making any noise; he will not even knock on your door, you will not even hear his footsteps. But when Bodhidharma comes to you he will shake the whole house from its very foundations.

Buddha will not shake you even if you are asleep. And Bodhidharma? He will wake you up from your grave! He hits hard, he is a hammer. He is just the opposite of Buddha in his expression, but his message is the same. He bows down to Buddha as his master. He never says, "This is my message." He simply says, "This belongs to the buddhas, the ancient buddhas. I am just a messenger. Nothing is mine, because I am not. I am only a hollow bamboo who has been chosen by the buddhas to be a flute for them. They sing; I simply let them sing through me."

Bodhidharma was born 14 centuries ago as a son of a king in the south of India. There was a big empire, the empire of Pallavas. He was the third son of his father, but seeing everything – he was a man of tremendous intelligence – he renounced the kingdom. He was not against the world, but he was not ready to waste his time in mundane affairs, in trivia. His whole concern was to know his self-nature, because without knowing it you have to accept death as the end.

All true seekers, in fact, have been fighting against death. Bertrand Russell has made a statement that if there were no death, there would be no religion. There is some truth in it. I will not agree totally, because religion is a vast continent. It is not only death, it is also the search for bliss, it is also the search for truth, it is also the search for the meaning of life; it is many more things. But certainly Bertrand Russell is right: if there were no death, very few, very rare people would be interested in religion. Death is the great incentive.

Bodhidharma renounced the kingdom saying to his father, "If you cannot save me from death, then please don't prevent me. Let me go in search of something that is beyond death." Those were beautiful days, particularly in the East. The father thought for a moment and he said, "I will not prevent you, because I cannot prevent your death. You go on your search with all my blessings. It is sad for me but that is my problem; it is my attachment. I was hoping for you to be the successor, to be the emperor of the great Pallavas Empire, but you have chosen something higher than that. I am your father so how can I prevent you?

"And you have put in such a simple way a question which I had never expected. You say, 'If you can prevent my death then I will not leave the palace, but if you cannot prevent my death, then please don't prevent me either.'" You can see Bodhidharma's caliber as a great intelligence.

And the second thing that I would like you to remember is that although he was a follower of Gautama Buddha, in some instances he shows higher flights than Gautama Buddha himself. For example, Gautama Buddha was afraid to initiate a woman into his commune but Bodhidharma got initiated by a woman who was enlightened. Her name was Pragyatara. Perhaps people would have forgotten her name; it is only because of Bodhidharma that her name still remains, but only the name – we don't know anything else about her. It was she who ordered Bodhidharma to go to China. Buddhism had reached China 600 years before Bodhidharma. It was something magical; it had never happened anywhere, at any time – Buddha's message immediately caught hold of the whole Chinese people.

The situation was that China had lived under the influence of Confucius and was tired of it. Because Confucius is just a moralist, a puritan, he does not know anything about the inner mysteries of life. In fact, he denies that there is anything inner. Everything is outer; refine it, polish it, culture it, make it as beautiful as possible.

There were people like Lao Tzu, Chuang Tzu, Lieh Tzu, contemporaries of Confucius, but they were mystics not masters. They could not create a countermovement against Confucius in the hearts of the Chinese people. So there was a vacuum. Nobody can live without a soul, and once you start thinking that there is no soul, your life starts losing all meaning. The soul is your very integrating concept; without it you are cut away from existence and eternal life. Just like a branch cut off from a tree is bound to die – it has lost the source of nourishment – the very idea that there is no soul inside you, no consciousness, cuts you away from existence. One starts shrinking, one starts feeling suffocated.

But Confucius was a very great rationalist. These mystics, Lao Tzu, Chuang Tzu, Lieh Tzu, knew that what Confucius was doing was wrong, but they were not masters. They remained in their monasteries with their few disciples.

When Buddhism reached China, it immediately entered to the very soul of the people ... as if they had been thirsty for centuries, and Buddhism had come as a rain cloud. It quenched their thirst so immensely that something unimaginable happened.

Christianity has converted many people, but that conversion is not worth calling religious. It converts the poor, the hungry, the beggars, the orphans, not by any spiritual impact on them but just by giving them food, clothes, shelter, education. But these have nothing to do with spirituality. Mohammedanism has converted a tremendous amount of people, but on the point of the sword: either you be a Mohammedan, or you cannot live. The choice is yours.

The conversion that happened in China is the only religious conversion in the whole history of mankind. Buddhism simply explained itself, and the beauty of the message was understood by the people. They were thirsty for it, they were waiting for something like it. The whole country, which was the biggest country in the world, turned to Buddhism. When Bodhidharma reached there 600 years later, there were already 30,000 Buddhist temples, monasteries, and 2 million Buddhist monks in China. And 2 million Buddhist monks is not a small number; it was 5 percent of the whole population of China.

Pragyatara, Bodhidharma's master, told him to go to China because the people who had reached there before him had made a great impact, although none of them were enlightened. They were great scholars, very disciplined people, very loving and peaceful and compassionate, but none of them were enlightened. And now China needed another Gautama Buddha. The ground was ready.

Bodhidharma was the first enlightened man to reach China. The point I want to make clear is that while Gautama Buddha was afraid to initiate women into his commune, Bodhidharma was courageous enough to be initiated by a woman on the path of Gautama Buddha. There were other enlightened people, but he chose a woman for a certain purpose. And the purpose was to show that a woman can be enlightened. Not only that, her disciples can be enlightened. Bodhidharma's name stands out amongst all the Buddhist enlightened people second only to Gautama Buddha.

There are many legends about the man; they all have some significance. One legend is that when he reached China – it took him three years – the Chinese emperor Wu came to receive him. His fame had reached ahead of him. Emperor Wu had done great service to the philosophy of Gautama Buddha. Thousands of scholars were translating Buddhist scriptures from Pali into Chinese and the emperor was the patron of all that great work of translation. He had made thousands of temples and monasteries, and he was feeding thousands of monks. He had put his whole treasure at the service of Gautama Buddha, and naturally the Buddhist monks who had reached China before Bodhidharma had been telling him that he was earning great virtue, that he will be born as a god in heaven.

Naturally, his first question to Bodhidharma was, "I have made so many monasteries, I am feeding thousands of scholars, I have opened a whole university for the studies of Gautama Buddha, I have put my whole empire and its treasures in the service of Gautama Buddha. What is going to be my reward?"

He was a little embarrassed seeing Bodhidharma, not thinking that the man would be like this. He looked very ferocious. He had very big eyes, but he had a very soft heart – just a lotus flower in his heart. But his face was almost as dangerous as you can conceive. Just the sunglasses were missing; otherwise he was a mafia guy!

With great fear, Emperor Wu asked the question, and Bodhidharma said, "Nothing, no reward. On the contrary, be ready to fall into the seventh hell."

The emperor said, "But I have not done anything wrong – why the seventh hell? I have been doing everything that the Buddhist monks have been telling me."

Bodhidharma said, "Unless you start hearing your own voice, nobody can help you, Buddhist or non-Buddhist. And you have not yet heard your inner voice. If you had heard it, you would not have asked such a stupid question.

"On the path of Gautama Buddha there is no reward because the very desire for reward comes from a greedy mind. The whole teaching of Gautama Buddha is desirelessness and if you are doing all these so-called virtuous acts, making temples and monasteries and feeding thousands of monks, with a desire in your mind, you are preparing your way towards hell. If you are doing these things out of joy, to share your joy with the whole empire, and there is not even a slight desire anywhere for any reward, the very act is a reward unto itself. Otherwise you have missed the whole point."

Emperor Wu said, "My mind is so full of thoughts. I have been trying to create some peace of mind, but I have failed and because of these thoughts and their noise, I cannot hear what you are calling the inner voice. I don't know anything about it."

Bodhidharma said, "Then, four o'clock in the morning, come alone without any bodyguards to the temple in the mountains where I am going to stay. And I will put your mind at peace, forever."

The emperor thought this man really outlandish, outrageous. He had met many monks; they were so polite, but this one does not even bother that he is an emperor of a great country. And to go to him in the darkness of early morning at four o'clock, alone … And this man seems to be dangerous – he always used to carry a big staff with him.

The emperor could not sleep the whole night: "To go or not to go? Because that man can do anything. He seems to be absolutely unreliable." And on the other hand, he felt deep down in his heart the sincerity of the man, that he is not a hypocrite. "He does not care a bit that you are an emperor and he is just a beggar. He behaves as an emperor, and in front of him you are just a beggar. And the way he has said, 'I will put your mind at peace forever.'

"Strange, because I have been asking," the emperor thought, "of many, many wise people who have come from India, and they all gave me methods, techniques, which I have been practicing, but nothing is happening – and this strange fellow, who looks almost mad, or drunk, and has a strange face with such big eyes that he creates fear … But he seems to be sincere too – he is a wild phenomenon. And it is worth the risk. What can he do – at the most he can kill me." Finally, he could not resist the temptation because the man had promised, "I will put your mind at peace forever."

Emperor Wu reached the temple at four o'clock, early in the morning in darkness, alone, and Bodhidharma was standing there with his staff, just on the steps, and he said, "I knew you would be coming, although the whole night you debated whether to go or not to go. What kind of an emperor are you – so cowardly, being afraid of a poor monk, a poor beggar who has nothing in the world except this staff. And with this staff I am going to put your mind to silence."

The emperor thought, "My God, who has ever heard that with a staff you can put somebody's mind to silence! You can finish him, hit him hard on the head – then the whole man is silent, not the mind. But now it is too late to go back."

And Bodhidharma said, "Sit down here in the courtyard of the temple." There was not a single man around. "Close your eyes, I am sitting in front of you with my staff. Your work is to catch hold of the mind. Just close your eyes and go inside looking for it – where it is. The moment you catch hold of it, just tell me, 'Here it is.' And my staff will do the remaining thing."

It was the strangest experience any seeker of truth or peace or silence could have ever had – but now there was no other way. Emperor Wu sat there with closed eyes, knowing perfectly well that Bodhidharma seemed to mean everything he said. He looked all around – there was no mind. That staff did its work. For the first time he was in such a situation. The choice ... if you find the mind, one never knows what this man is going to do with his staff. And in that silent mountainous place, in the presence of Bodhidharma, who has a charisma of his own ... There have been many enlightened people, but Bodhidharma stands aloof, alone, like an Everest. His every act is unique and original. His every gesture has his own signature; it is not borrowed.

He tried hard to look for the mind, and for the first time he could not find the mind. It is a small strategy. Mind exists only because you never look for it; it exists only because you are never aware of it. When you are looking for it you are aware of it, and awareness surely kills it completely. Hours passed and the sun was rising in the silent mountains with a cool breeze. Bodhidharma could see on the face of Emperor Wu such peace, such silence, such stillness as if he was a statue. He shook him and asked him, "It has been a long time. Have you found the mind?"

Emperor Wu said, "Without using your staff, you have pacified my mind completely. I don't have any mind and I have heard the inner voice about which you talked. Now I know whatever you said was right. You have transformed me without doing anything. Now I know that each act has to be a reward unto itself; otherwise, don't do it. Who is there to give you the reward? This is a childish idea. Who is there to give you the punishment? Your action is punishment and your action is your reward. You are the master of your destiny."

Bodhidharma said, "You are a rare disciple. I love you, I respect you, not as an emperor but as a man who has the courage just in a single sitting to bring so much awareness, so much light, that all darkness of the mind disappears."

Wu tried to persuade him to come to the palace. He said, "That is not my place; you can see I am wild, I do things I myself don't know beforehand. I live moment to moment spontaneously, I am very unpredictable. I may create unnecessary trouble for you, your court, your people; I am not meant for palaces, just let me live in my wildness."

He lived on this mountain whose name was Tai ... The second legend is that Bodhidharma was the first man who created tea – the name "tea" comes from the name Tai, because it was created on the mountain Tai. And all the words for tea in any language are derived from the same source.

The way Bodhidharma created tea cannot be historical but is significant. He was meditating almost all the time, and sometimes in the night he would start falling asleep. So, just not to fall asleep, just to teach a lesson to his eyes, he took out all his eyebrow hairs and threw them in the temple ground. The story is that out of those eyebrows, the tea bushes grew. Those were the first tea bushes. That's why when you drink tea, you cannot sleep. And in Buddhism it became a routine that for meditation, tea is immensely helpful. So the whole Buddhist world drinks tea as part of meditation, because it keeps you alert and awake.

Although there were 2 million Buddhist monks in China, Bodhidharma could find only four worthy to be accepted as his disciples. He was really very choosy. It took him almost nine years to find his first disciple, Hui Ko.

For nine years – and that is a historical fact, because there are ancientmost references, almost contemporary to Bodhidharma, which all mention that fact although others may not be mentioned – for nine years, after sending Wu back to the palace, he sat before the temple wall, facing the wall. He made it a great meditation. He would just simply go on looking at the wall. Now, looking at the wall for a long time, you cannot think. Slowly, slowly, just like the wall, your mind screen also becomes empty.

And there was a second reason. He declared, "Unless somebody who deserves to be my disciple comes, I will not look at the audience."

People used to come and they would sit behind him. It was a strange situation. Nobody had spoken in this way; he would speak to the wall. People would be sitting behind him but he would not face the audience, because he said, "The audience hurts me more, because it is just like a wall. Nobody understands, and to look at human beings in such an ignorant state hurts deeply. But to look at the wall, there is no question; a wall, after all, is a wall. It cannot hear, so there is no need to be hurt. I will turn to face the audience only if somebody proves by his action that he is ready to be my disciple."

Nine years passed. People could not find what to do – what action would satisfy him. They could not figure it out. Then came this young man, Hui Ko. He cut off one of his hands with a sword, and threw the hand before Bodhidharma and said, "This is the beginning. Either you turn, or my head will be falling before you. I am going to cut off my head too."

Bodhidharma turned and said, "You are really a man worthy of me. No need to cut off the head, we have to use it." This man, Hui Ko, was his first disciple.

Finally when he left China, or intended to leave China, he called his four disciples – three more he had gathered after Hui Ko. He asked them, "In simple words, in small sentences, telegraphic, tell me the essence of my teachings. I intend to leave tomorrow morning to go back to the Himalayas, and I want to choose, from you four, one as my successor."

The first man said, "Your teaching is of going beyond mind, of being absolutely silent, and then everything starts happening of its own accord."

Bodhidharma said, "You are not wrong, but you don't satisfy me. You just have my skin."

The second one said, "To know that I am not, and only existence is, is your fundamental teaching."

Bodhidharma said, "A little better, but not up to my standard. You have my bones; sit down."

And the third one said, "Nothing can be said about it. No word is capable of saying anything about it."

Bodhidharma said, "Good, but you have said already something about it. You have contradicted yourself. Just sit down; you have my marrow."

And the fourth was his first disciple, Hui Ko, who simply fell at Bodhidharma's feet, without saying a word, tears rolling down from his eyes. Bodhidharma said, "You have said it. You are going to be my successor."

But in the night Bodhidharma was poisoned by some disciple as revenge, because he had not been chosen as the successor. So they buried him, and the strangest legend is that after three years he was found by a government official, walking out of China towards the Himalayas with his staff in his hand and one of his sandals hanging from the staff – and he was barefoot.

The official had known him, had been to him many times, had fallen in love with the man, although he was a little eccentric. He asked, "What is the meaning of this staff, and one sandal hanging from it?" Bodhidharma said, "Soon you will know. If you meet my people just tell them that I'm going into the Himalayas forever."

The official reached immediately, as fast as he could, the monastery on the mountain where Bodhidharma had been living. And there he heard that he had been poisoned and he had died … and there was the tomb. The official had not heard about it, because he was posted on the boundary lines of the empire. He said, "My God, but I have seen him, and I cannot be deceived because I have seen him many times before. He was the same man, those same ferocious eyes, the same fiery and wild outlook, and on top of it, he was carrying on his staff one sandal."

The disciples could not contain their curiosity, and they opened the tomb. All that they could find there was only one sandal. And then the official understood why he had said, "You will find out the meaning of it; soon you will know."

We have heard so much about Jesus' resurrection. But nobody has talked much of the resurrection of Bodhidharma. Perhaps he was only in a coma when they buried him, and then he came to his senses, slipped out of the tomb, left one sandal there and put another sandal on his staff, and according to the plan, he left.

He wanted to die in the eternal snows of the Himalayas. He wanted that there should be no tomb, no temple, no statue of him. He did not want to leave any footprints behind him to be worshiped; those who love him should enter into their own being – "I am not going to be worshiped." And he disappeared almost into thin air. Nobody heard anything about him – what happened, where he died. He must be buried in the eternal snows of the Himalayas somewhere.

Gautama the Buddha

Gautama the Buddha represents the essential core of religion. He is not the founder of Buddhism – Buddhism is a by-product – he is the beginning of a totally different kind of religion in the world. He's the founder of a religionless religion, he has propounded not religion but religiousness, and this is a great radical change in the history of human consciousness. Before Buddha there were religions but never a pure religiousness. Man was not yet mature. With Buddha, humanity enters a mature age. All human beings have not yet entered into it, that's true, but Buddha has heralded the path; Buddha has opened the gateless gate.

It takes time for human beings to understand such a deep message. Buddha's message is the deepest ever. Nobody has done the work that Buddha has done, the way he has done it. Nobody else represents pure fragrance. Other founders of religions, other enlightened people, have compromised with their audience. Buddha remains uncompromised, hence his purity. He does not care what you can understand, he cares only what the truth is. He says it without being worried whether you understand it or not.

In a way this looks hard; in another way this is great compassion. Truth has to be said as it is. The moment you compromise, the moment you bring truth to the ordinary level of human consciousness it loses its soul, it becomes superficial, it becomes a dead thing. You cannot bring truth to the level of human beings; human beings have to be led to the level of truth. That is Buddha's great work.

Gautama the Buddha has started a spirituality that is non-repressive and non-ideological. That is a very rare phenomenon. The ordinary kind of spirituality, the garden variety, is very repressive. It depends on repression. It does not transform people, it only cripples them. It does not liberate people, it enslaves them. It is oppressive, it is ugly. Remember this: Buddha is non-repressive. And if you find Buddhist monks to be repressive, they have not understood Buddha at all. They have brought their own pathology into his teachings.

And Buddha is non-ideological. He gives no ideology because all ideologies are of the mind. And if ideologies are of the mind, they cannot take you beyond the mind. No ideology can become a bridge to reach beyond the mind. All ideologies have to be dropped, only then the mind will be dropped.

Buddha believes in no ideals either – because all ideals create tension and conflict in man. They divide, they create anguish. You are one thing and they want you to be something else. Between these two you are stretched, torn apart. Ideals create misery, ideals create schizophrenia. The more ideals there are, the more people will be schizophrenic, they will be split. Only a non-ideological consciousness can avoid being split. And if you are split how can you be happy? How can you be silent, how can you know anything of peace, of stillness?

The ideological person is continuously fighting with himself. Each moment there is conflict. He lives in conflict, he lives in confusion because he cannot decide who really he is – the ideal or the reality? He cannot trust himself, he becomes afraid of himself, he loses confidence. And once a man loses confidence he loses all glory. Then he is ready to become a slave to anybody – to any priest, to any politician. Then he is just ready, waiting to fall in some trap.

Why do people become followers? Why are people trapped? Why do they fall for a Joseph Stalin or an Adolf Hitler or a Mao Zedong? Why in the first place? They have become so shaky, the ideological confusion has shaken them from their very roots. Now they cannot stand on their own, they want somebody to lean on. They cannot move on their own, they don't know who they are. They need somebody to tell them that they are this or that. They need an identity to be given to them. They have forgotten their self and their nature.

Adolf Hitlers and Joseph Stalins and Mao Zedongs will be coming again and again until and unless man drops all ideologies. And remember, when I say all ideologies, I mean all ideologies. I don't make any distinction between noble ideologies and not so noble. All ideologies are dangerous. In fact the noble ideologies are more dangerous, because they have a more seductive power, they are more persuasive. But ideology as such is a disease, exactly a dis-ease, because you become two: the ideal and you. The "you" that you are is condemned, and the "you" that you are not is praised. Now you are getting into trouble. Now sooner or later you will be neurotic, psychotic or something.

Buddha has given a non-repressive way of life, and non-ideological too. That's why he does not talk about God, he does not talk about heaven, he does not talk about any future. He does not give you anything to hold on to, he takes everything away from you. He takes even your self. He goes on taking things away, and finally he takes even the idea of self, I, ego. He leaves only pure emptiness behind. And this is very difficult.

This is very difficult because we have completely forgotten how to give. We only know how to take. We go on taking everything. I "take" the exam and I "take" the wife. I even "take" the afternoon nap, a thing which cannot be taken, you have to surrender to it. Sleep comes only when you surrender. Even a wife, a husband, you go on taking. You are not respectful! The wife is not some kind of property. You can take a house – how can you take a wife or a husband? But our language shows our mind. We don't know how to give – how to give in, how to let go, how to let things happen.

Buddha takes all ideals away, the whole future away, and finally he takes the last thing that is very, very difficult for us to give – he takes your very self. Leaves a pure, innocent, virgin emptiness behind. That virgin emptiness he calls nirvana. Nirvana is not a goal, it is just your emptiness. When you have dropped all that you have accumulated, when you don't hoard anymore, when you are no longer a miser and a clinger, then suddenly that emptiness erupts. It has always been there.

That emptiness is there. You have accumulated junk so the emptiness is not visible. It is just like in your house you can go on accumulating things; then you stop seeing any space, then there is no more space. A day comes when even to move in the house becomes difficult; to live becomes difficult because there is no space. But the space has not gone anywhere – think of it, meditate over it – the space has not gone anywhere. You have accumulated too much furniture and the TV and the radio and the piano and all these things are there – but the space has not gone anywhere. Remove the furniture and the space is there; it has always been there. It was hidden by the furniture but it was not destroyed. It has not left the room, not for a single moment.

So is your inner emptiness, your nirvana, your nothingness.

Buddha does not give you nirvana as an ideal. Buddha liberates instead of coercing. Buddha teaches you how to live – not for any goal, not to achieve anything, but to be blissful here, now. He teaches how to live in awareness. Not that awareness is going to give you something – awareness is not a means to anything. It is the end in itself, the means and the end both; its value is intrinsic.

Buddha does not teach you otherworldliness. This has to be understood. People are worldly and the priests go on teaching the other world. The other world is also not very otherworldly, it cannot be, because it is just an improved model of the same world you live in now. From where will you create the other world? You know only this world. You can improve it, you can decorate the other world better, you can remove a few things that are ugly here and replace them with a few things you think will be beautiful, but it is going to be a creation out of your experience of this world. So your other world is not very different, it cannot be. It is a continuity. It comes out of your mind; it is a game of your imagination.

You will have beautiful women there – of course more beautiful than you have here. You will have the same kinds of pleasures there – maybe more permanent, stable, but they will be the same kinds of pleasures. You will have better food, more tasty – but you will have food. You will have houses – maybe made of gold, but they will be houses. You will repeat the whole thing again.

Just go into the scriptures and see how they depict heaven and you will find the same world improved upon. A few touches here and a few touches there, but it is not in any way "otherworldly". That's why I say the otherworldliness of other religions is not very otherworldly; it is this world projected into the future. It is born out of the experience of this world. There will not be misery and poverty and illness and paralysis and blindness and deafness. Things that you don't like here will not be there, and things that you like will be there, and in abundance. But it is not going to be anything new.

But all your scriptures talk about heaven – and their heaven or paradise is nothing but the same story. It may be printed on better art paper, with better ink, by an improved press, with more colorful illustrations, but the story is the same; it cannot be otherwise.

Buddha does not talk of otherworldliness or the other world. He simply teaches you how to be here in this world. How to be here alert, conscious, mindful, so that nothing impinges upon your emptiness; so that your inner emptiness is not contaminated, poisoned; so that you can live here and yet remain uncontaminated, unpolluted; so that you can be in the world and the world will not be in you.

The otherworldly spirituality is bound to be oppressive, destructive, sadomasochistic – in short, pathological. Buddha's spirituality has a different flavor to it – the flavor of no ideal, the flavor of no future, the flavor of no "other world". It is a flower here and now. It asks for nothing, all is already given. It simply becomes more alert so you can see more, you can hear more, you can be more.

Remember, you are only in the same proportion as you are conscious. If you want to be more, be more conscious. Consciousness imparts being. Unconsciousness takes being away. When you are drunk you lose being. When you are fast asleep you lose being. Have you not watched it? When you are alert you have a different quality – you are centered, rooted. When you are alert you feel the solidity of your being, it is almost tangible. When you are unconscious, just dragging by, sleepy, your sense of being is less. It is always in the same proportion as the consciousness.

So Buddha's whole message is to be conscious. And for no other reason, just for the sake of being conscious – because consciousness imparts being, consciousness creates you. And it creates a you so different from you that you are, that you cannot imagine. A you where "I" has disappeared, where no idea of self exists, nothing defines you ... a pure emptiness, an infinity, unbounded emptiness.

The word nirvana is a negative word. Literally it means "blowing out the candle".

Gautama Buddha used the word for the ultimate state of consciousness. He could have chosen some positive word, and in India there were many positive words for it. *Moksha* – freedom, liberation. *Kaivalya* – aloneness, absolute aloneness. *Brahmanubava* – the experience of the ultimate. But he chose a strange term, which has never been used in a spiritual context: "blowing out the candle". How can you relate it with a spiritual experience?

Buddha says your so-called self is nothing but a flame, and it is being kept burning through your desires. When all desires disappear the candle has disappeared. Now the flame cannot exist anymore; the flame also disappears – disappears into the vast universe, leaving no trace behind it; you cannot find it again. It is there but it has gone forever from any identity, from any limitation.

Hence Buddha chose the word nirvana rather than realization, because realization still can give you some egoistic superiority – that you are a realized person, that you are a liberated being, that you are enlightened, that you are illuminated, that you have found it. But you remain.

Buddha is saying "you" will be lost – who is going to find it? You disperse, you were only a combination of elements, now each element goes to its original source. The identity of the individual is no more. Yes, you will exist as the universe ...

So Buddha avoided any positive word, knowing the human tendency, because each positive word can give you a feeling of ego. No negative word can do that; that's why it remains unpolluted. You cannot pollute something which is not. And people were very much afraid to use the word. With a deep inner trembling ... nirvana. Thousands of times Buddha was asked, "Your word nirvana does not create in us an excitement, does not create in us a desire to achieve it. The ultimate truth, self-realization, the realization of God – all those create a desire, a great desire. Your word creates no desire."

And Buddha said again and again, "That is the beauty of the word. All those words that create desire in you are not going to help you, because desire itself is the root cause of your misery. Longing for something is your tension. Nirvana makes you absolutely free from tension; there is nothing to desire. On the contrary, you have to prepare yourself to accept a dissolution. In dissolution you cannot claim the ego, hence the word remains unpolluted."

No other word has remained unpolluted. Its negativity is the reason – and only a great master can contribute to humanity something which, even if you want, you cannot pollute. Twenty-five centuries ... but there is no way. Nirvana is going to dissolve you; you cannot do anything to nirvana.

It is certainly the purest word. Even its sound, whether you understand the meaning or not, is soothing, gives a deep serenity and silence, which no other word – god-realization, the absolute, the ultimate ... no other word gives that feeling of silence. The moment you hear the word nirvana it seems as if time has stopped, as if there is nowhere to go. In this very moment you can melt, dissolve, disappear, without leaving any trace behind.

When Buddha was born, the great astrologers said to the king, "We are afraid, but you have to be made aware of it: this newborn baby is either going to become a *chakravartin*" – a *chakravartin* means one who rules over the whole world – "or he is going to become a beggar who owns nothing." Two extremes …

The king was old and this was his only son, born in his old age. He asked the astrologers how to prevent him from becoming a beggar and renouncing the world. Those astrologers had no idea of the mind and psychology. Astrologers may have ideas about faraway stars, whose light takes millions of light years to reach the earth … And what foolishness, that man thinks his fate, his destiny, is determined by all these millions of stars so far away! There is a reason why astrology has remained significant: it gives you great satisfaction to think that the whole universe is interested in you. Even the faraway stars are trying their best to do something to you; you are not an ordinary person, you are not nothing.

Those faraway stars are not even aware of you, cannot be, but your ego feels tremendous satisfaction. Astrologers have been exploiting this since the very beginning of man. Of course, they exploit you, you have to pay for it, but it seems worth paying them; they are giving you a big ego. You are bigger, far more important, than the biggest star in the sky. They are all just revolving around you!

But those poor astrologers were not even as intelligent as Sigmund Freud. They told the king, "If you want your son not to renounce the world, then a few arrangements have to be made."

In India there are three clear-cut seasons in the year. Since the atomic explosions around the world, that has changed; otherwise, every year on the same day the rains would begin, and on the same day they would stop. On the same day the winter comes, and after four months on the same day it stops. For centuries it has been absolutely certain. Now it is not so, but in Buddha's time it was certain. Buddha's father made three palaces, one for each season. For summer, a palace in the hill station: cool, beautiful, green. Every care was taken that Buddha would never become disappointed with the world. For winter, a warm and cozy atmosphere was made in the palace.

The astrologers told the king, "From the very beginning let him be surrounded with beautiful girls, so by the time he becomes a young man he has all the beautiful girls of the land." They even went into details: that he should not see any old man, because in his seeing an old man the question could arise in him, "Is this the destiny for everyone?" Never allow him to see a dead body. Keep him absolutely unaware of the realities of life, keep him in a dreamland. Their argument was, when he has everything, why should he renounce?

The greatest physician of the country was looking after him. Even the gardeners in the king's garden were told that Buddha should not see a flower withering away or a leaf turning pale. In the night, everything that indicates death had to be removed. He should see only beautiful flowers that are always young. He should see only green leaves that are always green.

And this the king could manage. He managed it – and his management backfired. Those idiotic astrologers had no idea of a simple fact: that if you give a man everything and keep him unaware of all that is ugly around, soon he is going to be fed up. Soon he will start thinking, "Is this all? Then tomorrow is going to be the same, and the day after tomorrow is going to be the same. What is the point?" He will become bored. And that's what happened. Buddha became bored with unchanging beautiful women, unchanging beautiful flowers. How long can your mind keep silent? The astrologers were the reason why Buddha renounced the kingdom. If he had been allowed to live just the ordinary life of every man, perhaps there would have been no Buddha. In a way, the astrologers unknowingly did a great service to humanity.

The story is beautiful. There used to be an annual festival in the capital, and the prince who was going to be king used to inaugurate it, declare it open. It lasted for a few weeks – all kinds of things, all kinds of athletic games, shows. Buddha was going to inaugurate this youth festival in his 29th year. On the way to the festival, every care was taken – but existence has a way to reach you. You cannot remain completely closed in a grave, unless you are dead. If you are alive, there are bound to be loopholes from where existence will enter and make you aware of the reality. The astrologers and the kings could not be more intelligent than existence itself.

Every care was taken that on the way from the palace to the festival stadium, no old men should be seen, no dead bodies should be carried – nothing that could create a questioning in Buddha. But you cannot avoid reality for long. As the chariot was going towards the festival grounds, Buddha saw an old man. The old man was deaf and he had not heard that today he was not to pass on this road, he was to remain in the house or go somewhere else. He was deaf, he could not hear it, so just as usual he came out of his house; he was going to purchase something from the market.

Buddha, for the first time in 29 years, saw an old man just on the borderline of death. He asked his charioteer, "What is the matter? What has happened to this man? I have never seen anything like this!"

The charioteer loved Buddha just as his own son. He could not lie. He said, "Although it is going against the orders of your father, I cannot lie to you. You have been prevented from seeing people getting old. Everybody gets old – I will get old. This is the way of life."

Buddha immediately asked, "Am I also going to be old one day, just like this man?"

The charioteer said, "I have to say the truth to you: I would like that this should not happen to you, but it is the law of nature; nothing can be done. Just as from childhood you have become a young man, from youth you will become one day old too."

And then, just then, somebody died. Now you cannot prevent death. You cannot order death, "You are not to happen on this road, you can happen anywhere else." Death is not in your hands. Somebody died, people were crying, and the dead body was there.

Buddha asked, "What has happened? Why are people crying?" He had never seen anybody crying, he had never seen anybody with tears; he had never seen anybody dead. He asked, "What has happened to this man? He is not even breathing!"

The charioteer said, "This is the second stage. First you saw the old man. Soon death will come to him too. It has come to this man."

Buddha asked, "Am I also going to die one day?"

The charioteer – afraid of the king, but he must have been a man of some integrity – said, "Truth is truth, nobody can deny it. Your father the king is going to die, I am going to die, you are going to die. Death begins the day you are born. After birth there is no way to escape death."

And just then they passed a sannyasin, a wandering seeker. Astrologers had said to the king, "Your son should not be allowed any contact with sannyasins, because those are the people who have renounced everything. Those are the people who teach that this world is illusion, that all your desires are going to lead you nowhere, that you are simply wasting your life, and death is coming close by every moment. Sannyasins have to be avoided." And for 29 years Buddha had no notion that there were people who were trying to find something beyond life and death.

This red-clothed sannyasin looked very strange to him – a man who has not seen a sannyasin his whole life, for 29 years, is bound to be inquiring. He said, "And what about this man? I have seen people, but nobody wears a loose robe like this, with a begging bowl in his hand. What kind of man is he?"

The charioteer said, "This man has understood that beauty is going to turn into ugliness, that youth is going to turn into old age, that life is going to turn into death, and he is trying to find out – is there something eternal? Is there something which is not affected by youth, by old age, by death, by disease? He is a sannyasin, he has renounced the ordinary world. He is a seeker of truth."

They were just reaching the stadium. Buddha said to the charioteer, "Turn back – I am not going to the youth festival. If youth is finally going to become old age, disease, death, and if this is going to happen to me, then I have lost 29 years uselessly. I have lived in dreams. I am no longer young, and I am no longer interested in being the prince. Tonight I am going to renounce this world and be a seeker of truth."

What the astrologers had advised the king looked like common sense ... but common sense is superficial. They could not imagine a simple thing: that you cannot keep a man for his whole life unaware of reality. It is better to let him know from the very beginning; otherwise it will come as a big explosion in his life. And that's what happened. That very night Buddha escaped from the palace where everything was available.

❖

Buddha tried to find the truth for six years continuously, and no man has tried as totally as Buddha did. He made every effort possible, he went to every master available. There was not a single master Buddha did not go to. He surrendered to every master, and whatsoever was said he did so perfectly that even the master started feeling jealous. But every master finally had to say to Buddha, "This is all I can teach. And if nothing is happening I cannot blame you, because you are doing everything so perfectly. I am helpless. You will have to move to some other teacher."

This rarely happens because disciples never do everything so perfectly. So the master can always say, "Because you are not doing well, that's why nothing is happening." But Buddha was doing so well, so absolutely well, that no master could say to him, "You are not doing well." So they had to accept defeat. They had to say, "This is all we can teach, and you have done it and nothing is happening, so it is better you move to some other master. You don't belong to me."

Buddha moved for six years, and he followed even absurd techniques when they were taught to him. Somebody told him to fast, so for months he fasted. For six months he was continuously fasting, just taking a very small quantity of food every 15 days, only twice a month. He became so weak that he was simply a skeleton. All flesh disappeared, he looked like a dead man. He became so weak that he couldn't even walk. He finally became so weak that he would close his eyes to meditate and he would fall down in a fit.

One day he was taking a bath in the river Niranjana, just near Bodhgaya, and he was so weak that he couldn't cross the river. He fell down in the river and he thought that he was going to be drowned; it was the last moment, death had come. He was so weak he couldn't swim. Then suddenly he caught hold of a branch of a tree and remained there. And there for the first time the thought came to his mind, "If I have become so weak that I cannot cross this ordinary small river in summertime when the water has gone completely, when there is no more water and it is very small, just a little stream – if I cannot cross this little stream, how can I cross this big ocean of the world? How can I transcend this world? It seems impossible. I am doing something stupid."

What to do? He came out of the river in the evening and sat under a tree, which became the bodh tree, and that evening when the moon was coming up – it was a full-moon night – he realized that every effort is useless. He realized that nothing can be achieved, the very idea of achievement is nonsense. He had done everything. He was finished with the world, with the world of desires. He was a king and he had known every desire, he had lived every desire. He was finished with them, there was nothing to be achieved, there was nothing worthwhile. And then for six years he had been trying all austerities, all efforts, all meditations, yoga, everything, and nothing was happening. So he said, "Now there is nothing more except to die. There is nothing to be achieved, and every concept of achievement is nonsense; human desire is but futile."

So he dropped all effort that evening. He sat under the tree, relaxed, with no effort, no goal, nowhere to go, nothing to be achieved, nothing worth achieving. When you are in such a state of mind, mind relaxes – no future, no desire, no goal, nowhere to go, so what to do? He simply sat, he became just like the tree. The whole night he slept, and later on Buddha said that for the first time he really slept that night – because when effort is there it continues in sleep also. A person who is earning money and who is after money goes on counting even in his dreams, a person who is after power and prestige and politics goes on fighting elections in his dreams. You all know that when you are sitting for an examination in the university or college, in sleep also you go on doing the examination; again and again you are in the examination hall answering questions. So whatsoever effort is there it continues in sleep – and there is always some effort for something or other.

That night there was no effort. Buddha said, "I slept for the first time in millions of lives. That was the first night that I slept." Such a sleep becomes samadhi. And in the morning when he awoke he saw the last star disappear. He looked. His eyes for the first time must have been mirrorlike, with no content, just vacant, empty, nothing to project. The last star was disappearing, and Buddha said, "With that disappearing star I also disappeared. The star was disappearing and I also disappeared" – because the ego can exist only with effort. If you make some effort the ego is fed – you are doing something, you are reaching somewhere, you are achieving something. When there is no effort how can you exist?

The last star disappeared, "And," Buddha said, "I also disappeared. And then I looked, the sky was vacant; then I looked within, there was nothing – *anatta*, no self. There was no one."

It is said that Buddha laughed at the whole absurdity. There was no one who could reach. There was no one who could reach the goal, there was no one who could achieve liberation – there was no one at all, no entity. Space was without, space was within. "And," he said, "at that moment of total effortlessness I achieved, I realized."

But don't go to relax under a tree, and don't wait for the last star to disappear. And don't wait thinking that with the last star disappearing you will disappear. Those six years must precede the disappearance. So this is the problem: without effort no one has ever achieved, and with only effort no one has ever achieved. With effort coming to a point where it becomes effortlessness, realization has always been possible.

Buddha brings a totally new vision of meditation to the world. Before Buddha, meditation was something that you had to do once or twice a day, one hour in the morning, one hour in the evening, and that was all. Buddha gave a totally new interpretation to the whole process of meditation. He said: "This kind of meditation that you do one hour in the morning, one hour in the evening, you may do five times or four times a day, is not of much value. Meditation cannot be something that you can do apart from life just for one hour or 15 minutes. Meditation has to become something synonymous with your life; it has to be like breathing. You cannot breathe one hour in the morning and one hour in the evening, otherwise the evening will never come. It has to be something like breathing: even while you are asleep the breathing continues. You may fall into a coma, but the breathing continues."

Buddha says meditation should become such a constant phenomenon; only then can it transform you. And he evolved a new technique of meditation.

His greatest contribution to the world is vipassana.

The very word vipassana in Pali, the language in which Gautama Buddha spoke … he was perfectly acquainted with Sanskrit; as a prince he was well educated in the highest literature of those days. But when he started speaking he never used Sanskrit because Sanskrit was the language of the intellectuals, of the Brahmins, of the priests, not of the people. It has never been a living language. It has a uniqueness among all the languages of the world – it has been spoken only by the learned, by the scholarly amongst themselves; and because of its unknowability, the masses have been mystified by it. Translated, it contains nothing special, and sometimes it contains nothing but bullshit, but it has a very musical sound. Its construction is the most perfect of any language in the world. It is very exhaustive – 52 letters in the alphabet. English has only 26; it means the other 26 sounds are unavailable in English. Sanskrit is twice as rich because it can express all possible sounds, it has not left a single sound out of its alphabet. Subtle nuances have also been taken into account – sounds that are very difficult to pronounce, sounds that are rarely used by anyone, but which are possible to use, have been included.

But Gautama Buddha decided to speak in the language of the masses. It was a revolutionary step, because the languages of the masses are not grammatically right. Just by use, by ordinary people changing their tone, their sound, the words become easier; they are not complicated. Pali is a language of the simple and in a way, innocent and ignorant people. Vipassana is their word. The meaning – the literal meaning – of the word is "to look", and the metaphorical meaning is "to watch, to witness".

Gautama Buddha has chosen a meditation that can be called the essential meditation. All other meditations are different forms of witnessing, but witnessing is present in every kind of meditation as an essential part; it cannot be avoided. Buddha has deleted everything else and kept only the essential part – to witness.

There are three steps of witnessing – Buddha is a very scientific thinker. He begins with the body, because that is the easiest to witness. It is easy to witness my hand moving, my hand being raised. I can witness myself walking on the road, I can witness each step as I walk. I can witness while I am eating my food. So the first step in vipassana is witnessing the actions of the body, which is the simplest step. Any scientific method will always begin from the simplest. And while witnessing the body, you will be amazed at the new experiences. When you move your hand with witnessing, watchfulness, alertness, consciousness, you will feel a certain grace and a certain silence in the hand. You can do the movement without witnessing; it will be quicker, but it will lose the grace. Buddha used to walk so slowly that many times he was asked why he was walking so slowly. He said, "This is part of my meditation: always to walk as if you are walking in winter into a cold stream ... slowly, alert, because the stream is very cold; aware because the current is very strong; witnessing each of your steps because you can slip on the stones in the stream."

The method remains the same, only the object changes with each step. The second step is watching the mind. Now you move into a more subtle world – watching your thoughts. If you have been successful in watching your body, there is not going to be any difficulty. Thoughts are subtle waves – electronic waves, radio waves – but they are as material as your body. They are not visible, just as the air is not visible, but the air is as material as the stones; so are your thoughts, material but invisible. That is the second step, the middle step. You are moving towards invisibility, but still it is material … watching your thoughts. The only condition is, don't judge.

Don't judge, because the moment you start judging you will forget watching. There is no antagonism against judging. The reason it is prohibited is that the moment you start judging – "This is a good thought" – for that much space you were not witnessing. You started thinking, you became involved. You could not remain aloof, standing by the side of the road and just seeing the traffic. Don't become a participant, either by appraising, valuing, or condemning; no attitude should be taken about what is passing in your mind. You should watch your thoughts just as if clouds are passing in the sky. You don't make judgments about them – this black cloud is very evil, this white cloud looks like a sage. Clouds are clouds, they are neither evil nor good. So are thoughts – just a small wavelength passing through your mind.

Watch without any judgment and you are again in for a great surprise. As your watching becomes settled, thoughts will come less and less. The proportion is exactly the same: if you are 50 percent settled in your witnessing, then 50 percent of your thoughts will disappear. If you are 60 percent settled in your witnessing, then only 40 percent of thoughts will be there. When you are 99 percent a pure witness, only once in a while will there be a lonely thought – 1 percent, passing on the road – otherwise the traffic is gone. That rush-hour traffic is no longer there. When you are 100 percent non-judgmental, just a witness, it means you have become just a mirror, because a mirror never makes any judgments. An ugly woman looks into it – the mirror has no judgment. A beautiful woman looks into the mirror, it makes no difference. Nobody looks into it, the mirror is as pure as when somebody is being reflected in it. Neither reflection stirs it, nor no reflection. Witnessing becomes a mirror.

This is a great achievement in meditation. You have moved

halfway, and this was the hardest part. Now you know the secret, and the same secret has just to be applied to different objects.

From thoughts you have to move to more subtle experiences – emotions, feelings, moods. From the mind to the heart, with the same condition: no judgment, just witnessing. And the surprise will be that most of your emotions, feelings and moods which possess you … Now, when you are feeling sad, you become sad, you are possessed by sadness. When you are feeling angry, it is not something partial. You become full of anger; every fiber of your being is throbbing with anger. Watching the heart, the experience will be that now nothing possesses you. Sadness comes and goes; you don't become sad. Happiness comes and goes; you don't become happy either. Whatever moves in the deep layers of your heart does not affect you at all. For the first time you taste something of mastery. You are no longer a slave to be pushed and pulled this way and that way, where any emotion, any feeling, anybody can disturb you for any trivia.

When you become a witness of the third step, you will become, for the first time, a master: nothing disturbs you, nothing overpowers you, everything remains far away, deep below, and you are on a hilltop.

When you have become perfectly watchful of your body, mind and heart, then you cannot do anything more, then you have to wait. When perfection is complete on these three steps, the fourth step happens of its own accord as a reward. It is a quantum leap from the heart to the being, to the very center of your existence.

You cannot do it; it happens – you have to remember that. Don't try to do it, because if you try to do it your failure is absolutely certain. It is a happening. You prepare three steps, the fourth step is a reward from existence itself; it is a quantum leap. Suddenly your life force, your witnessing, enters into the very center of your being. You have come home.

You can call it self-realization, you can call it enlightenment, you can call it ultimate liberation, but there is nothing more than that. You have come to the very end in your search, you have found the very truth of existence and the great ecstasy that it brings as a shadow, by and around itself.

❖

There is a story: Buddha is going from one village to another, and on the way – it is a hot day, summer – he feels thirsty. He is old, so he asks his disciple Ananda, "Ananda, I am sorry but you will have to go back. Two or three miles back we have left a small stream of water, and I am very thirsty: you go and bring water."

Ananda said, "There is no need to feel sorry. This is my joy – to serve you in any way. I am obliged; you are not obliged. You rest under this tree, and I will go."

He went back. He knew exactly where the stream was; they had just passed it. And when they had passed by the side of the stream, it was crystal clear – a mountain stream has a clarity of its own. But when Ananda returned to take the water, two bullock carts had passed through it, and the whole stream was muddy; all the mud that was settled on the bottom had risen to the surface. Old leaves, rotten leaves, were floating on top. He could not think that he could take this water for Buddha to drink. So he came back and said to Buddha, "This is the situation. I could not bring that water for you, but don't be worried. Four miles ahead you can rest; I know a big river, and from there I will bring the water. Although it is getting late and you are thirsty, what else can I do?"

Buddha said, "No, I want the water from that stream. You unnecessarily wasted time; you should have brought the water."

"But," Ananda said, "the water is dirty and muddy; rotten leaves are floating all over it. How can I bring it?"

Buddha said, "You go and bring it."

When the master says so … Ananda went back reluctantly, but was surprised: by that time the leaves had moved. The water was continuously flowing, and it had taken the leaves away; the dust and the mud had settled down – just a little was left. But Ananda got the message; he sat by the side of the stream. That's what Buddha had meant: "Go back." And seeing that things had changed … If he had just waited, soon the crystal-clear water would have been there.

He waited, and soon the water was there. He brought some back. Buddha said, "Ananda, did you get the message?"

Ananda was crying. He said, "Yes, I got the message. In fact, I had not told you: when I went the first time and saw this whole thing – those two bullock carts passing just in front of me, disturbing the whole stream, I went into the stream to settle it. And the more I tried to settle it, the more it became unsettled. The more I walked into it, the more mud came up, more leaves. Seeing that it was impossible to settle it, I came back – I did not tell you this. I am sorry, I was foolish. That was not the way to settle the stream back into its natural way. I should have simply waited by the side, I should have simply watched.

"Things happen on their own. The leaves were going down the stream and the mud was settling. And just sitting there watching the stream, I got the message, that this stream is the stream of my mind – of all rotten thoughts, past, dead, mud – and I am continuously trying to settle it. Jumping into it makes it worse than before and creates a pessimistic attitude that 'perhaps in this life I am not going to attain what Buddha says – the state of no-mind.' But today, seeing that stream, a great hope has arisen in me: perhaps the stream of my own mind is also going to be settled in the same way. Just sitting there, I had a little glimpse."

Buddha said, "I am not thirsty, you are thirsty. And you were not sent to bring water for me, you were sent to understand a certain message. While we were coming I had seen those two bullock carts on top of the hill and I knew by what time they would be passing, so I sent you right in time to bring the water."

Just sit by the stream of your mind. Don't do anything; nothing is expected from you. You just keep quiet, calm, as if it is none of your business. What is happening in the mind is happening somewhere else. The mind is not you; it is somebody else: you are only a watcher. Buddha has called his whole philosophy *majjhim nikai* – he says remain in the middle always; no matter what the polarity, remain always in the middle. By witnessing one remains in the middle. The moment you lose your witnessing you either become attached or repulsed. If you are repulsed you will go to the other extreme; if you are attached you will try to remain at this extreme, but you will never be in between. Just be a witness. Don't be attracted, don't be repulsed. The headache is there; accept it. It is there as a fact. As a tree is there, as the house is there, as the night is there, the headache is there. Accept it and close your eyes. Don't try to escape from it.

You are happy; accept the fact. Don't cling to it, and don't try not to become unhappy. Don't try anything. If unhappiness comes, allow it. If happiness comes, allow it. Just remain a watcher on the hill, just seeing things. The morning comes, and then evening comes, and then the sun rises, and then the sun sets and there are stars and darkness, and again the sun rises – and you are just a watcher on the hill. You cannot do anything. You simply see. The morning has come; you note the fact, and you know that now the evening will come because the evening follows the morning. And when the evening comes you note the fact, and you know that now the morning will be coming because the morning follows the evening.

When pain is there, you are just a watcher. You know that pain has come, and sooner or later it will go, and the polar opposite will come. And when happiness has come, you know that it is not going to remain always. Unhappiness will be just hidden somewhere, it will be coming. You remain a watcher. If you can watch without attraction and without repulsion you will fall in the middle, and once the pendulum stops in the middle you can look for the first time at what the world is.

While you are moving, you cannot know what the world is; your movement confuses everything. Once you are not moving, you can look at the world. For the first time you know what reality is. A non-moving mind knows what reality is; a moving mind cannot know what reality is. Your mind is just like a camera: you go on moving and taking shots, but whatsoever comes is just a confusion because the camera must not move. If the camera is moving, the pictures are going to be just a confusion.

Your consciousness is moving from one pendulum to another, and whatsoever you know of reality is just a confusion, a nightmare. You don't know what is what; everything is confused, missed. If you remain in the middle and the pendulum has stopped, if your consciousness is focused now, centered, then you know what reality is. Only a mind that is unmoving can know what the truth is.

Gautama the Buddha's whole religion can be reduced to a single word. That word is freedom. That is his essential message, his very fragrance. Nobody else has raised freedom so high. It is the ultimate value in Buddha's vision, the *summum bonum*; there is nothing higher than that.

And it seems very fundamental to understand why Buddha emphasizes freedom so much. Neither God is emphasized nor heaven is emphasized nor love is emphasized, but only freedom. There is a reason for it: all that is valuable becomes possible only in the climate of freedom. Love also grows only in the soil of freedom; without freedom, love cannot grow. Without freedom, what grows in the name of love is nothing but lust. Without freedom there is no God. Without freedom what you think to be God is only your imagination, your fear, your greed. There is no heaven without freedom: freedom is heaven. And if you think there is some heaven without freedom, then that heaven has no worth, no reality. It is your fantasy, it is your dream.

All great values of life grow in the climate of freedom; hence freedom is the most fundamental value and also the highest pinnacle. If you want to understand Buddha you will have to taste something of the freedom he is talking about.

His freedom is not of the outside. It is not social, it is not political, it is not economic. His freedom is spiritual. By "freedom" he means a state of consciousness unhindered by any desire, unchained to any desire, unimprisoned by any greed, by any lust for more. By "freedom" he means a consciousness without mind, a state of no-mind. It is utterly empty, because if there is something, that will hinder freedom; hence its utter emptiness.

This word emptiness – *shunyata* – has been very much misunderstood by people, because the word has a connotation of negativity. Whenever we hear the word "empty" we think of something negative. In Buddha's language, emptiness is not negative; emptiness is absolutely positive, more positive than your so-called fullness, because emptiness is full of freedom; everything else has been removed. It is spacious; all boundaries have been dropped. It is unbounded – and only in an unbounded space, freedom is possible. His emptiness is not ordinary emptiness; it is not only absence of something, it is a presence of something invisible.

For example, when you empty your room: as you remove the furniture and the paintings and the things inside, the room becomes empty on the one hand because there is no longer any furniture, no more paintings, no more things, nothing is left inside; but on the other hand, something invisible starts filling it. That invisibleness is "roominess", spaciousness; the room becomes bigger. As you remove the things, the room is becoming bigger and bigger. When everything is removed, even the walls, then the room is as big as the whole sky.

That's the whole process of meditation: removing everything; removing yourself so totally that nothing is left behind – not even you. In that utter silence is freedom. In this utter stillness grows the 1,000-petaled lotus of freedom. And great fragrance is released: the fragrance of peace, compassion, love, bliss.

Gautama Buddha's emphasis on compassion was a very new phenomenon as far as the mystics of old were concerned. Gautama Buddha makes a historical dividing line from the past; before him meditation was enough, nobody had emphasized compassion together with meditation. And the reason was that meditation brings enlightenment, your blossoming, your ultimate expression of being.

What more do you need? As far as the individual is concerned, meditation is enough. Gautama Buddha's greatness consists in introducing compassion even before you start meditating. You should be more loving, more kind, more compassionate.

There is a hidden science behind it. Before a man becomes enlightened, if he has a heart full of compassion there is a possibility that after meditation he will help others to achieve the same beautitude, to the same height, to the same celebration as he has achieved. Gautama Buddha makes it possible for enlightenment to be infectious. But if the person feels that he has come back home, why bother about anybody else?

Buddha makes enlightenment for the first time unselfish; he makes it a social responsibility. It is a great change. But compassion should be learned before enlightenment happens. If it is not learned before, then after enlightenment there is nothing to learn. When one becomes so ecstatic in himself then even compassion seems to be preventing his own joy – it is a kind of disturbance in his ecstasy.

That's why there have been hundreds of enlightened people, but very few masters. To be enlightened does not mean necessarily that you will become a master. Becoming a master means you have tremendous compassion, and you feel ashamed to go alone into those beautiful spaces that enlightenment makes available. You want to help the people who are blind, in darkness, groping their way. It becomes a joy to help them, it is not a disturbance.

In fact, it becomes a richer ecstasy when you see so many people flowering around you; you are not a solitary tree who has blossomed in a forest where no other tree is blossoming. When the whole forest blossoms with you, the joy becomes a thousandfold; you have used your enlightenment to bring a revolution in the world.

Gautama Buddha is not only enlightened, but an enlightened revolutionary. His concern with the world, with people, is immense. He was teaching his disciples that when you meditate and you feel silence, serenity, a deep joy bubbling inside your being, don't hold onto it; give it to the whole world. And don't be worried, because the more you give it, the more you will become capable of getting it. The gesture of giving is of tremendous importance once you know that giving does not take anything from you; on the contrary, it multiplies your experiences. But the man who has never been compassionate does not know the secret of giving, does not know the secret of sharing.

It happened that one of his disciples, a layman – he was not a sannyasin, but he was very much devoted to Gautama Buddha – said, "I will do it ... but I want just to make one exception. I will give all my joy and all my meditation and all my inner treasures to the whole world – except my neighbor, because that fellow is really nasty."

Neighbors are always enemies. Gautama Buddha said to him, "You forget the world, you simply give to your neighbor."

He said, "What are you saying?"

Buddha said, "If you can give to your neighbor, only then will you be freed from this antagonistic attitude towards a human being."

Compassion basically means accepting people's frailties, their weaknesses, not expecting them to behave like gods. That is cruelty, because they will not be able to behave like gods and then they will fall in your estimation, and they will also fall in their own self-respect. You have dangerously crippled them, you have damaged their dignity. One of the fundamentals of compassion is to make everybody dignified, everybody aware that what has happened to you can happen to him; that he is not a hopeless case, that he is not unworthy, that enlightenment is not to be deserved, it is your very self-nature.

But these words should come from the enlightened man, only then can they create trust. If they come from unenlightened scholars, they cannot create trust. The word, through the enlightened man, starts breathing, starts having a heartbeat of its own. It becomes living, it goes directly into your heart – it is not intellectual gymnastics. But with the scholar it is a different thing. He himself is not certain of what he is talking about, what he is writing about. He is in the same uncertainty as you are.

Gautama Buddha is one of the landmarks in the evolution of consciousness; his contribution is great, immeasurable. And in his contribution, the idea of compassion is the most essential. But you have to remember that by being compassionate you don't become higher; otherwise you spoil the whole thing. It becomes an ego-trip. Remember not to humiliate the other person by being compassionate; otherwise you are not being compassionate, behind the words you are enjoying their humiliation.

Compassion has to be understood, because it is love come of age.

Compassion is not addressed to anybody. It is not a relationship, it is simply your very being. You enjoy being compassionate to the trees, to the birds, to the animals, to human beings, to everybody – unconditionally, not asking for anything in return.

A beautiful story for you:

Paddy came home an hour earlier than usual and found his wife stark naked on the bed. When he asked why, she explained, "I am protesting because I don't have any nice clothes to wear."

Paddy pulled open the closet door. "That's ridiculous," he said, "look in here. There is a yellow dress, a red dress, a print dress, a pantsuit ... Hi, Bill!" And he goes on, "A green dress ..."

This is compassion!

It is compassion to his wife, it is compassion to Bill. No jealousy, no fight, just simply, "Hi, Bill! How are you?" and he goes on. He never even inquires, "What are you doing in my closet?"

Compassion is very understanding. It is the finest understanding that is possible to man.

As he was approaching an intersection, a man's car lost its brakes and bumped into the rear of a car with "Just Married" written all over it. The damage was slight but the man sincerely offered his apologies to the newlywed couple.

"Aw, it doesn't matter," replied the husband. "It has been one of those days."

An understanding, a deep understanding that now everything is possible ... Once one is married, then he can expect all kinds of accidents. The greatest accident has already happened – now nothing matters.

A man of compassion should not be disturbed by small things in life, which are happening every moment. Only then, in an indirect way, are you helping your compassionate energies to accumulate, to crystallize, to become stronger, and to go on rising with your meditation.

So the day the blissful moment comes, when you are full of light, there will be at least one companion: compassion. And immediately a new style of life ... because now you have so much that you can bless the whole world.

The last words of Gautama the Buddha on the earth were: "Be a light unto yourself." Do not follow others, do not imitate, because imitation, following, creates stupidity. You are born with a tremendous possibility of intelligence. You are born with a light within you. Listen to the still, small voice within, and that will guide you. Nobody else can guide you, nobody else can become a model for your life, because you are unique. Nobody has there been ever who was exactly like you, and nobody is ever going to be there again who will be exactly like you. This is your glory, your grandeur – that you are utterly irreplaceable, that you are just yourself and nobody else.

The person who follows others becomes false, he becomes pseudo, he becomes mechanical. He can be a great saint in the eyes of others, but deep down, he is simply unintelligent and nothing else. He may have a very respectable character but that is only the surface, it is not even skin-deep. Scratch him a little and you will be surprised that inside he is a totally different person, just the opposite of his outside.

By following others you can cultivate a beautiful character, but you cannot have a beautiful consciousness, and unless you have a beautiful consciousness you can never be free. You can go on changing your prisons, you can go on changing your bondages, your slaveries. You can be a Hindu or a Mohammedan or a Christian or a Jain – that is not going to help you. To be a Jain means to follow Mahavira as the model. Now, there is nobody else like Mahavira nor can there ever be. Following Mahavira you will become a false entity.

You will lose all reality, you will lose all sincerity, you will be untrue to yourself. You will become artificial, unnatural, and to be artificial, to be unnatural, is the way of the mediocre, the stupid, the fool.

Buddha defines wisdom as living in the light of your own consciousness, and foolishness as following others, imitating others, becoming a shadow to somebody else.

The real master creates masters, not followers. The real master throws you back to yourself. His whole effort is to make you independent of him, because you have been dependent for centuries, and it has not led you anywhere. You still continue to stumble in the dark night of the soul.

Only your inner light can become the sunrise. The false master persuades you to follow him, to imitate him, to be just a carbon copy of him. The real master will not allow you to be a carbon copy, he wants you to be the original. He loves you! How can he make you imitative? He has compassion for you, he would like you to be utterly free – free from all outer dependencies.

But the ordinary human being does not want to be free. He wants to be dependent. He wants somebody else to guide him. Why? – because then he can throw the whole responsibility on the shoulders of somebody else. And the more responsibility you throw away onto somebody else's shoulders, the less is the possibility of your ever becoming intelligent. It is responsibility, the challenge of responsibility, that creates wisdom.

One has to accept life with all its problems. One has to go through life unprotected; one has to seek and search one's way. Life is an opportunity, a challenge to find yourself. But the fool does not want to go the hard way, the fool chooses the short cut. He says to himself, "Buddha has attained – why should I bother? I will just watch his behavior and imitate. Jesus has attained, so why should I search and seek? I can simply become a shadow to Jesus. I can simply go on following him wherever he goes."

But following somebody else, how are you going to become intelligent? You will not give any chance for your intelligence to explode. It needs a challenging life for intelligence to arise, an adventurous life, a life that knows how to risk and how to go into the unknown. And only intelligence can save you, nobody else – your own intelligence, mind you. Your own awareness can become your nirvana.

Be a light unto yourself and you will be wise; let others become your leaders, your guides, and you will remain stupid, and you will go on missing all the treasures of life – which were yours!

Life is a tremendously beautiful pilgrimage, but only for those who are ready to seek and search.

Chiyono

The nun Chiyono studied for years, but was unable to find enlightenment. One night she was carrying an old pail filled with water. As she was walking along, she was watching the full moon reflected in the pail of water. Suddenly, the bamboo strips that held the pail together broke and the pail fell apart. The water rushed out, the moon's reflection disappeared, and Chiyono became enlightened.

She wrote this verse:

This way and that way
I tried to keep the pail together,
Hoping the weak bamboo would never break.
Suddenly the bottom fell out ...
No more water,
No more moon in the water,
Emptiness in my hand.

Enlightenment happens when it happens: you cannot order it, you cannot cause it to happen. Still, you can do much for it to happen, but whatsoever you do is not going to function as a cause. Whatsoever you do is not going to bring enlightenment to you, but it prepares you to receive it. It comes when it comes. Whatsoever you do simply prepares you to receive it, to see it when it comes, to recognize it when it comes.

It happens ... but if you are not ready you go on missing it. It is happening every moment. Every breath that goes in and comes out brings enlightenment to you, because enlightenment is the very stuff that existence is made of. But to recognize it is the problem, to see that it is there is the problem.

God is. There is no question of God's being. The question is: we cannot see Him, we don't have eyes. All the meditations and the prayers and the purifications only help you, make you capable of seeing. Once you can see, you will be surprised – it has always been there. Day in, day out, year in, year out, it was showering on you, but you were not sensitive enough to catch hold of it, you were not empty enough to be filled by it. You were too much full of your own ego.

If one comes to fundamentals then this is the most fundamental thing: the moment you are not, enlightenment is. With emptiness, the matter is settled.

If you continue you will remain ignorant and full of darkness. You are darkness. Your presence is the "dark night of the soul". When you are, you are separate from existence. That's what darkness consists of: the idea of separation, that there is a gap between me and the whole. Then I am left alone. Then there is misery because fear surrounds me. I am so alone, and I am so tiny, and sooner or later death will come and destroy me. And I have no way to protect myself against death. Hence one lives in trembling and fear.

But we create the trembling and the fear. We cause it by the very idea of being separate from existence. The moment you drop this separation, the moment you see that you are not separate, that you cannot be separate, that there is no way to be separate, that you are part of the whole, intrinsic to the whole, that you are in the whole and the whole is in you, the matter is settled and settled forever. Death disappears, fear disappears, anguish disappears. And the whole energy that is involved in fear, in anxiety, in anguish, is released. That same energy becomes the celebration of the soul.

What is enlightenment? – the capacity to see oneself as one really is. We are utterly empty of the ego. The ego is just a make-believe. We have created it, we have projected it; it is our illusion, our dream. It exists not; in itself it is not there, so the more one becomes aware and looks within, the more one finds oneself not.

The more you become aware, the less you are. And the moment awareness is full, you have disappeared – no more water, no more reflection of the moon in the water, emptiness in your hands. And it is emptiness … therewith the matter is settled.

This happened to Chiyono. She had studied for years, she had practiced all kinds of meditations, she had cultivated all kinds of techniques but was unable to find enlightenment.

You cannot cause it, it is beyond you. If you could cause it, it would be below you. If you could cause it, then it would be again nothing but a new decoration for your ego. You cannot cause it. You cannot make it happen. You have to disappear for it to be.

So you can study all the scriptures of the world: you will become very learned, knowledgeable, but you will remain unenlightened. In fact you will become more unenlightened than you were before because the more knowledge you have the more ego you have; the more you practice ascetic techniques the more your ego is strengthened: "I am doing this and I am doing that, and I have done so much – so many fasts, so many bows." The more you do, the more you feel that now you are worthy and you can claim enlightenment.

Enlightenment cannot be claimed. One has to utterly disappear for it to be. The mind has to cease for God to be. Call it God or enlightenment – it is the same thing.

"Chiyono studied for years but was unable to find enlightenment."

Enlightenment is not something that you can find by searching; it comes to you when all search proves futile. And remember, I am not saying don't search, because unless you search you will never come to know that search is futile. And I am not saying don't meditate; if you don't meditate you will never come to understand that there is a meditation which you cannot do but which comes to you.

Your meditations will simply cleanse your eyes, will make you more perceptive. Your heart will become more alert, aware, loving, sensitive. Your being will start seeing things you had not seen before. You will start exploring new spaces within your being. Something new will happen every day, every moment. Your meditations are like a bath: they will give you a freshness – but that freshness is not enlightenment. That only prepares the way. You never reach to enlightenment; it is always the other way round – enlightenment reaches to you.

Prepare the way for God so that He can reach you. You cannot find Him; you can only wait, in deep trust, so that He can find you.

That's how Chiyono was missing: she was searching, seeking, she was too much involved in this inquiry. But this inquiry will also feed your ego, that "I am a seeker", that "I am no ordinary man", that "I am spiritual", that "I am religious", that "I am holy". And if that attitude of "holier than thou" arises, you are lost forever. That is the greatest sin you can commit in your life, the greatest fall. If the idea arises in you that you are holier than others, that you are a saint and others are sinners – "Look at my virtuous life" – if you become righteous you are lost, because this righteous ego will be the most subtle ego, and it will be very difficult for you to drop it. It is easier to drop iron chains. But if you can have golden chains studded with diamonds, it will become more and more difficult to drop them because they will not look like chains, they will look like valuable ornaments.

It is easy to get out of a dirty prison cell, but if it is a palace, who wants to get out of it? Really one wants to get into it, not out of it. The sinner is closer to God than the saint, because the sinner wants to get out of his bondage and the saint is enjoying an ego-trip.

Chiyono was a nun. She must have been enjoying subtle, righteous attitudes – knowledgeability, virtue. Her renunciation was great. It is said that she was one of the most beautiful women, so beautiful that when she went to one monastery they refused her, because to have such a beautiful woman in the monastery would create trouble for the monks. Then she had to disfigure her face to enter into another monastery. She must have been a very beautiful woman, but just think ... she disfigured her face, made it ugly, but deep down she must have been thinking, "Look at my renunciation. I was one of the most beautiful women. I have disfigured my face – nobody has done this before, or since. Look at my renunciation, look at my detachment from the body: I don't care a bit about beauty. I am bent upon finding enlightenment, whatsoever the cost." And she continued missing.

But one full-moon night it happened. It happened out of the blue, suddenly. It always happens out of the blue. It always happens suddenly.

But I am not saying that it could have happened to anybody else; it happened to Chiyono. All that she had done had not caused it, but all that she had done had caused one thing in her: the understanding that whatsoever you do, you fail, that man cannot succeed.

She must have come to a state of utter hopelessness. That hopelessness can be felt only when you have done all that you can do. And when that hopelessness comes, hope has arrived – because in that hopelessness the ego is shattered to the ground. One no longer claims.

The ego disappears only from the peak, when it has come to its crescendo. You cannot drop a lukewarm ego. No, that is not possible, because it still hopes. It says, "Who knows? A few efforts more, a few more practices, a little more renunciation … who knows? We have not looked in all the directions yet, there is still a possibility" – and the ego lingers. But when you have explored, searched in all possible directions and you have always failed; when nothing but failure has been your experience, how long can you continue searching, seeking? One day, searching and seeking drop.

So remember this paradox: enlightenment is possible only to those who stop seeking. But who can stop seeking? – only one who has searched deeply enough. This is the paradox. This is one of the great secrets to be understood; let it sink into your heart.

There is every possibility of choosing one. There are people who say, "Seek, and ye shall find." That is only half the truth: just by seeking, nobody has ever found. Then there are people who say, "If by seeking, God cannot be found, then why seek at all? Wait. It will happen through His grace." It never happens that way either. You have been waiting for centuries, for lives, and it has not happened: it is enough to prove that it doesn't happen that way.

Then how does it happen? It happens to a seeker when he drops his seeking. It happens to one who has searched with his total potential and has failed, utterly failed. In that failure, the first ray of light, and then it takes you by surprise! When you are completely feeling hopeless, when you are thinking to forget all about enlightenment, when the search has stopped, when even the desire to be enlightened has left you, suddenly it is there ... and therewith the matter is settled.

That's how it happened to Chiyono, that's how it happened to Buddha; that's how it always happens.

Chuang Tzu

Chuang Tzu is a rare flowering, rarer than a Buddha or a Jesus, because he achieved simply by understanding. There is no method, no meditation for Chuang Tzu. He says: simply understand the "facticity" of things. You are born – what effort have you made to be born? You grow – what effort have you made to grow? You breathe – what effort have you made to breathe? Everything moves on its own, so why bother? Let life flow on its own; then you will be in a let-go. Don't struggle and don't try to move upstream, don't even try to swim, just float with the current and let the current lead you wherever it leads. Be a white cloud moving in the sky – no goal, going nowhere, just floating. That floating is the ultimate flowering.

So the first thing to understand about Chuang Tzu is – be natural. Everything unnatural has to be avoided. Don't do anything that is unnatural. Nature is enough – you cannot improve upon it.

But the ego says, no, you can improve upon nature – that is how all culture exists. Any effort to improve upon nature is culture, and all culture is like a disease – the more a man is cultured the more dangerous he is. Chuang Tzu is not in favour of culture. He says nature is ultimate, and that ultimate nature he calls Tao. Tao means that nature is ultimate and cannot be improved. If you try to improve upon it, you will cripple it.

That is how we cripple every child. Every child is born in Tao, then we cripple him with society, civilization, culture, morality, religion ... we cripple him from every side. Then he lives, but he is not alive.

I have heard that a small girl was going to a party, a friend's birthday party. She was very small, just four years old. She asked her mother, "Were there such parties and dances when you were alive?"

The more cultured and civilized, the more dead. If you want to see perfectly dead men and yet still alive go to the monks in the monasteries, go to the priests in the churches, go to the Pope in the Vatican. They are not alive – they are so afraid of life, so afraid of nature that they have suppressed it from everywhere. They are already in their graves. You can paint the grave, you can even make a marble grave, very valuable – but the man inside is dead.

Culture kills you, culture is a murderer, culture is a slow poison – it is a suicide. Chuang Tzu and his old master, Lao Tzu, are against culture. They are for nature, pure nature. Trees are in a better position than you, even birds, fishes in the river, are in a better position because they are more alive, they dance more to the rhythm of nature.

You have completely forgotten what nature is. You have condemned it to the very root. And if you want to condemn nature you have to start by condemning sex, because the whole of nature arises out of it. The whole of nature is an overflowing of sex energy, of love. The birds sing, the trees flower – this is all sexual energy, exploding. Flowers are sex symbols, the singing of the birds is sexual, the whole of Tao is nothing but sex energy – the whole of nature propagates itself, loves itself, moves into deeper ecstasies of love and existence. So if you want to destroy nature, condemn sex, condemn love, create moral concepts around life. Those moral concepts, howsoever beautiful they look, will be like marble graves and you will be there inside them. Some drunkard may think that you know what life is, that you know how to live, but anyone who is in his state of awareness cannot even call you alive. Your morality is a sort of death: before death kills you, the society kills you.

That is why Chuang Tzu's message is one of the most dangerous, the most revolutionary, the most rebellious – because he says: allow nature! And don't give any goal to nature. Who are you to create goals and purposes? You are just a tiny part, an atomic cell. Who are you to force the whole to move according to you? This is most dangerous for people who are religious, for people who are moralistic puritans. This is a most dangerous message. This means break all the barriers, allow nature to erupt – dangerous it is.

Priests are afraid of health because health is immoral in their eyes. You may or may not have heard of one of the thinkers of the 20th century, a German thinker, very famous in his day – Count Keyserling. He was thought to be a great religious philosopher and he wrote in his diary: "Health is the most immoral thing." Because health is energy, and energy is delight, energy is enjoyment, energy is love, energy is sex, energy is everything that is natural. Destroy the energy, make it feeble and dim. Hence so many fasts – just to destroy the energy, just to prevent so much energy from arising that it starts overflowing. Religious people have always thought that health is dangerous. Then to be unhealthy becomes a spiritual goal.

I repeat again, Chuang Tzu is very rebellious. He says nature, energy and the ecstasy that comes by overflowing, and the balance that happens spontaneously, is enough. There is no need for effort. So much beauty happens all around in nature without any effort: a rose is beautiful without any effort, a cuckoo goes on singing without any effort ... Look at a deer, alive, full of energy, fast. Look at a hare, so alert, so aware, that even a buddha may become jealous.

Look at nature – everything is so perfect. Can you improve upon a rose? Can you improve on nature in any way? Only man has gone wrong somewhere. If the rose is beautiful without any effort on its part, why not man? What is wrong with man? If stars remain beautiful without any effort, without any yoga postures, why not man? Man is part of nature, just as stars are. So Chuang Tzu says: be natural, and you will flower. If this understanding enters you, deeper and deeper and deeper, then all effort becomes meaningless. Then you are not constantly making arrangements for the future, then you live here and now, then this moment is all, then this moment is eternity. And buddhahood is already the case, you are already a buddha. The only thing that is missing is that you have not given it any chance to flower because you are so engaged in your own projects.

A flower flowers without any effort because the energy is not dissipated in any projects; the flower is not planning for the future, the flower is here and now. Be like a flower, be like a bird, be like a tree, a river, or the ocean – but don't be like a man. Because man has gone wrong somewhere.

Nature and to be natural – effortlessly natural, spontaneously natural – that is the essence of all the teaching that Chuang Tzu gives to you.

Chuang Tzu says:

Easy is right. Begin right and you are easy.
Continue easy, and you are right.
The right way to go easy is to forget the right way
And forget that the going is easy.

Chuang Tzu is very rare – in a way the most unique mystic in the whole history of man. His uniqueness is that he talks in absurdities. All his poems and stories are just absurd. And his reason to choose absurdity as his expression is very significant: the mind has to be silenced. With anything rational, it cannot stop; it goes on and on. Anything logical and the mind finds nourishment through it. It is only the absurd that suddenly shocks the mind – it is beyond the mind's grasp.

His stories, his poems and his other statements were so absurd that either people simply left him, thinking that he was mad ... Those who were courageous enough to remain with him found that no other meditation was needed. Just listening to his absurd statements, the mind stops functioning. And that is the meaning of meditation.

Meditation is not of the mind. Meditation means the mind has been put aside. There is no concentration, there is no contemplation, there is no "meditation upon" something. It is a state of no-mind; it is absolute silence, not even a small stirring of any thought.

In the East, so many devices have been tried ... how to stop the mind chattering continuously, how to bypass it, how to stop it, how to go beyond it. Chuang Tzu has his own, unique contribution. He talks in absurdities, and the mind cannot tackle them. The mind needs something reasonable, rational, logical; that is its territory. The absurd is beyond it.

There is a famous story about Chuang Tzu: one morning he woke up with tears in his eyes, so sad and so depressed. His disciples had never seen him sad or depressed or with tears; he is an enlightened master ... what has happened? They all rushed and enquired, "Can we be of some help?" Chuang Tzu said, "I don't think so." They said, "Still, we want to know what is the problem that is torturing you so much. You are beyond problems!"

Chuang Tzu said, "I used to be, but last night I saw a dream and it has disturbed my whole attainment, achievement, self-realization, enlightenment – everything has gone down the drain."

They said, "Just a dream?" He said, "It was not just a dream, it has shattered me into pieces." They said, "Still, please tell us the dream!"

The dream was that Chuang Tzu saw that he had become a butterfly. All the disciples laughed. They said, "Unnecessarily being depressed and crying and tears and thinking that your enlightenment and self-realization have all gone down the drain ... It is an ordinary dream, nothing to be worried about. In dreams people see themselves becoming many things, but a dream is a dream."

Chuang Tzu said, "I understand that a dream is a dream. The problem is that I am worried, who am I? If Chuang Tzu in his sleep can dream that he has become a butterfly, a butterfly in her dream can see she has become Chuang Tzu. And now I am puzzled. Who am I? – Chuang Tzu or a butterfly?

"If Chuang Tzu is capable of dreaming himself to be a butterfly, you cannot cancel the possibility of a butterfly taking a nap on the rose bushes and dreaming that she has become Chuang Tzu. Who can prevent her? And the question is, have I awakened, or is the butterfly dreaming that she is Chuang Tzu? You tell me who I am! – the butterfly or Chuang Tzu."

They were all at a loss ... what to say? This man goes on finding such absurd things. Millions of people for millions of years have been dreaming, but nobody has raised this question. You have been dreaming, but have you ever raised this question – that when you wake up perhaps it is the beginning of a new dream?

What makes you so certain that you are not dreaming? In the dream you were so certain that you were a butterfly, and now you are so certain that you are Chuang Tzu. There is no difference in certainty. In fact when you are awake the possibility of suspicion is there, you can doubt; but when you are dreaming, there is even no doubt at all, no suspicion, no question mark – you are simply a butterfly.

He said, "Sit down and meditate and find out the answer – who am I?" They looked at each other – how to meditate upon it, how to think about it? It is unthinkable, it is beyond the mind. His closest disciple, Lieh Tzu, had gone out to the nearest village. He returned; he saw the whole scene: Chuang Tzu in tears sitting on his bed, all the disciples with closed eyes, their minds completely stuck.

What can the mind say about it? The question is absurd. He asked one of the disciples who was near the door, "What is the matter? It seems to be really serious! I have never seen such seriousness here. And why is our master crying? Has somebody died or something?"

The disciple said, "He has created a new absurdity. Nobody has died and nothing has happened; he is torturing us and nothing else! Now we have to meditate upon it." And he told him the problem. Lieh Tzu said, "Don't be worried. You meditate; I am coming." He went out, brought a bucket full of ice-cold water and poured it on Chuang Tzu. And Chuang Tzu said laughingly, "If you had been here before you would have saved all these idiots! They are looking so serious, as if they are really thinking. And you would have saved my tears and my misery. Just wait; don't pour the water, it is too cold."

Lieh Tzu said, "Has your problem been solved or not?" Chuang Tzu said, "It is solved – you are my successor!"

It is not a question to be solved by the mind. The mind is absolutely impotent.

Chuang Tzu has hundreds of stories and he must have had a very strange kind of genius – even to invent those stories is not easy – but his teaching was very simple. And those who remained with him, all became enlightened. That is a rare phenomenon. He defeated even his own master Lao Tzu – a few people became enlightened, but most of Lao Tzu's disciples remained in their old ignorance. He defeated Gautama Buddha – a few of his disciples became enlightened, but that was a very small proportion, because he had thousands of disciples and not more than a dozen became enlightened. Chuang Tzu has a rare position in the history of mystics. All his disciples became enlightened ... he would not leave you alone unless you had become enlightened! He was so much after you that finally people decided that it was better to become enlightened. Every day a new torture ... the only way to save yourself was to become enlightened. But his method was very simple, and this poem tells in a very aphoristic way his whole approach.

"Easy is right." Nobody has dared to say it ever. On the contrary, people make the right as difficult as possible. To you, who have all been conditioned by different traditions, the wrong is easy, and the right is arduous. It needs training, it needs discipline, it needs repression, it needs renouncing the world, it needs renouncing the pleasures ...

Lies are easy, truth is difficult – that is the common conditioning of humanity. But Chuang Tzu is certainly a man of tremendous insight. He says, easy is right. Then why have people been making right difficult? All your saints have been making right very difficult. There is a psychology behind it: only the difficult is attractive to your ego. The more difficult is the task, the more the ego feels challenged.

Climbing Everest was difficult; hundreds of people had died before Edmund Hillary reached the top alive. For the whole century groups upon groups of mountaineers had been coming, and when Edmund Hillary reached, there was nothing to be found! Just at the very peak there is not even space enough ... only one person can stand there, on the highest point. He was asked, "What prompted you? Knowing perfectly well that hundreds of mountaineers have lost their lives during 100 years, and not even their bodies have been found … why did you try this dangerous project?"

He said, "I had to try. It was hurting my ego. I am a mountaineer, I love climbing mountains, and it was humiliating that there is Everest and nobody has been able to reach there. It is not a question of finding anything, but I feel so immensely happy."

What is this happiness? You have not found anything! The happiness is that your ego has become more crystallized. You are the first man in the whole history who has reached Everest; now nobody can take your place. Anybody who will reach there will be second, third … but you have made a mark on history; you are the first. You have not found anything, but you have found a deep nourishment for your ego. Perhaps Edmund Hillary himself is not aware of it.

All the religions are making the right difficult, because the difficult is attractive – attractive to the ego. But the ego is not the truth; the ego is not right. Do you see the dilemma? The ego is attracted only towards the difficult. If you want people to become saints you have to make your right, your truth, your discipline very difficult. The more difficult it is, the more egoists will be attracted, almost magnetically pulled.

But the ego is not right. It is the worst thing that can happen to a man. And it cannot deliver to you the right, the truth; it can only make your ego stronger. Chuang Tzu is saying in a simple statement the most pregnant statement: easy is right. Because for the easy, ego has no attraction.

If you are going towards the easy, the ego starts dying. And when there is no ego left, you have arrived to your reality – the right, the truth. And truth and right have to be natural. Easy means natural; you can find them without any effort. Easy is right means natural is right, effortlessness is right, egolessness is right.

"Begin right and you are easy. Continue easy and you are right." They are just two sides of the same coin. If, beginning to live a right life, you find it difficult, then remember, it is not right. If, living the right, your life becomes more and more easy, more and more a let-go, flowing with the stream …

Going against the stream is difficult, but going with the stream is not difficult. So either choose the easiest things in life, the most natural things in life, and you will be right; or if you want to begin the other way, remember the criterion that the right has to produce easiness in you, relaxedness in you.

"Continue easy, and you are right." Never forget for a moment that the difficult is the food for the ego, and the ego is the barrier that makes you blind to see, makes you deaf to hear, makes your heart hard to open, makes it impossible for you to love, to dance, to sing.

Continue easy. Your whole life should be an easy phenomenon. Then you will not be creating the ego. You will be a natural being, just ordinary. And to Chuang Tzu, and to me also, the ordinary is the most extraordinary. The people who are trying to be extraordinary have missed the goal. Just be ordinary, just be nobody.

But all your conditionings are so corrupting; they corrupt you. They say: to be easy is to be lazy, to be ordinary is humiliating. If you don't try for power, for prestige, for respectability, then your life is meaningless – that has been forced into your mind.

Chuang Tzu in these simple statements is taking away all your conditionings. "Continue easy, and you are right." Never for a moment get attracted towards the difficult. It will make you somebody – a prime minister, a president – but it will not make you divine. Easy is divine.

And the last part is something never to be forgotten. "The right way to go easy is to forget the right way" – because even to remember it is an uneasiness. "The right way to go easy is to forget the right way and forget that the going is easy." What is the need of remembering these things? Relax to such a point ... be as natural as the trees and the birds. You will not find in the birds that somebody is a saint and somebody is a sinner; you will not find in the trees that somebody is virtuous and somebody is full of vices. Everything is easy – so easy that you need not remember it. I agree with Chuang Tzu. I would have loved to meet him. If I were given the opportunity to meet one of the mystics of the whole human history, Chuang Tzu would be my choice.

He was very much misunderstood. It is obvious … because he was destroying all the so-called great commandments for being right, and destroying them so easily. He was one of the most natural men the world has seen. He has not given any discipline, he has not given any doctrine, he has not given any catechism. He has simply explained one thing: that if you can be natural and ordinary, just like the birds and the trees, you will blossom, you will have your wings open in the vast sky.

You don't have to be saints. Saints are very tense – more tense than sinners. I have known both, and when there is a choice I will choose the sinners as company rather than the saints. Saints are the worst company, because their eyes are full of judgment about everything: you should do this and you should not do that. And they start dominating you, condemning you, humiliating you, insulting you, because what they are doing is right and what you are doing is not the right thing. They have poisoned your nature so badly that if real criminals have to be found they will be found in your saints, not in your sinners. Your sinners have not done much harm to anybody.

Chuang Tzu says that if you feel any tension, then remember, whatever you are doing is not right. And he is the only man who has given such a beautiful criterion: "Easy is right. Begin right and you are easy. Continue easy, and you are right. The right way to go easy is to forget the right way and forget that the going is easy." Relax into nobodiness. Become part of this relaxed universe – so relaxed that you forget all about easiness and you forget all about rightness. To me, this is enlightenment.

Chuang Tzu's wife died. The emperor came to pay his respects. Chuang Tzu was a great sage, so even the emperor came. He was also a friend; the emperor was a friend to Chuang Tzu, and sometimes he would call Chuang Tzu to his palace to learn his wisdom. Chuang Tzu was just a beggar, but a great sage. The emperor came and he rehearsed in his mind what to say because Chuang Tzu's wife had died. He thought of every good thing to console him, but the moment he saw Chuang Tzu he became very uneasy. Chuang Tzu was singing. He was sitting under a tree playing an instrument, singing loudly. He looked very happy, and just in the morning his wife had died. The emperor became uneasy and he said, "Chuang Tzu, it is bad enough that you are not weeping, but the singing is too much. It is going too far!"

Chuang Tzu asked, "But why should I weep?"

The emperor said, "It seems you have not heard that your wife is dead."

Chuang Tzu said, "Of course, my wife is dead. Why should I weep? If she is dead, she is dead. And I never expected that she was going to live forever. You weep because you expect. I never expected that she was going to live forever. I always knew she was going to die any day, and this day it happened. This was going to happen any day. And any day is as good for death as any other, so why should I not sing? If I cannot sing when there is death, then I cannot sing in life, because life is a continuous death. Every moment death will occur somewhere to someone. Life is a continuous death. If I cannot sing at the moment of death, I cannot sing at all.

"Life and death are not two things. They are one. The moment someone is born, death is born with him. When you are growing in life you are also growing in death, and whatsoever is known as death is nothing but the peak of your so-called life. So why should I not sing? And, moreover, the poor woman has lived so many years with me, so will you not allow me to sing a little in gratitude when she has left? She must go in peace, harmony, music and love. Why should I weep?

"You weep only when you expect and the expected doesn't happen. I never expected that she was going to be here forever. When you do not expect, when you do not desire, you cannot be discontented."

Look at the difference. We go on desiring, then there are failures. Then we try to cultivate contentment. This sutra means that you do not desire and you see also the futility of desire. So the second difference: you cultivate contentment only when you fail. If you succeed, then you are overjoyed. That shows your contentment was false. When you are a failure, you say, "I am contented." When you succeed, you are filled with joy. That is impossible. Behind your contentment, under your contentment, there must have been some sadness. Otherwise, in your success this joy is not possible. If in success you feel happy, then it is impossible not to feel unhappy when you fail.

With a person like Chuang Tzu or a person like Buddha, whether they succeed or fail is immaterial. It is irrelevant. They remain contented. Your false contentment will be broken by your success. You use it only as a center when you are in failure, in misery. When you succeed, you come off the center into the open sky, dancing and jumping, happy and enjoying. This is impossible. That shows that your center was a false one. It was just an emergency arrangement. It was not your nature. The person who is in contentment will not feel any difference between success and failure. He cannot. Now there is no difference. Whatsoever happens he is contented. Whether he succeeds or fails is not his concern, because there is no desire to have a particular result, to have a particular future. Whatsoever happens, his future is liquid. He is ready to absorb it, whatsoever it is.

I remember another anecdote about Chuang Tzu. Whenever someone would say something to him, even before he had said it Chuang Tzu would say, "Good, very good!" This was a habit. So sometimes the situation would become very awkward, because someone would say something which was not good and he would not even hear. He would just say, "Good, very good!" Someone was saying, "My wife has died," and Chuang Tzu said, "Good, very good!" as if he had not heard. Someone would say, "My house has been broken into during the night, burglarized." But Chuang Tzu would say, "Good, very good!"

One day someone said, "Your son has fallen from the tree and broken both his legs." He said, "Good, very good!" So people began to think that he didn't know the meaning of "good" – because if there is nothing bad, if everything is good, then you are crossing the boundaries of language. So the whole village gathered, and they asked him, "Please be kind enough to tell us what you mean by 'good' – because we have been reporting all kinds of things, even misfortunes and deaths have been reported, and you have said 'good'. And this morning your own son has fallen from the tree, both legs broken. He was your help in old age, your only help. He was serving you up until now, and now you will have to serve him. In your extreme old age it is a misfortune, but you said 'good'."

Chuang Tzu said, "Wait! Life is a very complex affair."

And the next day it happened that the country was involved with the neighbouring country, at war, and it was compulsory that every young man be recruited into the military. Only Chuang Tzu's son was left because his legs were crippled. So they said, "You have a very deep insight into things it seems. You said 'good', and it has turned out to be 'good'."

Chuang Tzu said. "Wait! Don't be in a hurry. Life is very complex and things go on happening!"

The son was just engaged to a girl, but the next day the family refused to let her marry him because now there was no hope that he would even be able to walk again; his legs were very much injured. So again the people said, "It seems to be a bad thing after all."

Chuang Tzu said, "Wait! Don't be in a hurry. Life is very patient."

After a week, the girl who was going to be his son's wife, whom the family denied to him, died suddenly. So the villagers came and said again, "What are you doing! You have a very uncanny insight. Did you see that she was going to die?"

But Chuang Tzu went on saying, "Wait! Wait!"

Chuang Tzu had said that everything is good if you do not have any expectation. And life is infinite, but our patience is so small.

Dionysius

Whenever the Eastern scholar by any chance, if at all, comes across a person like Dionysius, he starts thinking that he must have borrowed from the East. That seems to be a tacit assumption: that the East has some monopoly over spirituality. Nobody has any monopoly. East and West cannot make any difference in man's spiritual growth. Jesus could become a buddha in Jerusalem, Lao Tzu could become a buddha in China, Dionysius could become a buddha in Athens. There is no need to borrow from anybody.

Yes, in scientific experimentation we have discovered very recently a strange phenomenon: that whenever one scientist discovers something, almost simultaneously many people all around the earth discover the same thing in different ways. Albert Einstein is reported to have said, "If I had not discovered the theory of relativity, then within two years somebody else was bound to discover it."

Why does it happen that some scientist working somewhere far away in Soviet Russia discovers something almost simultaneously with some other scientist who is working in England or in America or in India or in Japan – not knowing anything of the other, not even being aware of the existence of the other, not knowing that somebody else is also working on the same problem?

Now it is becoming more and more clear that with all the great discoveries, although the initial effort is made by the conscious mind, the ultimate result always comes through the unconscious. And the deepest layer of the unconscious mind is collective. I am different from you as a person, you are different from me as persons – as far as conscious mind is concerned. If you go a little deeper, we are not so different in the unconscious mind. If you go a little deeper still, we come even closer in the collective unconscious.

And the mystics say there is even a little more than the collective unconscious; they call it the universal unconscious. That is the very center. At that center we all meet and we all are one. All the great insights come from that center. It is only a question of who is looking in that direction – he will get the insight first. Otherwise the insight starts happening to many people; they may not be looking at it and therefore they will miss it.

Alan Watts, writing on a small treatise of tremendous beauty, the *Theologia Mystica* of St Dionysius, says that one is tempted, greatly tempted, to think that Dionysius must have visited the East; if not, then some Eastern mystic must have traveled to Athens.

In those days, when Dionysius lived, many Western travelers had started coming to India. With the coming of Alexander the Great many barriers were broken, many bridges were made. And it was not one-sided: Eastern mystics also started traveling towards the West. Even Jain monks went to Alexandria, to Athens, to the farthest corners of the known world. The Jains are referred to in ancient Athenian treatises as "gymnosophists". Sophist means one who is searching for the truth and gymno comes from Jain. "Gymnosophist" is the name for the Jain mystics who had penetrated Athens. There was also trade going on between India and Greece, so with the businessmen, the traders coming and going, there was a great exchange of thoughts.

Alan Watts thinks either Dionysius visited India – because the way he speaks is so Eastern, the insight that he reveals is so Eastern; even his words remind one of the Upanishads – so Watts thinks either he visited the East or somebody from the East or many influences from the East somehow became available to him. But I am not tempted that way at all.

My own experience and understanding is this: that great truths erupt in many places in almost similar ways. Lao Tzu never came to India and nobody from India ever visited Lao Tzu. China and India were divided by the great Himalayan mountains; there was no trade going on between India and China, no communication of any kind. Still, what Lao Tzu says is so similar to the Upanishads, is so synonymous with the teachings of Buddha, that there is a great temptation to believe that there must have been some communication – either Buddha has borrowed from Lao Tzu or Lao Tzu has borrowed from Buddha.

But I say to you, nobody has borrowed from anybody else, they have all drunk from the same source. And when you taste the ocean, whether you taste it on an Indian shore or on the Chinese shore, it makes no difference; it always has the same salty taste. So is truth: it has the same taste, the same flavor, the same fragrance. Maybe in expressing it there is a possibility of a few differences of language, but that does not matter much. Sometimes even those differences are not there.

Dionysius is a Christian, and one of the real Christians. It seems Friedrich Nietzsche was not aware of Dionysius; otherwise he would not have said that the first and the last Christian died on the cross 2,000 years ago. In fact, there have been a few more Christs in the tradition of Christ. Dionysius is one of the most beautiful of them all. Then there is Meister Eckhart, St Francis, Jacob Boehme and a few more – not many, of course, because Christianity became such an organized religion that it became impossible for mystics to exist, or even if they existed they went underground. They had to; there was no other way.

Christianity destroyed all possibilities of mysticism. There were only two ways to avoid being persecuted. One was to go underground or escape to some desert, to some mountains. And the second possibility was to exist as a formal Christian on the surface, use the Christian language, and go on doing your inner work privately. That's what Dionysius did.

You will be surprised to know: he was the first bishop of Athens. He must have been a man of rare intelligence. To remain a bishop of Athens and yet to penetrate the deepest mysteries of life like Buddha, Lao Tzu, Zarathustra, he must have been a man of rare intelligence.

He managed a facade. He deceived the Christian organization.

His treatise was not published while he was alive. He must have managed it in such a way that it was published only when he was dead. If the treatise had been published while he was alive he would have been expelled from the Church, persecuted, tortured. And a man of understanding, a man who is not suicidal in some way, would not like to be persecuted unnecessarily. If it becomes a necessity he accepts the challenge. But he is not looking for it; he is not in some way hankering to be a martyr. He is not suicidal; he is not violent towards himself.

Dionysius is a rare man: living with Christianity and its rigid organization, being a bishop and still being able to reach to the ultimate peaks of consciousness is something worthy of praise. He must have been a very intelligent man; he managed well. He deceived the Vatican, he deceived the popes. After all, he himself was a bishop – he knew all the inside tricks! His treatise is thought to be Christian; it is not Christian at all. It has nothing to do with Christianity. Jesus would have agreed with it, but not the Christian organization.

Kahlil Gibran

Kahlil Gibran is pure music, a mystery such that only poetry can sometimes grasp it, but only sometimes. Centuries have passed; there have been great men but Kahlil Gibran is a category in himself. I cannot conceive that, even in the future, there is a possibility of another man of such deep insight into the human heart, into the unknown that surrounds us.

He has done something impossible. He has been able to bring at least a few fragments of the unknown into human language. He has raised human language and human consciousness as no other man has ever done. Through Kahlil Gibran, it seems all the mystics, all the poets, all creative souls have joined hands and poured themselves.

Although he has been immensely successful in reaching people, still he feels it is not the whole truth, but just a glimpse. But to see the glimpse of truth is a beginning of a pilgrimage that leads you to the ultimate, to the absolute, to the universal.

Another beautiful man, Claude Bragdon has said about Kahlil Gibran, a few beautiful words. He says, "His power came from some great reservoir of spiritual life, else it could not have been so universal and so potent. But the majesty and beauty of the language with which he clothed it were all his own." I have always loved this statement of Bragdon, even though not agreeing with it.

One need not agree with a beautiful flower; one need not agree with the sky full of stars – but one can still appreciate. I make a clear-cut distinction between agreement and appreciation – and a man is civilized if he can make the distinction. If he cannot make the distinction, he's still living in a primitive, uncivilized state of consciousness.

I agree in a sense, because what Bragdon is saying is beautiful; hence, my appreciation. But I cannot agree because what he is saying is simply guesswork. It is not his own experience.

Have you noted? – he says, "His power came from some great reservoir of spirituality, of spiritual life, else it could not have been so universal and so potent." It is rational, logical, but it has no roots in experience. He feels that something beyond the grasp of mind has come through Kahlil Gibran but he is not certain. And he cannot be certain, because it is not his experience. He is immensely impressed by the beautiful language; each word is a poetry unto itself. But he himself is unaware of that great reservoir of spirituality. He himself has not tasted it. He has loved Kahlil Gibran but he has not lived him.

Kahlil Gibran is certainly a great poet, perhaps the greatest that has ever been born on the earth, but he is not a mystic; and there is a tremendous difference between a poet and a mystic. The poet, once in a while, suddenly finds himself in the same space as the mystic. In those rare moments, roses shower over him. On those rare occasions, he is almost a Gautama Buddha – but remember, I'm saying almost.

These rare moments come and go. He's not the master of those rare moments. They come like the breeze and the fragrance and by the time you have become aware – they are gone.

A poet's genius is that he catches those moments in words. Those moments come into your life too. They are free gifts of existence – or in other words, glimpses to provoke in you a search, to come to a moment when this space will become your very life, your blood, your bones, your marrow. You will breathe it, your heart will beat it. You will never be able to lose it, even if you want to.

The poet is for moments a mystic, and the mystic is a poet forever.

But this has always created a very difficult question, and nobody been able to solve it.

I have a humble solution. The problem has been posed again and again, thousands of times all over the world: if the poet gets only glimpses, yet creates so much beauty, so much poetry – words start becoming alive the moment he touches them – why have the mystics not been able to produce the same kind of poetry? They are 24 hours a day, day and night in that creative state, but their words don't carry that beauty. Even the words of Gautama Buddha or Jesus Christ fall very much short of the words of people like Kahlil Gibran, Mikhail Naimy, Rabindranath Tagore. It certainly seems to be strange; because the people who have only moments create so much and the people who have the universal consciousness available to them, waking or sleeping … what happens? Why have they not been able to produce Kahlil Gibrans? And nobody has answered it.

My own experience is that if a beggar finds a gold mine, he will sing and he will dance and he will go mad with joy – but not an emperor.

A poet once in a while becomes the emperor – but only once in a while; that's why he cannot take it for granted. But the mystic is not just for a moment merged with the universal consciousness – he is merged. There is no way of coming back.

Those small glimpses may be translated into words, because they are only dewdrops. But the mystic has become the ocean; hence, silence becomes his song. All words seem so impotent, nothing seems to be capable of bringing his experience into any kind of communication. And the ocean is so vast and he is continuously one with it; naturally, he himself forgets that he is separate.

To create, you have to be there to create. To sing a song, you have to be there. But the mystic has become the song. His presence is his poetry. You cannot print it, you cannot paint it, you can only drink it.

To communicate with a poet is one thing but to be in communion with a mystic is totally different. But it is good to begin with poets, because if you are not able even to absorb dewdrops, the ocean is not for you. Or better to say, you are not for the ocean.

To you, even the dewdrop will appear like a vast ocean.

The real painter dissolves himself into his painting, and the real poet disappears into his poetry. But that kind of creativity is of the mystic – and because the mystic disappears in his creativity, he has no time even to sign his painting, or his poetry. The poets can do that, because for a moment the window opens, they see the beyond, and the window closes.

Kahlil Gibran has written almost 30 books. *The Prophet*, his first, is a jewel; the remaining are rubbish. This is a strange phenomenon – what happened to the man? When he wrote *The Prophet*, he was just young – 21 years of age. One would have thought that now more and more would be coming. And he tried hard; for his whole life he was writing but nothing came even close to the beauty and the truth of *The Prophet*. Perhaps the window never opened again.

A poet is accidentally a mystic. It is just by accident ... a breeze comes, you cannot produce it. And because he became world-famous – this is one book which must have been translated into almost all the languages of the world – he tried hard to do something better, and that's where he failed. It is unfortunate that he never came across a man who could have told him a simple truth: "You had not tried when you created *The Prophet*; it happened. And now you are trying to do it."

It has happened; it is not your doing. You may have been a vehicle. Something that was not yours ... just like a child is born of a mother. The mother cannot create the child, she is simply a passage. *The Prophet* belongs to the category of a very small number of books which are not dependent on your action, your intelligence, on you; on the contrary, they are possible only when you are not, when you allow them to happen, when you don't stand in the way. You are so relaxed that you don't interfere.

It is one of those rarest of books. In it, you will not find Kahlil Gibran – that's the beauty of the book. He allowed the universe to flow through him; he is simply a medium, a passage, just a hollow bamboo which does not hinder the flute player.

In my experience, books like *The Prophet* are holier than your so-called holy books. And because these books are authentically holy, they have not created a religion around themselves. They don't give you any ritual, they don't give you any discipline, they don't give you any commandments. They simply allow you to have a glimpse of the same experience which happened to them.

The whole experience cannot come into words, but something … perhaps not the whole rose, but a few petals. They are enough proof that a rose exists. Your window just has to be open, so a breeze sometimes can bring petals.

Those petals coming through a breeze into your being are really invitations of the unknown. God is calling you for a long pilgrimage. Unless that pilgrimage is made, you will remain meaningless, dragging somehow, but not really living. You will not have laughter in your heart.

Kahlil Gibran avoids his own name by creating a fictitious name, Almustafa. Almustafa is the prophet. Kahlil Gibran, in the name of Almustafa, is giving the very essence of mysticism. He is not preaching any religion in particular, he is preaching religion as such.

Almustafa is just a name. It is Kahlil Gibran who is speaking through him – and for a special reason. He could have spoken directly in his own name; there was no need for Almustafa to be a medium. But Kahlil Gibran does not want to create a religion, although whatever he has said is the fundamental religiousness. To avoid it … because in the name of religion so much inhumanity to human beings has been done, so much bloodshed …

Millions of people have been killed. Thousands have been burned alive. The moment any religion becomes organized and crystallized it becomes a danger to all that is valuable in life. Then it is no longer the path to God, it becomes an excuse for war.

Kahlil Gibran keeps himself hidden behind Almustafa so people don't start worshiping him, so people don't continue the ugly past. Rather than saying directly what he wants to say, he has created a device, "Almustafa". Because of Almustafa, his book is not counted as a holy book – although it is one of the most holy books in the world. Compared to it, all other holy books will appear unholy.

He created Almustafa so that his book would be taken as fiction, as poetry. This is his compassion, and this is his greatness. You can look in all the holy scriptures; you will not find words so alive that they go directly like arrows into your heart. And you will find much that is inhuman, unworthy of remaining in those holy scriptures. But man is so blind – just the small fiction of Almustafa, and people have forgotten a simple fact: that these truths cannot be asserted unless you have experienced them, unless they are your own.

George Gurdjieff

George Gurdjieff is one of the most significant masters of this age.

He is unique in many ways – nobody has said things in the contemporary world the way Gurdjieff has said them. He is almost like another Bodhidharma or Chuang Tzu, apparently absurd but in reality giving great indications towards the liberation of human consciousness. He often used to say, "You are in prison." Sometimes he was even deeper into the reality, and instead of saying, "You are in prison," he would say, "You are the prison." That is truer.

If you wish to get out of prison – or better to say, if you don't want to be a prison – the first thing you must do is realize that you are in prison ... or you are the prison. This is something to be always remembered as one of the first principles for any seeker of truth.

The tendency of the human mind is to deny those things which are ugly, to hide those things which he does not want others to know – to hide in such a way, in such depths of the unconscious that even he himself becomes unaware of them. This way he maintains his superficial personality.

Gurdjieff had a story about it ...

There was a magician who used to live in faraway deep forests, and he had many sheep because that was his only food. In those deep forests he was keeping all those sheep just to kill them every day, one by one. Naturally, the sheep were very afraid of the man, and they used to run into the forest, being afraid that any day can be their day. Their friends are gone, there is no reliability ... tomorrow they may be gone. Out of fear they used to go far away, deep into the forest. And to find them was a tedious job every day.

Finally, the magician did a trick. He hypnotized all the sheep, and told every sheep, "You are an exception; everybody may be killed but you can never be killed. You are no ordinary sheep; you have a divine privilege." To some he said, "You are not sheep at all; you are lions, you are tigers, you are wolves. Only sheep are killed. You need not hide yourself in the forest; that is very embarrassing, because a lion hiding himself in the forest in the fear that he will be killed … only sheep are killed." And in this way, he managed to hypnotize all the sheep in different ways.

He even said to a few sheep, "You are men, human beings, and human beings don't kill each other. You are just like me. Never be afraid and never escape out of fear." Since that day, no sheep escaped and hid in the forest, although they all saw every day that one sheep was being killed, slaughtered. But naturally everybody thought, "That must be a sheep; I am a tiger, a lion, a human being. I am special and exceptional, I have a divine privilege …" So many different stories he put in their minds.

Gurdjieff says that unless you realize the first thing – that you are in prison, that you are the prison – then there is no hope for freedom. If you already believe that you are free, you are a hypnotized sheep which believes himself to be a lion – exceptional, there is no need to be afraid – which even believes he is a human being. He goes on seeing other sheep being killed, and still remains in a hypnotized state, never being aware of his actuality. To be free, if you already know that you are free, there is no problem.

All the religions together, perhaps unintentionally, have created a tremendous hypnotic state. People believe they have immortal souls. I am not saying that they don't have, I am simply saying that they don't know what they are believing. And because they believe they have an immortal soul, they never discover that they already have it. They have been told, "You are the very kingdom of God" … and it is so comfortable and so consoling to believe. But then there is no way to seek and search and find whether your hypothetical belief has any truth in it, or is just a hypnotic trick used by the society to keep you unafraid of death, to keep you unafraid of disease, old age, to keep you unafraid of your loneliness.

Your god may be just a psychological hypnosis. It is not your discovery. That is true – that much is absolutely true. It has been implanted in your mind, and because you go on believing in it, your belief prevents any adventure in seeking the truth.

Ordinarily, you have been told continually that unless you believe, you will not find. But the truth is just the contrary. Belief is a barrier, it is not a bridge. Those who believe never find, because they never even begin the search; there is no need.

You are in prison and you think you are free.

You are in chains but you think they are ornaments. You are a slave but you have been told that you are humble, that you are simple, that this is the way a religious person should be. You are surrounded by many hypnotic strategies developed by society down the ages. And those hypnotic strategies are the root cause of your ignorance, of your misery, of your unenlightened state.

Hence the first thing to realize is that you are in prison. The moment you recognize that you are in prison, you cannot tolerate the prison. Nobody can tolerate it; it goes against human dignity. You will start finding ways to get out of it. You will start finding people who have already got out of it. You may start seeking and searching for outside help beyond the walls, because there are people beyond the walls ready with every kind of help. But they are absolutely helpless if you believe that you are living in absolute freedom.

If you believe this imprisonment is your home, then of course it is absolute nonsense even to think of getting rid of it. The wall that keeps you a prisoner, you think is a protection. Then there is no question of making a hole in the wall and getting out, or finding a ladder, or taking some help from the outside. A rope can be thrown from the outside, a ladder can be arranged from the outside, but this is possible only if the basic thing, that you are in prison, is recognized. George Gurdjieff was consistently insisting, "This is a basic realization. Without it, there is no progress towards enlightenment. If you think you are free, you can't escape."

George Gurdjieff helped more people in this century than anybody else, because he created a great longing: "Don't die before you have created a soul; otherwise nothing will survive the death. Crystallize your being so that death cannot destroy it. But you are not born with it, you have to create it."

The idea of all the religions, although true, has not been helpful; it has become a hindrance. Gurdjieff's compassion is great. All the religions were against him, obviously, because that is the one point they all agree on – that everybody is born with a soul. But Gurdjieff's point is more psychological, and more effective in creating liberation. He says you are just empty, and you will remain empty unless you make the effort, with a determined will, to create a center within you. There is possibility, potential, but you have to make it an actuality.

His insight was great.

And since Gurdjieff, people have forgotten it completely. He was alive just a few decades ago and just within a few years people have forgotten the great teacher who was compassionate enough even to lie, just to make you shocked; just to create an opening in you so that you can start searching whether what all the religions have been saying has any truth in it or not.

The first thing he says is to realize you are in prison. The first thing that can also be said is, you have to realize that you are not yet. You have to be. You are a seed, but you have to find the right soil, and nobody else can do it for you. If you go on depending on priests and your so-called saints, you will miss this great opportunity that life has given to you. And one does not know whether a second chance is being given or not. It has to be made emphatically clear to you that there is a possibility – once missed, you have missed it forever.

Gurdjieff created a great turmoil in a few intelligent people, and he put them to great work in finding themselves. I don't agree with George Gurdjieff as far as his methods are concerned, but as far as this statement is concerned I agree totally. It is simply a psychological fact.

George Gurdjieff's father died and at that time he was only nine years old. The father was poor but a very integrated man, a man of tremendous awareness. He called Gurdjieff and said, "Listen. You are too young to understand what I am saying, but remember it. Soon

74

you will be able to understand it, and if you can start acting accordingly, start acting so that you don't forget. I don't have anything else to give to you; no money, no house, no land." He was a nomad. "I am handing you over to my friends, but remember, this is the only treasure that I can give you as an inheritance. And listen carefully; these are the last words of your father – his whole life's experience."

A nine-year-old boy … he came close to listen to the old father and the father said, "It is a very simple thing: if somebody insults you, listen silently, carefully, in detail to what he is saying – what are the implications. And then tell the person, 'I am grateful that you have taken so much interest in me. After 24 hours I will come and reply to you. I cannot help it, because my dying father has made it a condition to me that only after 24 hours' consideration am I allowed to answer.'"

And in his own old age, Gurdjieff said to his disciples, "This simple principle helped me tremendously, because after 24 hours who remains angry? And after considering 24 hours, either one finds he is right – and if he is right there is no need to bother, it is better to change yourself – or he is wrong. Then too there is no need to be bothered. It is his problem, not your problem."

A man who is fully awakened remains undefiled by whatsoever he does, because it is a response. It is a pure reflection from a mirror, with no judgment. It does not come from the past, it comes from the present consciousness. But anything that comes from your past experiences is going to create a chain for you.

Gurdjieff has only one thing to teach to his disciples and that is not to be identified. His whole school, all his techniques, methods, situations, are based on one single base, and that base is: not to be identified.

You are crying; when you are crying, you have become one with the crying. There is nobody to watch it, there is nobody to see it; be alert and aware of it – you are lost in crying. You have become the tears and the red, swollen eyes and your heart is in a crisis. Teachers like Gurdjieff, when they say not to be identified, they say, "Cry, nothing is wrong in it, but stand by the side and look at it – don't be identified." And it is a wonderful experience if you can stand by the side. Cry, let the body cry, let the tears flow, don't suppress it because suppression helps nobody, but stand by the side and watch.

This can be done – because your inner being is a witness, it is never a doer. Whenever you think it is a doer there is an identification. It is never a doer. You can walk the whole earth – your inner being never walks a single step. You can dream millions of dreams – your inner being never dreams a single dream. All movements are on the surface. Deep in the depth of your being there is no movement. All movements are on the periphery, just like a wheel moves, but at the center nothing moves. At that center everything remains as it is, and on the center the wheel moves.

Remember the center! Watch your behavior, your actions, your identifications, and a distance is created; by and by a distance comes into existence – the watcher and the doer become two. You can see yourself laughing, you can see yourself crying, you can see yourself walking, eating, making love; you can act many things, whatsoever is going on around – and you remain the seer. You don't jump and become one with whatsoever you are seeing.

This is the trouble. Whatsoever happens you start saying: you are hungry, you say, "I am hungry" – you have become identified with the hunger. But just look inside; are you hunger, or is hunger happening to you? Are you hunger or are you simply aware of the hunger happening in the body? You cannot be hunger; otherwise, when the hunger has disappeared, where will you be? When you have eaten well and the belly is full and you are satiated, where will you be if you are hunger? Evaporated? No, then immediately you become the satiety. Before the hunger disappears a new identification has to be created; you become the satiety.

You were a child and you thought you were a child; now where are you because you are no more a child? You have become a young man or you have become old – who are you now? Again you are identified with youth or old age.

The innermost being is just like a mirror. Whatsoever comes before it, it mirrors, it simply becomes a witness. Disease comes or health, hunger or satiety, summer or winter, childhood or old age, birth or death – whatsoever happens, happens before the mirror, it never happens TO the mirror.

This is non-identification, this is cutting the root, the very root – to become a mirror.

❖

Gurdjieff had many exercises. One exercise was to deny the mechanism sometimes. You are hungry: just deny and let your body suffer. You be just calm and quiet, and remember that the body is hungry. Don't suppress it; don't force it not to be hungry. It is hungry; you know. But at the same time say to it, "I am not going to fulfill this hunger today. Be hungry, suffer! Now, I am not going to move today in this supplied groove. I will remain aloof."

And, suddenly, if you can do this, you begin to feel a gap. The body is hungry, but somewhere there is a distance between you and it. If you try to occupy your mind, then you have missed the point. If you go to the temple and begin to do kirtan and singing just to forget the hunger, then you have missed the point. Let the body be hungry. Don't occupy your mind to escape from hunger. Remain hungry, but just tell the body, "Today I am not going to fall in the trap." You remain hungry, you suffer.

There are persons who are doing fasting, but meaninglessly because whenever they fast they try to occupy the mind so that the hunger should not be known and should not be felt. If the hunger is not felt, the whole point is missed! Then you are playing tricks. Let the hunger be there in its totality, in its intensity. Let it be there; don't escape from it. Let the fact of it be there, present, and remain aloof and tell the body, "Today I am not going to give you anything." There is neither conflict nor suppression nor any escape.

If you can do this, then suddenly you become aware of a gap. Your mind asks for something. For example, someone has become angry. He is angry with you, and the mind begins to react, to be angry. Just tell the mind, "I am not going to fall in the trap this time." Be aloof.

Let the anger be there in the mind, but be aloof. Don't cooperate, don't be identified, and you will feel that anger is somewhere else. It surrounds you, but it is not in you, it doesn't belong to you. It is just like smoke around you. It goes on, goes on, and waits for you to come and cooperate.

There will be every temptation. This is what is really meant by temptation. Mm? No devil is there to tempt you. Your own mind tempts you, because that's the most convenient way to be and to behave. Convenience is the temptation; convenience is the devil. The mind will say, "Be angry!" The situation is there and the mechanism is just on. Always, whenever this situation was there, you have been angry, so the mind supplies you again with the same reaction.

As far as it goes it is good because the mind makes you ready to do something you have always been doing; but sometimes just stand off, off the track, and tell the mind, "Okay, anger is there outside. Someone is angry with me. You are supplying me with an old reaction, a stereotyped reaction, but this time I am not going to cooperate. I will just stand here and observe and see what happens." Suddenly the whole situation changes.

If you don't cooperate the mind falls dead, because it is your cooperation which gives it dynamism, energy. It is your energy, but you only become aware when it is used by the mind. Don't give it any cooperation, and the mind will just fall down as if without a backbone – just a dead snake with no life. It will be there, and for the first time you will become aware of a certain energy in you which doesn't belong to the mind but belongs to you.

This energy is pure energy, and with this energy one can move into the unknown. Really, this energy moves into the unknown if it is not associated with the mind. If it is associated with the mind, then it moves into the known. If it moves into the known, then it takes the shape of desire. If it moves into the unknown, then it takes the shape of desirelessness. Then there is sheer movement – a play of energy, a sheer dance of energy, an overflowing energy moving into the unknown.

❖

Gurdjieff has written three books – only one was published in his lifetime – and his writing is a nightmare. I don't think anybody who is not as mad as I am is going to read his book, *All and Everything*. Yes, it is all and everything! But 1,000 pages of all and everything … He himself was suspicious about whether anybody could understand it or not. And how long he took! He took years to write it, and his way of writing was also strange.

He would be sitting in a cafe in Paris, where people were coming and going. That was really a method. If you sit in the Himalayas and you write something, that's nothing; it doesn't show that you are writing with full awareness. You may have fallen asleep and gone on writing; you may be dreaming and writing – because there is no disturbance. So all the writing Gurdjieff did was in different cafes in Paris where much was going on: music, dance, customers coming, shouting, talking … everything was going on. And cafes, particularly in Paris, are meeting places of artists and poets, who are all argumentative. He was sitting in the middle of such a crowd, writing *All and Everything*.

It was a method on Gurdjieff's part. His disciples said, "You can find a better place – you have a beautiful place outside Paris." His commune was in a beautiful place. "There, in silence, you can write. You come from the commune to sit in these crowded cafes where nobody has ever written books before; at least religious books have never been written in such circumstances." But he insisted on writing there. And his writing was such that he would write one chapter, then his disciples would read it. One disciple would read, and Gurdjieff would watch the other disciples: what impact was it having? How much deeper … ? No book had been written this way.

If they were understanding it too easily, then Gurdjieff had to change it because that meant, "If these idiots can understand it, then it is not worth printing." It took him 20 or 30 years, working continually; again he would write the chapter, again it would be read. Again somebody would be yawning, somebody would be sleeping, and he would have to change it. If it created yawning, if it created sleep, then what was the point of writing it? Again and again, hundreds of times, a single chapter was rewritten, and the disciples were tired of reading the same chapter again and again.

In this way he wrote 1,000 pages, but still he was not sure that anybody was going to get it, its meaning. So he told the publisher, "The first hundred pages should be cut and the remaining 900 pages should remain uncut, with a note: 'You can read 100 pages. If you still feel ready to go ahead, then you can cut the remaining pages; otherwise you can return the book and take your money back' – just a sample of 100 pages."

It is a well-known fact that almost all the books that were sold came back. Not even 100 pages could people read. And the publisher was at a loss, but there was no question: the money was given by Gurdjieff, so there was no question, it was his publication. He said, "This is nothing to do with you. Whatever your service charge is, you can have it, but this is how my book is going to be. Unless a person reads 100 pages, he is not qualified to have it. After reading 100 pages, if he is ready to open the rest … once you open the remaining 900 pages, even a single page, then the book cannot be returned."

And he was costing the book with no reason – no rhyme, no reason. There was no price printed on it: the price varied according to the customer. That was a great idea of Gurdjieff's. From one person he would ask $1,000; to somebody else he would give it free. It was according to the customer – the price was not to be according to the book.

That man always had some good ideas. From a man who is really into the book you should not ask for money. The book has to be given as a gift; he deserves it. And from somebody who has too much money, and is going to waste it anyhow in Monte Carlo or in some other gambling place, why not ask $10,000? And there are people who will purchase it only if it is $10,000; otherwise it is below them – it is not worthwhile.

His disciples were continually asking, "Books have prices; you can fix any price. But this seems to be strange, that you are sitting in the bookshop, and you judge the customer. Are you selling the book or purchasing the customer?" And the book is really written in such a way … No other book has ever been written like that – and I hope no other book is ever written again that way.

Gurdjieff makes strange words, mixing many languages. He knew many languages, nomadic languages which don't have alphabets even. You cannot find dictionaries of them because those languages don't have any dictionary, they don't have any alphabet. They are only dialect, not languages; they are only spoken. And one word does not mean one language: one word means two or three languages joined together. And a long word may run a full sentence – one word! He is really taxing you as much as he can – your patience, your intelligence – but if you can go through the whole book it is really paying: slowly you start getting the knack of his almost impossible words.

When you come across them again and again in different places you can start feeling a certain meaning. You may not be able to say what it is but you start having a sense of it. And if you go through the whole book you are absolutely certain what it is about although you cannot say, because it is only a feeling that it has left within you. His whole effort is somehow to bypass your intellect. Intellectually, you cannot move even one paragraph into it. Your intellect will say, "Stop! This is nonsense." And it is nonsense as far as intellect is concerned.

When, for the first time, P. D. Ouspensky was allowed to be brought to George Gurdjieff – one of Gurdjieff's inner circle of disciples had been trying for months, saying that he wanted to bring a friend. Finally he was given permission. On a cold night in Russia – the snow was falling – Ouspensky, with great excitement, thousands of questions and words passing through his mind … he was a world-famous man, one of the most significant mathematicians of his time. And as far as writing is concerned I don't see anybody comparable to him; he writes magically. His books were already translated into many languages. And nobody knew Gurdjieff; just a small group of 20 people was all that he had. Ouspensky was thinking that this was the same way that he had been introduced into other societies, clubs, meetings ... but this was something totally different.

By dim candlelight Gurdjieff was sitting looking at the floor, and 20 people around him were sitting in the same posture looking at the floor. These two also joined in, and Ouspensky – seeing everybody, what they were doing ... neither was he introduced nor was anything done. The man who had brought him simply sat in the posture and started looking at the floor.

Ouspensky, thinking that perhaps this was the way, also sat in the same posture and started looking at the floor. But whatever he would do his mind was working: "What am I doing here? And he has brought me to introduce me to George Gurdjieff. This is the fellow, it seems, who is sitting in the middle; but he has not even looked at me. And what are they searching for on the floor? There is nothing – a clean floor. And all the 20 are just sitting!"

Minutes passed – and minutes seemed like hours. A silent night, just the flickering light of a small candle, and the sound of the snow falling outside ... And those people went on sitting. Half an hour passed, and his mind was running like mad: "What is happening, and what am I doing here?"

At that moment Gurdjieff looked at him and said, "Don't be worried. Soon you will be sitting here with these people in the same way, without disturbance. They have learned how to sit with a master ... to sit in such a way that the consciousnesses start merging and melting into each other. Twenty-one people are not sitting here, just 21 bodies and one soul, and no thought. But it will take time for you. Forgive me for making you wait for half an hour; it must have seemed to you as if days passed.

"Now take this paper, go to the other room. On one side write what you know. On the other side write what you do not know. And remember that whatever you write down as knowing, we will never discuss; that is finished. You know it and it is none of my business to interfere in it. What you do not know, that will be the only part that I will teach you."

With trembling hands – for the first time Ouspensky became aware of thinking about what he knows. He has written about God, and he has written about heaven and hell, and he has written about the soul and the transmigration of the soul – but does he KNOW?

He went into the other room and sat there with the paper and the pencil. And as he checked in his mind what he knows, what he does not know – for the first time in his whole life he was checking it; otherwise nobody bothers about what one knows, what one does not know. And after a few minutes he came out with the empty paper, and he said, "I do not know anything. You will have to teach me everything."

Gurdjieff said, "But you have written so many books. I have seen your books and I did not think that a man who knows nothing could write so well."

Ouspensky said, "Just forgive me. I am not acquainted with the way you work, but within a few minutes you have made me aware of my utter ignorance. And I want to begin from the very scratch. Forgive me for those books. They were written certainly in sleep, because now I can see I don't know anything about God. I have read about God but that is not knowing. Just one thing I want to know: what is happening here?"

And Gurdjieff said, "This is a way of creating hollow bamboos. All these people are waiting here to become empty. When they become empty, that is their entrance to the school. This is just outside the school, a school is inside. When they become empty, when I am satisfied that they are empty, they will be taken in. We are not here to teach you anything. We are here to help you to know. We will create situations in which you yourself come to know."

The Westerners came like a fashion. To be with Gurdjieff was fashionable; they came, and after a few days they left him – because to be with him was not an easy job. He was a difficult man, and very irrational in his methods; but his methods are very valid under his system.

So your logic may think that it is absolutely wrong. For example, to Bennett he said, "Today you dig a trench 20 feet long, 4 feet deep, 2 feet wide, non-stop." Not even a coffee break, no food. "You cannot go anywhere, not even to the toilet. You have to dig the ditch non-stop."

So he tried hard: "The quicker it is done, the better, so I am freed." By the evening it was complete. Gurdjieff came and he said, "Good. Now fill it up exactly the same as it was before you started digging. Then you will be free."

He said, "My god, this is stupid. If it was to be filled exactly as it was, then it was exactly as it was in the morning. Why this whole torture?" The logical mind cannot understand it.

But Bennett remained with him a long time, and understood a little bit later on what he was doing – because he felt it himself. When he came to a point digging the ditch where he felt so tired that it seemed he would fall down, suddenly at that very moment there was a great rush of energy, a fresh energy became available. And he was surprised – from where? He had not even taken his tea. And with this fresh energy he started digging again.

By the evening he was exhausted, was again on the verge of falling down, and then a second release within his own being – the strongest that he had ever felt in his whole life. But unless you listen to his inner experience, the exercise seems to be absolutely absurd. No sane person is going to remain around Gurdjieff if he has to do such a thing.

Only later on when Bennett was lying down in his bed – he could not sleep the whole night because the second release of energy was so much that it kept him awake, it wanted to do something – he said, "This is absolute madness. The whole day I have been doing. I have never done such work. I am a writer, not a gravedigger."

Next day he asked Gurdjieff. He said, "That's what I wanted you to understand, that there are layers of energy in you. The first layer is the routine daily work. It is enough for your routine daily work. If you go beyond it, you will come to a point where you will feel exhausted, almost feeling that you will die if you continue; but that is the point to continue, because only then will the second layer start functioning.

"It functions only when you are stubborn enough to provoke it, to challenge it to function. That is your emergency layer. You are tired and you are going to sleep and your house catches fire, and suddenly all tiredness is gone and the whole night you are putting the fire out, and you don't feel tired at all. The emergency layer has taken over.

"And the third layer is the cosmic layer, which is inexhaustible; once you have touched it, you know it, and you can reach it. Then you can work miracles – which will look like miracles to others, but not to you because you know that you have these possible layers."

Almost everybody dies working in the first layer.

So Gurdjieff has a system of his own which is not of the routine, traditional religions – they don't have anything. And he should not be judged by other people's criteria; he should be judged by his own criteria. So first try to understand his system and then judge – if you are bent upon judging.

He was one of the most misunderstood men in the world, for the simple reason that everybody was judging according to his prejudiced mind, and here was a man who was trying to bring a secret doctrine into the open for the first time; but he could not succeed.

He failed utterly, not because of himself – you cannot conceive a better man than him. But the thick skulls of the mediocre men who inhabit the earth are really too thick.

Heraclitus

Heraclitus is really beautiful. Had he been born in India, or in the East, he would have been known as a buddha. But in the Greek context, he was a stranger, an outsider. He is known in Greece not as an enlightened person but as Heraclitus the Obscure, Heraclitus the Dark, Heraclitus the Riddling. Aristotle, the father of Greek philosophy and of Western thought, didn't think that Heraclitus was a philosopher at all. Aristotle said, "At the most he is a poet," but even that was difficult for him to concede. So later on he said in other works, "There must be some defect in Heraclitus' character, something wrong biologically; that's why he talks in such obscure ways, and talks in paradoxes." Aristotle thought he was a little eccentric, a little mad – and Aristotle dominates the whole Western mind. If Heraclitus had been accepted, the whole history of the West would have been totally different. But he was not understood at all. He became more and more separate from the main current of Western thinking and the Western mind.

Heraclitus was like Gautama Buddha or Lao Tzu. The Greek soil was absolutely not good for him. He would have been a great tree in the East: millions would have profited, millions would have found the way through him. But for Greeks he was just outlandish, eccentric, something foreign, alien; he didn't belong to them. That's why his name has remained just on the side, in a dark corner; by and by he has been forgotten.

At the moment when Heraclitus was born, precisely at that moment, humanity reached a peak, a moment of transformation. It happens with humanity just as with an individual: there are moments when changes happen. Every seven years the body changes, and it goes on changing – if you live for 70 years, then your total biophysical system will change ten times. And if you can use those gaps when the body changes, it will be very easy to move into meditation.

For example, at 14 for the first time sex becomes important. The body goes through a biochemical change, and if at that moment you can be introduced into the dimension of meditation, it will be very, very easy to move because the body is not fixed, the old pattern has gone and the new has yet to come in – there is a gap. At the age of 21, again deep changes happen, because every seven years the body completely renovates itself: all the old cells drop and the new cells come in. At the age of 35 again it happens, and this goes on. Every seven years your body comes to a point where the old goes and the new settles – and there is a transitory period. In that transitory period everything is liquid. If you want some new dimension to enter into your life, that is precisely the moment.

In the same way exactly it happens also in the history of humanity as a whole. Every 25 centuries there comes a peak – and if you can use that moment, you can easily become enlightened. It will not be so easy in other times because at that peak the river itself is flowing in that direction; everything is fluid, nothing is fixed.

Twenty-five centuries ago Gautama Buddha and Mahavira the Jain were born in India; in China, Lao Tzu and Chuang Tzu; in Iran, Zarathustra, and in Greece, Heraclitus. They are the peaks. Never before were such peaks attained, or if they were attained they are not part of history … because history starts with Jesus.

You don't know what happened 25 centuries ago. Again the moment is coming, we are again in a fluid state: the old is meaning-less, the past doesn't have any significance for you, the future is uncertain – the gap is here. And again humanity will achieve a peak, the same peak as there was in Heraclitus' time. If you are a little aware, you can use this moment – when things are liquid, transfor-mation is easy. When things are fixed, then transformation is difficult.

Heraclitus is a really rare flowering, one of the most penetrating souls, one of those souls who become like Everest, the highest peak of the Himalayas. Try to understand him. It is difficult; that's why he is called Heraclitus the Obscure. He is not obscure, but to understand him is difficult; to understand him you will need a different type of being – that is the problem. So it is easy to categorize him as obscure and then forget him.

There are two types of people. If you want to understand Aristotle you don't need any change in your being, you simply need some information. A school can provide information about logic, philosophy; you can collect some intellectual understanding and you can understand Aristotle. You need not change to understand him, you need only a few more additions to your knowledge. The being remains the same, you remain the same. You need not have a different plane of consciousness; that is not the requirement. Aristotle is clear. If you want to understand him, a little effort is enough; anybody of average mind and intelligence will understand him. But to understand Heraclitus is going to be rough terrain, difficult, because whatsoever you collect as knowledge will not be of much help; just a cultivated head won't be of any help. You will need a different quality of being, and that is difficult. You will need a transformation. Hence, he is called obscure.

When Heraclitus is talking he looks as if he is riddling, he looks as if he is enjoying riddles, because he talks in paradoxes.

All those who have known always talk in paradoxes. There is something to it – they are not riddling, they are very simple. But what can they do? If life itself is paradoxical, what can they do? Just to avoid paradoxes you can create neat and clean theories, but they will be false, they will not be true to life. Aristotle is very neat, clean; he looks like a man-managed garden. Heraclitus looks like riddles – he is a wild forest.

With Aristotle there is no trouble; he has avoided the paradox, he has made a neat and clean doctrine – it appeals. You will be scared to face Heraclitus because he opens the door of life, and life is paradox-ical. Buddha is paradoxical, Lao Tzu is paradoxical; all those who have known are bound to be paradoxical. What can they do? If life itself is paradoxical, they have to be true to life. And life is not logical. It is a *logos*, but it is not logic. It is a cosmos, it is not a chaos – but it is not logic.

The word *logos* has to be understood because Heraclitus will use it. And the difference between *logos* and logic also has to be understood. Logic is a doctrine about what is true, and *logos* is truth itself. *Logos* is existential, logic is not existential; logic is intellectual, theoretical. Try to understand. If you see life you will say there is death also. How can you avoid death? If you look at life, it is implied. Every moment of life is also a moment of death; you cannot separate them. It becomes a riddle.

Life and death are not two separate phenomena; they are two faces of the same coin, two aspects of the same coin. If you penetrate deeply you will see that life is death and death is life. The moment you are born, you have started dying. And if this is so, then when you die you will start living again. If death is implied in life, then life will be implied in death. They belong to each other, they are complementary.

Life and death are just like two wings or two legs: you cannot move only with the right leg or the left leg. In life you cannot be a rightist or a leftist, you have to be both together. With doctrine you can be a rightist, you can be a leftist. Doctrine is never true to life and cannot be, because doctrine, of necessity, needs to be clean, neat, clear, and life is not that – life is vast.

Somewhere, one of the greatest poets of the world, Whitman, has said, "I contradict myself because I am vast."

Through logic you will attain to a very tiny mind – you cannot be vast. If you are afraid of contradiction you cannot be vast. Then you will have to choose, then you will have to suppress, then you will have to avoid the contradiction, then you will have to hide it – but by your hiding, can it disappear? By just not looking at death, are you going to not die?

You can avoid death, you can have your back towards it, you can forget completely about it ... That's why we don't talk about death; it is not good manners. We don't talk about it, we avoid it. Death happens every day, everywhere it is happening, but we avoid it. The moment a man dies we are in a hurry to be finished with him. We make our graveyards outside of the town so nobody goes there. And there also we make graves with marble and write beautiful lines on them. We go and put flowers on the grave. What are you doing? You are trying to decorate it a little.

In the West, how to hide death has become a profession. There are professionals who help you to avoid it, to make the dead body beautiful, as if it is still alive. What are you doing? Can this help in any way? Death is there. You are headed towards the graveyard; wherever you put it makes no difference – you will reach there. You are already on the way, you are standing in the queue waiting for the moment, just waiting in the queue to die. Where can you escape to from death?

But logic tries to be clear, and just to be clear it avoids. It says life is life, death is death – they are separate. Aristotle says A is A, it is never B. That became the foundation stone of all Western thought: avoid the contradiction – love is love, hate is hate; love is never hate. This is foolish because every love implies hate, has to; that's how nature is. You love a person and you hate the same person, you have to; you cannot avoid it. If you try to avoid it everything will become false. That's why your love has become false: it is not true, it is not authentic. It cannot be sincere, it is a facade.

Why is it a facade? – because you are avoiding the other. You say, "You are my friend and a friend cannot be an enemy. And you are my enemy, you cannot be my friend." But these are two aspects of the same coin – the enemy is a hidden friend, and the friend is a hidden enemy. The other aspect is hidden, but it is there. But it will be too much for you. If you see both it will be unbearable. If you see the enemy in the friend you will not be able to love him. If you see the friend in the enemy you will not be able to hate him. The whole life will become a riddle.

Heraclitus is called "the Riddler." He is not, he is true to life. Whatsoever it is, he simply reports it. He has no doctrine about life, he is not a system-maker – he is simply a mirror. Whatsoever life is, he represents it. Your face changes, the mirror represents it; you are loving, the mirror represents it; next moment you become hateful, the mirror represents it. The mirror is not riddling, it is true.

Aristotle is not like a mirror, he is like a dead photograph. It doesn't change, it doesn't move with life. That's why Aristotle says there is some defect in this man Heraclitus, some defect in his very character. For Aristotle mind should be clear, systematic, rational; logic should be the goal of life and you should not mix the opposites. But who is mixing them? Heraclitus is not mixing them. They are there, mixed. Heraclitus is not responsible for them. And how can you separate them if they are mixed in life itself? Yes, in your books you can try, but your books will be false. A logical statement is basically going to be false because it cannot be a life statement. And a life statement is going to be illogical because life exists through contradictions.

Illness is not bad: it is through illness that you regain health. Everything fits in the harmony – that's why Heraclitus is called the Riddler. Lao Tzu would have understood him deeply, but Aristotle could not understand him. And, unfortunately, Aristotle became the source of Greek thought. And Greek thought, even more unfortunately, became the whole base of the Western mind.

What is the message of Heraclitus, the deepest message? Understand so you can follow.

He does not believe in things, he believes in processes – process is God to him. And if you watch closely, you will see that things don't exist in the world; everything is a process. In fact to use the word "is" is existentially wrong, because everything is becoming. Nothing is in a state of isness, nothing!

You say, "This is a tree." By the time you say it, it has grown; your statement is already false. The tree is never static, so how can you use the word "is"? It is always becoming, becoming something else. Everything is growing, moving, in a process. Life is movement. It is like a river – always moving. Says Heraclitus, "You cannot step in the same river twice," because by the time you come to step into it the second time, it has moved.

It is a flow. Can you meet the same person twice? Impossible! You were here yesterday morning also – but am I the same? Are you the same? Both rivers have changed. You may be here again tomorrow, but you will not find me; somebody else will be here.

Life is changing. "Only change is eternal," says Heraclitus – only change never changes. Everything else changes. He believes in a permanent revolution. Everything is in revolution. It is how it is there. To be means to become. To remain where you are means to move; you cannot stay, nothing is static. Even the hills, the Himalayas, are not static; they are moving, moving fast. They are born, then they die. The Himalayas is one of the youngest mountain ranges in the world, and it is still growing. It has not reached its peak yet, it is very young – every year it grows one foot. There are old mountains whose peaks have been attained; now they are falling down, old, their backs are bent.

The walls you see around you, every particle of them is in movement. You cannot see the movement because the movement is very subtle and fast. Now physicists agree with Heraclitus, not with Aristotle, remember. Whenever any science reaches nearer to reality, it has to agree with Lao Tzu and Heraclitus. Now physicists say everything is in movement. Eddington has said that the only word which is false is "rest". Nothing is at rest, nothing can be; it is a false word, it doesn't correspond to any reality. "Is" is just in the language. In life, in existence, there is no "is"; everything is becoming. Heraclitus himself, when he says about the river – and the symbol of the river is very, very deep with him – that you cannot step in the same river twice, he also says that even if you do, you are the same and you are not the same. Just on the surface you look the same. Not only has the river changed, you have also changed.

This is the deepest message of Heraclitus: everything flows and changes; everything moves, nothing is static. And the moment you cling, you miss reality. Your clinging becomes the problem, because reality changes and you cling.

No, you cannot step in the same river twice. It is impossible. Don't cling; if you cling you create a hell. Clinging is hell, and a non-clinging consciousness is always in heaven. One moves with the mood, one accepts the mood, one accepts the change; there is no grudge, no complaint about it because this is how life is, things are. You can fight, but you cannot change.

Be true to your changing self, because that is the only reality.

Life moves through one opposite to another. And Heraclitus says this is the secret, the hidden harmony; this is the hidden harmony.

A story:

When some visitors unexpectedly found Heraclitus warming himself by the cooking fire, he said to them: "Here, too, are the gods."

He never went to a temple, because if you are a man of perception, if your eyes are open, if you can hear and feel, then what need is there to go to a temple? Here also are gods.

God is not a person. God is all that is the case. God is existence.

Just imagine the picture: Heraclitus sitting by the fireside, warming himself. The cracking of the wood, the flames rising towards heaven, the warmth ... It must have been a cold winter night – unexpectedly some visitors come and they ask, "What are you doing?" And he says, "Here also are gods." What he is saying is that this is a prayer, this warming yourself is a prayer – if the fire becomes a divine phenomenon.

It reminds me of a Zen master, Ikkyu. He was journeying and he was staying in a temple, just overnight. The night was very, very cold, so he made a fire. But not finding wood anywhere, he took a statue of Buddha – a wooden statue that was in the temple – and burnt it. The priest was fast asleep ... noise, the fire, and this Ikkyu moving here and there. He looked – he opened his eyes and looked – and he was aghast, he couldn't believe it, because this was a Buddhist monk, and not only a monk but a very famous master. The priest jumped out of his bed, he came running and he said, "What are you doing? You have burnt a Buddha!"

Ikkyu took out a small piece of wood and searched in the ashes for the Buddha – the statue was almost gone, nothing was there.

The priest said, "What are you searching for? It is no longer there."

Ikkyu said, "I am searching for the bones – Buddha must have bones."

The priest laughed and said, "Now I am completely certain you are mad. How can a wooden Buddha have bones?"

Ikkyu said, "Then bring the other two Buddhas also, because the night is still long and very cold, and the buddha within me needs a little warmth. These Buddhas are just wooden, so don't worry. Here inside are bones, and a real buddha, and this buddha needs a little warmth. These Buddhas are no good anyway, they have no bones, so don't worry."

The priest threw him out of the temple. The night was very cold, but there are people who will worship a wooden Buddha and throw out a real buddha. In the morning he looked out to see what had happened to Ikkyu: he was sitting just outside the temple near a milestone – and worshiping it. The sun was rising, it was a beautiful morning and he had found a few flowers from somewhere. He had put those flowers on the milestone and he was worshiping. The priest came running and he said, "What are you doing? You are really completely mad! During the night you burnt a Buddha and now you are worshiping a milestone."

Said Ikkyu, "Here, also, is a god."

Heraclitus: "Here, too, are gods."

If you can feel, every moment is divine and everything is divine, and all that exists is holy. If you cannot feel, go to the temples, go to the mosques and churches, but you will not find anything there either – because it is you who need a transformation, it is not the situation that needs change. The situation remains the same: in the temple, outside the temple, everywhere God is. It is you who cannot see and so you change places: from the house you go to the temple in search of God.

You need an inner transformation.

The change in the situation won't help. You need a psychological reorientation. You need a totally new way of looking at things, then suddenly the whole world becomes the temple, then there is nothing else.

For Heraclitus, fire became the symbol – and fire is really a beautiful symbol. Heraclitus says fire is the basic substance of life. It is! Now physicists agree with Heraclitus. They agree that electricity is the base of all existence, that everything is nothing but modes of electricity. Heraclitus says it is fire. What is the difference? And fire is a more beautiful word than electricity. Fire gives a sense of more aliveness than electricity does, fire is more wild than electricity. When you say electricity is the base, it looks as if the universe is somehow mechanical because electricity has become associated with a mechanism, and then God looks like an engineer – but electricity is fire.

Hindus have called this basic element *prana*, vitality – but vitality is fire. When you are vital, alive, you are fiery, aflame. Henri Bergson has called the base of all *elan vital*, just like *prana*. Those who have been seeking, somehow or other they come near fire. Deep down this existence is fire. Fire is life. And Zarathustra is right: he made fire the suprememost god. He must have agreed with Heraclitus – they were contemporaries, Zarathustra and Heraclitus. Fire became the supreme god for the followers of Zarathustra.

Fire has many things deep in it. You will have to understand the phenomenon of fire, the symbol, because it is a way of speaking, it is a metaphor, something deep Heraclitus wants to indicate when he says that fire is the substratum. Watch fire some day on a winter's night; sit also by the side of a fire and just watch, just feel it, the warmth. Cold is death, warmth is life. A dead body is cold, a live body is warm – and you have to maintain a certain warmth continuously. An inner mechanism exists in man to keep the warmth always within a certain limit, because only between those certain degrees is life possible.

That's why we say, "A warm welcome", not "A cold welcome"; warm love, not cold love – because cold symbolizes death, warmth symbolizes life. The sun is the source, solar energy is fire. Just watch: in the evening everything becomes sad. Even trees, birds become completely silent; no song, all songs disappear. Flowers close and the whole earth waits for the morning. And in the morning, the sun has not yet risen and the earth starts becoming ready to welcome. The birds start singing even before the sun has arisen – that is a welcome sign. Flowers start flowering again; everything becomes again alive, movement enters.

Fire is a very, very meaningful symbol in other ways also. If you watch fire you will see a continuous upward movement. Water flows downwards, fire flows upwards – that's why the Hindus talk about "the fire of kundalini". When you rise upwards you are not like water, you are like a flame of fire. When your inner being changes, you feel a flame going upwards. Water, even water, in contact with fire starts evaporating upwards.

In a very, very old Tibetan scripture it is said that a master is like fire and the disciple is like water. If the disciple comes in deep contact with the master, the quality of the disciple changes – it becomes the quality of fire, just like water heated evaporates. Water without fire moves downwards. With fire immediately a change comes in. Beyond 100 degrees the fire has made the water ready to move upwards; the dimension changes.

Fire always moves upwards. Even if you hold a lamp upside down the flame will go upwards, the flame cannot go downwards. Fire is an effort to reach the highest peak, the omega point.

Heraclitus has found the right symbol. It is not a philosophical statement, but in Greek histories of philosophy they think Heraclitus is proposing an essential element, like others – like Thales, Anaxagoras, Anaximenes, other Greek philosophers. There are four elements – earth, water, fire, air – so there have been philosophers who proposed that earth is the basic element; somebody else proposed that water is the basic element; somebody else fire; somebody else air. Heraclitus proposes that fire is the basic element, but he should not be understood in the way Thales is understood, no. It is not a statement. It is not a statement about a philosophical theme or theory, he is not proposing any doctrine. He is a poet, he is not a philosopher at all. He is giving a symbol, and the symbol means much more than the word "fire".

Watch fire outside, then watch fire inside, and become as much of a flame as possible.

That's why when some visitors unexpectedly found Heraclitus warming himself by the cooking fire, he said to them: "Here, too, are the gods."

"I have searched myself," he says. "So I am not just saying this because others have said it – I have known it myself." He says: "Time is a child moving counters in a game; the royal power is a child's."

The royal power is a child's, and time is a child moving counters in a game – the whole concept of *leela*, play, he condenses in just a few sentences. Life is like a play – don't make it a business, otherwise you will miss it. You miss it because you make a business out of it and it is a play. Play well, but don't think in terms of achieving something out of it. Just be like a child: he plays, he is not worried about what he achieves out of it. Small children, even if they are defeated in a game, jump and feel very happy. Failure is not a failure if it is a play; defeat is not a defeat if it is a play. Otherwise, if it is a business, even victory is a defeat. Ask Napoleons, Alexanders: even victory is defeat. What do you find finally? You are victorious, and nothing has been achieved. You longed for this goal so much and now you have reached it – and you simply feel frustrated and your whole life is lost.

Remember, your life will be lost if you are after some goals, because life has no goal. It is a purposeless play. It is not going anywhere, it is simply enjoying itself.

This is the most difficult thing to understand because the mind is mathematical. It says, "Then what is the meaning of it, then what is the purpose?" There is no purpose and no meaning. Then the mind immediately says, "If there is no meaning then why live, then why not commit suicide?" But see: if there is meaning the whole thing will become ugly, then it will be like a business. If there is purpose, then all life will lose the poetry.

The poetry is there because there is no purpose. Why does the rose flower? Ask the rose; it will say, "I don't know – but flowering is so beautiful, what is the need to know? Flowering in itself, intrinsically, is so beautiful." Ask a bird, "Why do you sing?" and he will be simply puzzled at what nonsense questions you ask. Singing is so beautiful, it is such a benediction – why raise the question? But the mind looks for the goal, the mind is an achiever – it cannot simply enjoy. Something must be there in the future to be achieved, some goal must be reached, then mind feels good. If there is nothing to be achieved, it flops. But that is what the whole effort is – let it flop!

There is no purpose, there is no goal. This moment, the whole existence is celebrating – all except you. Why not participate? Why not be like a flower, purposelessly flowering? And why not be like a river, meaninglessly flowing? Why not be like the ocean, roaring, just enjoying?

This is what Heraclitus says: "Time is a child moving counters in a game; the royal power is a child's."

And every child is a king. Just watch a child – every child is simply a king, an emperor. Look at the movement: even if the child is naked, no emperor can compete with him. Why is a child so beautiful? Every child, without any exception, is beautiful. What is the beauty of a child? He is still uncontaminated by the mind, which seeks purpose, meaning, goal. He simply plays, he doesn't bother about the next day.

A small child came home. His mother was very angry and she said, "I have heard from neighborhood children that you threw mud in a small girl's mouth, and you have been punished – you were standing outside the class the whole day!"

He said, "Yes."

His mother was horrified; she said, "Why? Why did you throw that mud?"

The small child shrugged his shoulders and said, "Well, the mouth was open."

The why is meaningless. It is enough: he had mud in the hand and the mouth was open, so what to do? It simply happened.

We are asking why. Why is irrelevant for a child – it is how it happened! The mouth was open and he had the mud. He did not do it really. We punish him wrongly, he did not do it – it happened, it simply happened this way. It was a coincidence that the girl was standing with an open mouth. He didn't mean anything, he didn't mean any harm, he didn't mean any insult. He simply welcomed the opportunity, he enjoyed it. But we ask why.

Between a child and a grown-up exists an abyss; they are poles apart. The child cannot understand what the adults are saying because he lives in a totally different dimension – the dimension of play. And the adults cannot understand what the child is doing because the adult is a businessman, he lives in the world of whys, reasons, causes. They never meet, they cannot meet, there is no possibility of understanding – unless the adult again becomes a child. Only a saint, a real sage, can understand a child, because he is also a child. He can understand.

If you can become a child again, you have achieved all. If you cannot become a child again, you have missed all. A sage is a twice-born child. And firstborn children are not real children because they will have to grow up. The second birth is the real birth, because when somebody is twice-born he has given birth to himself. It is a transformation, he has again become a child. He does not ask for reasons and whys, he simply lives. Whatsoever the moment presents, he moves with it; he has no plans, he has no projections. He lives without demanding anything, and that is the only way to live; otherwise, you simply appear to be living, you are not alive.

For a child there is nothing bad, nothing good, there is no God, no Devil; a child accepts everything. Again, a sage accepts everything. That's why he can say God is winter and summer, God is peace and war, God is Devil and good – both. For a sage, again all morality disappears, all distinctions fall down; everything is holy and every place is sacred.

A man who can be blissful need not pray – prayer is a poor substitute. A man who is blissful need not meditate. A man who is blissful can live the moment blissfully, has done all that can be done. Everything is holy and sacred. You can eat your food in such a way that it becomes prayer. You can love a man in such a way that it becomes prayer. You can dig a hole in the garden in such a way that it becomes prayer. Prayer is not a formal thing – it is the quality of prayerfulness that you bring to something.

"The royal power is a child's." Why? – because the royal power means innocence. God comes to you when you are innocent. When you are cunning the door is closed. Never destroy anybody's innocence, never create doubts in somebody who is innocent, because innocence is the royal power. Never create doubt in anybody, because once trust is destroyed and innocence is broken, then it is very, very difficult – it is just like a broken mirror.

"Time is a child moving counters in a game; the royal power is a child's."

And about time, also, Heraclitus has no mathematical theory. About time, also, he says that it is just like a child moving counters in a game: the day and night, they move. Heraclitus does not believe that time is going somewhere. It is moving, it is moving in a circle. It is not linear, it is like a wheel. And this is something to be understood: all the scientists think that time is linear, that it is moving in a line; and all the knowers of the inner say it is a wheel – it is not linear, it is circular. There seems to be some reason for it. Scientists cannot see the whole, they see just a part. The scientific mind is a specific mind, specialized. The scientist can see only a part, and he also divides the part to see an even smaller part. He goes on dividing – the scientist cannot see the whole. The very discipline of science makes him capable of seeing the part more clearly. He goes on seeing more and more clearly, but less and less. His vision becomes clear and penetrating, but his object becomes smaller and smaller. He comes to the atom, the smallest; and in time also he comes to the moment, the smallest.

If you see a small sector of a circle it will look like a line, but the circle is vast – just like on the earth. We are sitting here, and if we draw a line and you think it is a straight line then you are wrong – because on a circular earth, how can you draw a straight line? If you go on drawing that line, continue it, it will become a circle, it will encompass the whole earth. So all straight lines are just fragments of a vast, big circle.

Science cannot see the whole, that is why time seems to be line. Religion sees the whole – science misses the forest, it looks at the tree; religion misses the tree, looks at the forest. And when you look at the whole, everything is circular. All movement is circular, and time is also a circular movement. It is a game, not going anywhere, moving. If you can see that time is not going anywhere, but moving in a circle, then the whole tension of the mind to reach somewhere drops. Then to reach somewhere in the future becomes useless, meaningless – then you start enjoying the moment.

Life is not an effort to attain, it is a celebration. Heraclitus says, "Bigotry is the sacred disease."

But even this you should not make into a theory, because the moment you make a theory and you say, "This is right," you will start converting people. The moment you say, "This is right," your ego has taken it. Now it is not a question of this being right – you are right. How can you be wrong? – then the sacred disease enters. Whenever a person becomes religious, this disease is possible. Whenever one becomes religious one becomes vulnerable to this disease, bigotry. It is very difficult to find a religious man and not bigoted.

It happened: I saw Mulla Nasruddin drinking in a bar and asked, "Nasruddin, what are you doing? Just yesterday you told me that you have left all drinking and you have become an absolute teetotaller, so what are you doing?"

Nasruddin said, "Yes I am an absolute teetotaller – but not a bigoted one."

Whatsoever you are, remain flexible. Don't create a fixed frame around you, remain moving and flowing. Sometimes one has to go out of the discipline also. Life is bigger than your discipline and sometimes one has to go completely against one's own rules – because God is both summer and winter.

Don't be a victim of bigotry. Be religious, but don't be a Hindu, a Mohammedan, a Christian. Let the whole earth be your church, let the whole existence be your temple. And when the whole God is available, why be satisfied with a fragment? Why say Christian, why say Hindu? When you can be a human being, why choose labels? Drop all labels and drop all beliefs.

Jesus

Who is Jesus Christ? The question has been asked down the centuries again and again, and it has been answered too. But the questioners were wrong, and so were those who have answered it, because the question was out of a certain prejudice, and so was the answer. They were not essentially different; their source was one and the same.

The question was asked by those who were suspicious of Jesus' godhood. And the question was answered by those who were not ready to believe Jesus' manhood. They were only ready to believe half of him. The Jews were ready to believe that he was a man. And the Christians were ready to believe that he was God. The Jews were denying half of him – the Christ part. And the Christians were denying the other half – the Jesus part.

Who is Jesus Christ? Christians don't want to see him as Jesus, Son of man – man of flesh, blood and bones, man as other men are. And the Jews did not want to believe in him as God, as divine – made of pure consciousness, not of flesh, blood and bones.

Nobody has been ready to believe Jesus in his totality. And that is not only the case with Jesus, that is the case with all the masters – Buddha, Krishna, Zarathustra. And unless you allow Jesus in his totality to penetrate you, you will not be transformed. Unless you allow him as he is, you will not be in contact with him. Jesus is both Jesus and Christ, and he is not ashamed of it.

In the Bible many times he says "I am the Son of man", and as many times he also says "I am the Son of God." And he seems to have no idea that there is any contradiction between these two. There is none. The contradiction exists in our minds. It doesn't exist in Jesus' being. His being is bridged. His being is bridged between time and eternity, body and soul, this world and that. His being is bridged between the visible and the invisible, the known and the unknown. He is utterly bridged, he is at ease with both, because he is both. Jesus and Christ are like two shores, and the river is only possible if there are two shores. Jesus is the river that flows between these two shores: both shores are his. He exists between them, he is a river.

Who is Jesus Christ – God or man? And I say all the questions that have been asked were wrong, and so were the answers. Why? – because the questions came either from Judaic knowledge or from Muslim knowledge or from Hindu knowledge. And the answers came from Christian knowledge, and knowledge cannot answer it. Knowledge cannot even ask it! Knowledge is impotent. Such questions of such importance can be asked only out of innocence, not out of knowledge. The distinction has to be understood.

When you ask a question out of knowledge, you are not really asking, because you already know. Your question is false, inauthentic. Your heart is not there. You are asking for asking's sake – maybe for a discussion, a debate, an argument. But you know the question beforehand – the answer is there a priori. So you cannot receive the answer, you are not open for it, you are not available for it. You are not ready to move, to explore; you already have the answer. And the question is arising out of that answer.

The Jews had the answer. They knew that he was not the Messiah, that he was not God. Why? – because they had the idea that when the Messiah came, everybody would recognise him! Everybody – without any exception. That was their idea of the Messiah, that everybody would recognise him.

And if Jesus was not recognised by everybody, how could he be the Messiah? They have a definition. They had also believed – that has also been their knowledge – that when Jesus, the real Jesus, the Christ, the Messiah came, everybody would be liberated immediately. All past sins, present sins would disappear in that light, and it had not happened. "Christ is there but people are not liberated yet, they are still living in sin, they are still living in misery. So this man cannot be the Messiah, cannot be the Christ." This was not the man they were waiting for.

These are prejudices. They had never seen any messiah. How could they define what would happen when the Messiah came?

For example, if in the dark night of your soul you have an idea that when the morning comes, money will shower from the sky: when the sun rises, everybody will become rich. And then in the morning when the sun rises, how can you accept that this is the sun? – because the money is not falling and everybody has not become rich, people are still poor. And you go on looking at the sky and no money is coming. And because you are too concerned with the money, you don't see what is coming from the sun – the light, the life, the ecstasy. You cannot see that because your eyes are completely covered with your prejudice, with your idea. And then you ask "Who is this Jesus Christ?" You already know how the Messiah should be. That is hindering, that is an obstruction. That's why the Jews missed. It was for this man that they had been waiting for centuries, and when he came and knocked on their doors, they missed. They denied him. How could they have denied? Were they bad people? No, they were people as good as you are, they were as good as Hindus and Mohammedans and Buddhists; there was nothing wrong with them. Then what was the problem? The problem was their knowledge. They had a prejudice. And when Christians answer that Jesus is the only begotten son of God, again it is knowledge.

The Jews were very disturbed because Jesus was claiming that he was God, or God's son. For 2,000 years Christians have been defending Jesus – that he was God, that he is God.

And they have been trying to efface all the possibilities with which it can be proved that he is man. That's why they say he was born out of a virgin mother – that is the beginning. So they deny his manhood, so he is not just like you; he is special. Even in his birth he is special. Then they try to make his life in such a way that no indications are left that he was human. He was very human, utterly human. He was a total man. He was not a perfectionist. When it was needed to be angry he became really angry. He threw the money-changers out of the temple and he said to them "What are you doing here in my Father's home, in my Father's temple? Get out from here!" And he was in such a rage, that alone, single-handed, he threw many people outside.

He loved people. He had friends, he mixed with people. He ate with people, drank with people, he moved with people. He lived like an ordinary man. He had no pretensions of being anything extraordinary. And even if something extraordinary happens, he always says, "It is your faith that has performed the miracle. It is God's mercy on you. It is something between you and your God." He does not even expect gratitude. Somebody is very grateful because a miracle has happened and he has been cured, and he wants to touch his feet and thank him, and he says "No." And the man says "You are a great man, you are so good!" and Jesus says "Nobody is good except God. You thank him. Forget about me. It is your faith that has cured you, not I. And if you have to be thankful, you have to be thankful to God. Forget about me. Don't allow me to be between you and your God."

That's exactly what Buddha is reported to have said to his disciples: "If you meet me on the way, kill me immediately. Never allow me to stand between you and the reality. Hold my hand as far as you are not capable of walking alone and on your own. The moment you are capable of walking alone and on your own, just forget about me. Go ahead. Then don't cling to me. Then don't try to remain a shadow of me. If you meet me on the way, kill me immediately!" he says. That's what Jesus goes on saying again and again: "Forget about me. Let your thanks go directly to God. Who am I?"

Christians have been trying to efface all traces of his humanity; so he is born out of the Virgin Mary, a virgin mother, which is absolutely absurd. Then he lives a life in which all human traits are removed. Christians only talk about his miracles, not about his ordinary life. They are afraid. Christians say that Jesus never laughed! Now this seems to be the ultimate in stupidity. Jesus … and never laughed? Then who else can laugh? But laughter seems too human, too mundane: they cannot allow Jesus to laugh.

But Jesus' life is such that he must have been laughing. He must have been really laughing. He must have been a man of laughter, because he says again and again "Rejoice! Be merry! Celebrate!" These words cannot come from a man who has never laughed. And a man who has never laughed, why should he go to parties? Why should he drink with people? Why should he be mixing with people? And he was a mixer. Every day, every night, he was moving with people. He was not secluded. He must have been really laughing, enjoying. But Christians say he never laughed.

They have made his picture very sad-looking, long-faced, burdened. This is not possible! This is utterly wrong, because it goes against the basic realisation of a Christ, of a Buddha. Because a man who has attained to ultimate consciousness will be completely blissful, cheerful. His life will be a song and a dance. It will have the quality of flowers and stars. It can't be sad. Why should he be sad? It is his Father's world, it is his God's world. Why should he be sad? He has come home. When is he going to be happy? If you are not happy by knowing God, then there is no possibility.

Jesus looks so sad. He has been painted sad. He has been painted as "the Saviour". He has been painted as if he is carrying the burdens of everybody and sins of everybody. He forgives you! He does not carry your burden, he simply forgives you.

This is a wrong standpoint, that he takes your burden upon himself. If it is not of worth, why should he take it upon himself? And if it is so valuable, why should he take it from you? He will put some more on you. No, he is not taking anybody's burden, he is simply helping everybody to drop it. Because it is you who are holding and clinging to it, it is valueless. When he says you are forgiven, he says, "Forget all about your sadnesses and forget all about hell. It is your Father's world, and he is compassion and he is love. How can love punish you? How can love throw you in hell? How can love torture you? God is not a sadist!"

And then Christians say: resurrection. Their whole Jesus depends on three things. First: a virgin birth; second: a non-laughing, non-enjoying monotonous, sad life of miracles; and third: resurrection. These are the three things that seem to be important to them, and these are all useless because they miss the whole point. The real Jesus is missed. This is a myth that Christians have created around him, and because of this myth the real Jesus is lost.

I would like to tell you, he is a real man, an authentic man. He lived like a man, and he loved living like a man. He lived in all the dimensions of manhood, and yet he is God.

Jesus Christ is both Jesus and Christ. He is Christ in Jesus, and he is Jesus in Christ. He is the meeting point where two worlds meet, where two utterly polarized worlds meet. And hence the beauty, and hence the ecstasy of Jesus.

Ecstasy always arises when two polarities meet. The bigger the polarities, the bigger the distance between the polarities, the bigger the ecstasy. That's why while you are making love to a woman there is great joy, because two polarities meet. Not very big polarities, because a man and woman are not very far away – not very distant, but still distant. When a man and woman meet and are lost in love there is great ecstasy, there is great joy because they are dissolved, the egos are lost. Boundaries are no more valid – they are overlapping, overflowing into each other. Their ordinary mundane worries don't make any sense in this moment of joy. This orgasmic moment, how does it arise? It is the meeting of the polarities. What to say about Jesus meeting Christ, Gautama meeting Buddhahood, man meeting God – those are the ultimate polarities as far away as possible – finite meeting infinite. The very meeting is the ultimate in celebration.

Jesus must have been ecstatic. Because of the Christian painting, Christian ideology, he looks very sad. He must have been a man of great joy, overflowing with delight. What else is possible when the light has happened inside? – delight has to happen outside. They go together. When the house is lit – even with closed windows – travelers can see the light falling outside, from the curtains, from the doors. That is delight! When light has happened inside, from the outside people can see something immensely valuable flowing.

That is the definition of ecstasy: polarities meeting.

Ordinary man is like a person living in sleep. not aware of who he is. When God's energy touches him, when he is available to God's energy, when he is receptive to God's energy, when that stirring energy comes dancing into him, there is ecstasy. There is no ecstasy unless we join the mundane with the supramundane, the mud with the sun, the earth with sky, the body with the soul, matter with mind – only then, when sun and the mud meet, is the lotus born, the lotus of ecstasy. Unless reality is as miraculous as the supposedly miraculous, we are frozen in ice.

Man as man is a frozen thing. And let me say to you: God as God is also a frozen thing. So it is not only that you are seeking God, God is also seeking you. It is not that without God you are sad, God is ALSO sad without you. And when you meet with God, and God meets with you, it will not be only YOUR ecstasy, it will be his ecstasy too. The whole existence will feel ecstatic. Whenever a single human being becomes a Christ or a Buddha, the whole existence dances, the whole existence is overjoyed – goes mad with ecstasy!

Meeting is the melting of the divisions. Thinking of yourself as man is creating a division. And if you don't drop this division, this category that you have created around you, that "I am a man", you will not allow God to enter in you. You have to be completely free from boundaries, from all boundaries – the boundary of the Hindu, the boundary of the Christian, the boundary of man, the boundary of richness, poorness, education, uneducation, the boundary of white and black, the boundary of the Brahmin and the Sudra – all the boundaries have to be dropped. In that very dropping the eternal enters into your time world. Into your dark night of the soul comes that light, floods that light. And suddenly, you are no more the same. And let me repeat: God is also no more the same!

God was never so rich as he became after Christ. He was never so rich as he became after Buddha. He is not so rich as he will become when you meet him, because you will pour into him. I know you only have a small energy, but an ocean is created by small drops falling,

falling, falling … Small rivers flow into the ocean and create the ocean. No single river can create the ocean, but each single river goes on creating it, goes on helping it. God is bigger than ever every day, because some water, some river again flows into him, again brings a new life, a new thrill.

God is evolving, God is not a static thing. God is evolving every moment.

Meeting is the melting of the boundaries, blurring of the divisions, overlapping, overflowing. This is what is called trust or faith or surrender. At absolute zero, absolute surrender, life takes over once more and we are returned to God or to Tao or to dhamma, to free-flowing totality. God is the free-flowing totality, God is not a person. We return to our pure being only when we become a free-floating totality. In this state everything is okay, right.

In yoga they call it a certain state of *nadam*, a certain state of harmony, accord. When man disappears into God and man's conflict with God disappears, there is *nadam*, there is harmony – what Heraclitus calls "the hidden harmony". *Nadam* is homeostatis – harmony, rhythm. You are out of rhythm, out of tune with God, that is your misery. Jesus is in tune with God, that is his joy. If he is also miserable, if he is also sad, then what is the difference between you and him? The difference is that he feels for you, that he feels all compassion for you, but he himself is in utter joy. In fact, because he is in utter joy, he feels sorry for you, he feels compassion for you. He wants to bring you also to this utter joy, and he knows it is yours just for the asking. Hence he says, "Ask, and it shall be given you; seek, and ye shall find; knock, and it shall be opened unto you."

Jesus never died on the cross. It takes at least 48 hours for a person to die on the Jewish cross; and there have been known cases where people have existed almost six days on the cross without dying. Because Jesus was taken down from the cross after only six hours, there is no possibility of his dying on the cross. It was a conspiracy between a rich sympathizer of Jesus and Pontius Pilate to crucify Jesus as late as possible on Friday – because on Saturday, Jews stop everything; their Sabbath does not allow any act. By the evening of Friday everything stops.

The arrangement was that Jesus would be crucified late in the afternoon, so before sunset he would be brought down. He might have been unconscious because so much blood had flowed out of the body, but he was not dead. Then he would be kept in a cave, and before the Sabbath ended and the Jews hung him again, his body would be stolen by his followers. The tomb was found empty, and Jesus was removed from Judea as quickly as possible. As he again became healthy and healed, he moved to India and he lived a long life – 112 years – in Kashmir.

It is a coincidence, but a beautiful coincidence, that Moses died in Kashmir and Jesus also died in Kashmir. I have been to the graves of both. The graves are ample proof, because those are the only two graves that are not pointing towards Mecca. Mohammedans make their graves with the head pointing towards Mecca, so in the whole world all the graves of Mohammedans point towards Mecca, and Kashmir is Mohammedan.

These two graves don't point towards Mecca, and the writing on the graves is in Hebrew, which is impossible on a Mohammedan grave – Hebrew is not their language. The name of Jesus is written exactly as it was pronounced by the Jews, "Joshua". "Jesus" is a Christian conversion of the Jewish name. The grave is certainly of Jesus.

A family has been taking care of both the graves – they are very close together in one place, Pahalgam – and only one family has been taking care of them down the centuries. They are Jews – they are still Jews – and I had to take their help to read to me what is written on the graves.

Moses had come to Kashmir to find a tribe of Jews who were lost on the way from Egypt to Jerusalem. When he reached Jerusalem his deep concern was the whole tribe that had got lost somewhere in the desert. When his people were established in Jerusalem, he went in search of the lost tribe, and he found the lost tribe established in Kashmir. Kashmiris are basically Jewish – later on Mohammedans forcibly converted them – and Moses lived with them and died there.

Jesus also went to Kashmir, because then it was known that Moses had found the lost tribe there. The doors of Judea were closed – he would be hanged again – and the only place where he would find the people who spoke the same language, the people who have the same kind of mind, where he would not be a foreigner, was Kashmir. So it was natural for him to go to Kashmir.

But he had learned his lesson. He had dropped the idea of being the only begotten son of God; otherwise these Jews would crucify him too. He dropped the idea of being a messiah. He lived with his few intimate friends and followers in Pahalgam.

Pahalgam is named after Jesus, because he used to call himself "the shepherd" – Pahalgam means "the town of the shepherd". So it was a small colony of Jesus and his friends, surrounding the grave of their forefather and the founder of Judaic tradition. Jesus remained a Jew to the very end; he never heard about Christianity.

But the followers who were left in Judea managed to create the story of resurrection. And there was no way to prove it this way or that. Neither could they produce Jesus – if he was resurrected then where was he? Nor could the other party prove what had happened. They had put such a big rock on the mouth of the cave that it was impossible for Jesus to have removed it, and there was a Roman soldier on duty 24 hours, so there was no possibility of anybody else removing the rock and taking the body.

But because Pontius Pilate was from the very beginning against crucifying Jesus … He could see the man was absolutely innocent. "He has some crazy ideas, but they are not criminal. And what harm does it do to somebody? If someone thinks he is the only begotten son of God, let him enjoy it. Why disturb him, and why get disturbed? If somebody thinks he is the Messiah and he has brought the message of God … if you want to listen, listen; if you don't want to listen, don't listen. But there is no need to crucify the man."

But Jesus learned his lesson – learned the hard way. In Kashmir he lived very silently with his group, praying, living peacefully, no longer trying to change the world. And Kashmir was so far away from Judea that in Judea the story of resurrection, amongst the followers of Jesus, became significant.

So I say a kind of resurrection certainly happened – it was a conspiracy more than a resurrection. But certainly Jesus did not die on the cross, he did not die in the cave where he was put; he lived long enough.

Up to now, for 2,000 years, Christianity has depended on the miracles of Jesus. Those were its basic foundations to prove it a superior religion to any other religion – because Gautama Buddha does not walk on water, Mahavira cannot revive a dead man, Krishna cannot heal the sick just by touching them, Mohammed cannot make wine out of water.

These miracles have been, for 2,000 years, the superiority of Christianity over all religions; otherwise what has Christianity got? But it is ready to drop the miracles because now they are continuously hammered. Nobody is ready to believe in them – they go against the very way things are. And nature does not change its rules, its laws, for anybody; it does not take anybody as an exception. So the new theologian feels embarrassed. He knows himself that it is impossible to prove the miracles.

I asked the Archbishop in Bombay, "You represent Jesus, the Pope represents Jesus. You should do at least some little miracles as evidence that you are really representatives; otherwise what have you got to prove that you are the representative? Walk on water, and the whole world will become Christian. And you say faith in Jesus can do miracles – then try it! You must have faith."

But no theologian, nor any pope, is ready to walk on water. They all know that nature does not change its laws for anybody.

The priest is the most cunning part of humanity – and clever. He is a businessman, he sees the opportunity of a great business. While Jesus is alive, it is dangerous to be with him. No businessman will come close to him – only gamblers may risk it and be with him. It is dangerous to be with him: he can be crucified, you can be crucified.

But once he is dead it is a great opportunity for business. Then a new kind of people starts gathering around: those are the priests, the popes, the imams, the rabbis – learned, scholarly, argumentative, dogmatic. They create the dogma, the creed. They create the cult.

On the dead body of a religious person, a cult is created.

Christianity is a cult.

Friedrich Nietzsche used to say … and I feel that he has the tremendous quality of seeing certain things which others go on missing. The man was mad, but sometimes mad people have a very sharp intelligence. Perhaps that is the reason that they go mad. Friedrich Nietzsche says, "The first and the last Christian died on the cross 2,000 years ago. Since then there has been no Christian at all." And he is absolutely right.

Jesus was the only Christian, although he never knew the word "Christian". He knew only Aramaic, the language which he spoke, and a little bit of Hebrew, the language which the rabbis spoke. But he had no idea of Greek. The word "Christ" is a Greek word, and the word Christian comes out of Christ. Jesus never in his life heard the words Christ or Christian. The Hebrew word for Christ is "messiah", so Jesus knew "messiah".

But once he died … And it was very strange that when he was alive, overflowingly alive, and was ready to give, to share, to pour his being into their being, the people were avoiding him. But once he was dead, the priests were not going to miss the opportunity.

The priests immediately gather around the dead body of a Buddha, of a Jesus, of a Lao Tzu, and they immediately make the catechism.

They start making a church on the dead body.

If Jesus comes back, the pope will be the first person to ask for his crucifixion again, because Jesus will disturb the whole business. That's what he was doing the last time he was here.

Why were the rabbis angry? The business was going so well, everything was settled, everybody was satisfied and suddenly this man Jesus comes and starts disturbing people's minds. He starts people thinking, enquiring, seeking … The establishment cannot tolerate such a person, because if you start seeking and searching, soon you will find that the establishment is standing on a dead body.

Jesus has promised in the Bible, "I will be coming," but I can tell you authoritatively that he is not going to come – one experience was enough. Who wants to be crucified again? And that time at least there was a consolation: that these were Jews, orthodox, traditional; they could not understand the revolution that he had brought.

This time, even that consolation will not be there. These will be the Christians, his own people, who will crucify him.

Last time, Jesus had prayed to God, "Forgive these people because they don't know what they are doing." What is he going to do this time? He will have to pray, "Forgive these people – they know perfectly well what they are doing." But they will do exactly the same thing.

A cult is a business, a religious kind of business. It has a religious jargon. It has no experience. Yes, once somewhere in the past there may have been a flower, but it is gone. Centuries have passed, and since then the priest goes on pretending that he is the representative of that fragrance. Nobody can represent fragrance: it comes with the flower and goes with the flower. But the priest can create a plastic flower, can even put French perfume on it. And that's what he has been doing in all the religions.

Religion is rebellious, is bound to be so, because religion starts saying things which the tradition will oppose, because only one of these two can exist: either the mass, unintelligent crowd – mind which makes the tradition, or a man like Jesus or Buddha or Mahavira.

They are alone. And what they are saying can be understood only by the chosen few. What they bring to the world is something so otherworldly, that unless you can have a heart-to-heart contact with them, there is no way of understanding them – you will misunderstand. Jesus is misunderstood, Socrates is misunderstood, Al-Hillaj Mansoor is misunderstood. Whenever you find a religious man, it will be simply certain that all around him there will be misunderstanding. But once he dies, things settle down. Once he dies the priesthood makes a new business.

Now, Jews have been suffering almost a heart attack for nearly 2,000 years, for the simple reason that they missed the business. Christianity is now the biggest business in the world ... and they missed. And Jews are not the people to miss when there is a business; they have an eye for business opportunities.

I have heard a story ... it has been happening for centuries that every year on a particular day in the Vatican, the chief rabbi of the city comes with roll in his hand to St Peter's Square where the pope waits for him. Jews and Christians gather in thousands to see this meeting of the pope and the chief rabbi, but what transpires between them, nobody knows. The rabbi bows down, gives the roll to the pope. The pope bows down – that's all.

The next morning, the roll is sent back to the rabbi to keep for the next year. For 2,000 years no pope bothered to look into it, but this pope became curious: what is this? What kind of convention is this that has been going on and on? And every time the rabbi gives it to the pope and the next morning it has to be sent back, ceremoniously – the same roll goes back. What exactly is in it? He opened the roll. It was very ancient – 2,000 years old. And do you know what he found? It was the bill for the Last Supper! The Jews were still asking, "Pay for it at least." And of course Jesus died without paying.

Kabir

Much is not known about Kabir – fortunately, because when you know too much about the person, it creates more complexities in understanding him. When you don't know anything about the person himself, then there is less complexity. That's why in the East it has been one of the most cherished old traditions not to say much about the mystics, so that it never hinders people. We don't know much about Krishna and we don't know much about Buddha; or all that we know about them is more mythological than historical, not true, fictitious. But about Kabir, even fiction does not exist. And he is not very ancient, yet he lived in such a way that he has effaced himself completely. He has not left any mark.

Only politicians leave marks on time – only politicians are that foolish. The mystics live in the timeless. They don't leave any marks on time, they don't leave any signatures on time. They don't believe in signing the sands of time. They know it will be effaced, so there is no point in it.

Kabir has not said much about himself, and nothing much is known about him. Not even this much is known – whether he was a Hindu or a Mohammedan.

The story goes that he was born a Mohammedan but was brought up by a Hindu. And this is beautiful; this is how it should be. Hence his richness. He has the heritage of two rich traditions, Hindu and Mohammedan. If you are just a Hindu, of course, you are poor. If you are just a Mohammedan you are poor. Look at my richness – I am a Hindu and a Mohammedan and a Christian and a Sikh and a Parsi. Not only that, I am a theist and I am an atheist too. I claim the whole heritage of humanity! I claim all; I don't reject anything. From Charvakas to Buddhas, I claim all.

The whole humanity is yours, the whole evolution of human consciousness is yours, but you are so miserly. Somebody has become a Hindu; he claims only a corner and lives in that corner, crippled and paralyzed. In fact, the corner is so narrow you cannot move. It is not spacious enough. A religious person will claim all – Buddha, Mahavira, Christ, Zarathustra, Lao Tzu, Nanak, Kabir ... he will claim all. They are all part of me; they are all part of you. Whatsoever has happened to human consciousness, you carry the seeds of it in you.

This is the one thing to be understood about Kabir: that he was born as a Mohammedan and brought up by a Hindu, and it never became conclusive to whom he had really belonged. Even at the time when he was dying it was a dispute among his disciples. The Hindus were claiming his body, the Mohammedans were claiming his body, and there is a beautiful parable about it. Kabir had left a message about his death. He knew it was going to happen – people are foolish, they will claim the body and there is going to be conflict – so he had left a message: "If there is any conflict, just cover my body with a sheet and wait, and the decision will come." And the story says that the body was covered and the Hindus started praying and the Mohammedans started praying and then the cover was removed, and Kabir had disappeared – only a few flowers were there. Those flowers were divided.

This parable is beautiful. I call it a parable, I don't say it really happened, but it shows something. A man like Kabir has already disappeared. He is not in his body. He is in his inner flowering. You are in the body only to a certain extent. The body has a certain function to fulfill; the function is that of consciousness flowering. Once the consciousness has flowered, the body is nonexistential. It does not matter whether it exists or not. It is simply irrelevant.

The parable is beautiful. When they removed the cover there were only a few flowers left. Kabir is a flowering – only a few flowers were left. And the stupid disciples even then wouldn't understand. They divided the flowers.

Remember one thing: all ideologies are dangerous. They divide people. You become a Hindu, you become a Mohammedan, you become a Jain, a Christian – you are divided. All ideologies create conflict. All ideologies are violent. A real man of understanding has no ideology; then he is undivided, then he is one with the whole of humanity. Not only that, he is one with the whole of existence. A real man of understanding is a flowering. This flowering we will be discussing.

The songs of Kabir are tremendously beautiful. He is a poet; he is not a philosopher. He has not created a system. He is not a theoretician or a theologian. He is not interested in doctrines, in scriptures. His whole interest is in how to flower and become a god. His whole effort is how to make you more loving, more alert.

It is not a question of learning much. On the contrary, it is a question of unlearning much. In that way he is very rare. Buddha, Mahavira, Krishna, Rama, they are very special people. They were all kings, and they were well educated, well cultured. Kabir is a nobody, a man of the masses, very poor, very ordinary, with no education at all, with no culture. And that is his rarity. Why do I call it his rarity? Because to be ordinary in the world is the most extraordinary thing. He was very ordinary, and he remained ordinary.

The natural desire of the human mind is to become special – to become special in the ways of the world, to have many degrees, to have much political power, to have money, wealth. To be special, the mind is always ready to go on some ego-trip. And if you are fed up with the world, then the ego starts finding new ways and new means to enhance itself – it becomes spiritual. You become a great mahatma, a great sage, a great scholar, a man of knowledge, a man of renunciation; again you are special.

Unless the desire to be special disappears, you will never be special. Unless you relax into your ordinariness, you will never relax.

The really spiritual person is one who is absolutely ordinary. Kabir is very normal, you would not have been able to find him in a crowd. His specialness is not outward. You cannot just find him by looking at his face. It is difficult. Buddha was special, a very beautiful man, a charismatic personality. Jesus is very special, throbbing with revolution, rebellion. But Kabir? Kabir is absolutely ordinary, a normal person.

Remember, when I say normal, I don't mean the average. The average is not the normal. The average is only "normally" abnormal; he is as mad as all others are. In fact, in the world, normal persons don't exist.

I have heard: A famous psychiatrist conducting a university course in psychopathology was asked by a student, "Doctor, you have told us about the abnormal person and his behavior, but what about the normal person?"

The doctor was a little puzzled, and then he said, "In my whole life I have never come across a normal person. But if we ever find him, we will cure him!"

Kabir is really that normal person that you never come across in life, with no desire to be special. When he became enlightened, then too he remained in his ordinary life. He was a weaver; he continued to weave.

His disciples started growing in numbers – hundreds, and then thousands, and then many more thousands were coming to him. And they would always ask him to stop weaving clothes – "There is no need. We will take care of you." But he would laugh and say, "It is better to continue as God has willed me. I have no desire to be anything else. Let me be whatsoever I am, whatsoever God wants me to be. If he wants me to be a weaver, that's why I am a weaver. I was born a weaver and I will die as a weaver."

He continued in his ordinary way. He would go to the marketplace to sell his goods, he would carry water from the well. He lived very, very ordinarily. That is one of the most significant things to be understood. He never claimed that he was a man of knowledge – because no man of knowledge ever claims it. To know is to know that to know is not to know and that not to know is to know. A real man of understanding knows that he does not know at all. His ignorance is profound. And out of this ignorance arises innocence. When you know, you become cunning. When you know, you become clever. When you know, you lose that innocence of childhood.

Kabir says he is ignorant, he does not know anything. And this has to be understood, because this will create the background in your mind for his poetry. From where is this poetry coming? It is coming out of his innocence, flowering out of his innocence. He says he does not know.

Have you ever observed the fact that in life we go on claiming that we know, but we don't know? What do you know? Have you known anything, ever? If I ask why the trees are green, will you be able to answer it? Yes, the best answer that I have heard is from D. H. Lawrence. A small child was walking with him in a garden and the child asked – as children are prone to ask – "Why are the trees green?" D. H. Lawrence looked at the trees, looked into the eyes of the child, and said, "They are green because they are green." That's the truest answer ever given. What else can you say? Whatsoever else you say will be foolish; it will not make any sense. You can say trees are green because of chlorophyll, but why is chlorophyll green? The question remains the same. I ask you one question, you give me an answer, but the question is not really answered.

You have lived with a woman for 30 years, and you call her your wife, or with a man, for 50 years; do you know the man or the woman? A child is born to you; do you know him? Have you looked into his eyes? Can you claim that you know him? What do you know?

Do you know a piece of rock? Yes, scientists will give many explanations, but they don't become knowledge. They will say electrons and protons and neutrons. But what is an electron? And they shrug their shoulders; they say, "We don't know." They say, "We don't know YET," in the hope that someday they will be able to know. No, they will never be able to know, because first they said, "The rock is made of atoms," and when it was asked what is an atom, they said, "We don't know yet." Then they said, "The atom consists of electrons." Now we ask what is an electron; they say, "We don't know yet." Someday they will say the electron consists of this and that, x, y, z; but that doesn't make any difference.

The ultimate remains irreducible to knowledge. The ultimate

remains a mystery. If the ultimate is a mystery, then life becomes a life of wonder. If the ultimate is not known, then poetry arises. If the ultimate is known – or you think that it is known – then philosophy arises. That is the difference between philosophy and poetry.

And Kabir's approach is that of a poet, of a lover, of one who is absolutely wondering what it is all about. Not knowing it, he sings a song. Not knowing it, he becomes prayerful. Not knowing it, he bows down. The poet's approach is not that of explanation. It is that of exclamation. He says, "Aha, aha! So here is the mystery."

And wherever you find mystery there is God. The more you know, the less you will be aware of God; the less you know, the closer God will be to you. If you don't know anything, if you can say with absolute confidence, "I don't know", if this "I don't know" comes from the deepest core of your being, then God will be in your very core, in the very beat of your heart. And then poetry arises … then one falls in love with this tremendous mystery that surrounds you.

That love is religion. Religion is not after any explanations. Religion is not a quest for the explanation. Rather, it is an exploration of love, a non-ending journey into love.

I invite you to come with me into the innermost realm of this madman Kabir. Yes, he was a madman – all religious people are. Mad, because they don't trust reason. Mad, because they love life. Mad, because they can dance and they can sing. Mad, because to them life is not a question, not a problem to be solved but a mystery into which one has to dissolve oneself.

So in the beginning of the journey I would like to say to you, be innocent; only then will you be able to understand Kabir. Don't bring your mind in, don't start arguing with him, because he is not a logician. When you go to see a painting you don't argue with the painting. You enjoy it. When you go to listen to a musician playing on his guitar you don't argue. When you go to a poet you don't argue. You listen to the poetry; there is no argument in your head.

But about religion, there is difficulty. When you come to listen to a religious person you argue. And the responsibility lies with the so-called religious people themselves because they have been arguing. There have been foolish people who have even tried to prove God through argument. As if God depends on your argument. As if, if you cannot argue, he will not be able to be there; he will become nonexistential. As if God is a syllogism.

Kabir is not going to give you any argument. His assertions are just like the Upanishads, or Mohammed's assertions in the Koran or Jesus' assertions in the Bible – just statements. He feels ... he sings about his feeling. Please feel him. There is no question of your head. Put your heads aside.

If you want to understand, you will have to silence your mind. Listen to Kabir as one listens to poetry; he is a poet. So don't listen to the words. Listen to the silence that surrounds the words. Don't listen to the words. Listen to the poetry that surrounds the words, listen to the rhythm, the song. Listen to Kabir's celebration. He is not here to preach anything to you. He is like a cherry tree. In the full-moon night the cherry tree has blossomed. Flowers have no arguments; they are simply there. This is an explosion. Kabir has burst into song.

And these are the two possibilities: whenever enlightenment happens, either a person becomes absolutely silent or he bursts into song. These are the two possibilities. When Meher Baba attained he became silent. Then his whole life he remained silent. When Meera attained she started dancing and singing. These are the two possibilities: either one becomes absolutely silent or one's whole life becomes a song. Kabir's life is that of song.

But remember, in his song there is silence. And always remember also, in Meher Baba or people like that there is song in their silence. If you listen attentively to Meher Baba's silence, you will be full of a song, you will feel it showering on you. And if you listen to Kabir silently, you will see that his song is nothing but a message for silence.

Kabir is one of the most rare human beings who has ever been on this earth. He belongs to the highest category of mystics. And strangely enough he was absolutely uneducated, uncultured, an orphan. But although living the poor life of a weaver, he has also woven some golden poems of tremendous beauty. His words are raw but very pregnant. He says:

Ignorance shuts the iron gates ...

This word "ignorance" has a beauty. Ordinarily you may not have thought about it in this way. You have always thought about ignorance as absence of knowledge; but its true meaning is, ignoring yourself, ignoring that which can become your knowing, which can become your wisdom. And the whole day, the whole life, you are continuously ignoring yourself.

You are taking care of everything, every trivia, but never taking any note of the most precious thing that you have – yourself. And Kabir is using the word in the same sense. Ignoring yourself is the only ignorance. It shuts the iron gates.

... but love opens them.

These are the words of a man who knows. If he was only a learned man he would have said that knowledge opens the doors. But instead of knowledge, only a man who knows can say, but love opens them.

The mind is going to remain in ignorance; it cannot get out of it. The iron gates are closed. The mind can become knowledgeable, but it cannot become wise. It is only the heart which opens the gates. It is only love that makes you wise.

The sound of the gates opening wakes the beautiful woman asleep.

Now these are symbolic words. According to Kabir, your soul is the sleeping woman. He is using the word "woman" for your soul, your consciousness, because only the feminine qualities are authentically spiritual qualities. Beauty is feminine, honesty is feminine, sincerity is feminine; all that is great within your consciousness is feminine. Even the word "consciousness" is feminine.

In English it is difficult, because in English you don't make a difference in words, you don't make a difference between male and female in each word. But in any language that is born in the East, each word has the distinction: consciousness, awareness, samadhi, *sambodhi*, all are feminine. And the man of love and compassion starts having a feminine beauty and a feminine grace. The male is a little barbarous. His qualities are that of a warrior, fighter, egoist, chauvinist, fanatic, fascist. The male qualities are qualities of a Nazi.

It is not strange that Germany is the only country which calls its own land the fatherland. The whole world calls their countries the motherland – Germany is a special case. It is time they should change it; they should stop calling it the fatherland because that gives male qualities the priority.

Friedrich Nietzsche was thought of by Adolf Hitler as his master, although Adolf Hitler had not the intelligence to understand Friedrich Nietzsche – whatever he understood was simply misunderstanding. But there were a few points for which Friedrich Nietzsche was also responsible.

He said in a letter that the most beautiful experience of his life was when he saw, one day in the early morning when the sun had risen, a batallion of soldiers with their shining guns, and heard the harmonious sound of their steps: "I have never seen such a beautiful scene, nor have I heard such beautiful music as the music of the soldiers and their boots going in harmonious parade." Nietzsche also is responsible; these types of pieces Adolf Hitler collected from Nietzsche. The soldier became the real human being, and all the qualities of a warrior became the qualities of a superman.

But the East has always been aware that man and his qualities may be utilitarian, useful, but they don't have the sensitivity, the softness, the lovingness, the compassion of the woman. That is why Kabir says, "The sound of the gates opening wakes the beautiful woman asleep."

Kabir says, "Don't let a chance like this go by."

I also say to you, don't let a chance like this go by. We are making every effort here to wake up your woman, to wake up your consciousness, to wake up your grace, to wake up your beauty. Don't let a chance like this go by.

Kabir is a harbinger, a herald of the future, the first flower that heralds the spring. He is one of the greatest poets of religion. He is not a theologian, he does not belong to any religion. All religions belong to him, but he is vast enough to contain all. No particular religion defines him. He is a Hindu and a Mohammedan and a Christian and a Jain and a Buddhist. He's a great beauty, a great poetry, a great orchestra.

And the man was utterly illiterate. The man was a weaver, a poor man. In India he is rare – Buddha was the son of a king, so was Mahavira, so was Rama and so was Krishna. India has been always interested too much in riches – notwithstanding what its leaders go on saying to the world, that it is spiritual. It has been too materialistic, and not even honest about it. Even when Indians talk against material things they are materialists. If they praise Buddha they praise because he renounced the kingdom – the value is still in the kingdom. Because he renounced such wealth, that's why he's worshiped.

Kabir is rare, he is a poor man. In Kabir, for the first time a poor man is recognized as a man of God. Otherwise it was a monopoly of kings and princes and rich people.

Kabir is the Christ of the East. Christ was also illiterate – the son of a carpenter – and Christ also speaks in the same way as Kabir. They have great similarities. They belong to the same earth, they are very earthy, but both have great insights. Unsophisticated they are, uncultured, uncivilized. Maybe that is the reason why their sayings are so potent. Their wisdom is not that of the universities, they have been never to any school. Their wisdom comes from the masses, their wisdom is out of their own experience. It is not learned, it is not scholarly, they are not pundits and rabbis. They are ordinary people. In Kabir, in the East, for the first time a poor man has come to declare the beauties of God.

It is very difficult for a poor man to declare the grace of God, it is very difficult for a poor man to be religious. This is my understanding – that if you find a rich man and not religious, then he is stupid. A religious consciousness is bound to happen if you are rich. Much awareness is not needed for it, your very riches will prove to you the futility of this world. If you have all, you have to become religious, that is inevitable – because when you have all you will be able to see, even a stupid person will be able to see, great intelligence is not needed, that "I have got all, and I have nothing inside me." If this does not happen to a rich man then he is really very, very foolish, utterly stupid.

To be religious for a poor man is very difficult, great intelligence is needed – because a poor man has nothing. To see that the world is meaningless is very difficult when you are poor. You have not experienced the world – great insight is needed to see that which you don't have, to see its futility. Because of that, my appreciation for a Christ or a Kabir is far more than for a Buddha or a Mahavira. They had all; they went through the world. Buddha had all the beautiful women of his kingdom available to him. If he became aware that there is nothing in physical beauty, that it is a dream, it is natural. He had all the luxuries possible to a man 25 centuries ago. If he became alert that they don't satisfy, much intelligence is not needed for it. They don't satisfy – the actual experience proves that they don't satisfy, that the discontent remains the same.

But for a Kabir or a Christ it is very difficult. They are not kings, they are poor people; even their necessary needs are not fulfilled. There is every possibility of hoping and dreaming and desiring. To see that the world is meaningless will need a great genius. So Kabir is illiterate but a man of great intelligence – of eyes so penetrating that he can even see the futility of that which he has not got. He can SEE it without having it in his own hands, his perception is so clear. He brings the first glimpse of a future religion.

Whatsoever Kabir is saying has not been written – it is addressed to his disciples. This is a spontaneous outpouring of his heart. He was a singer, he was a poet: somebody would ask something and he would sing a song spontaneously. And nobody has ever sung such songs.

The enlightened man is none other than the fool. Remember, while moving in the company of Kabir, that the enlightened man is none other than the fool. What makes a man enlightened is the realization that he is as a fool. "My mind is that of a fool" says Lao Tzu. Kabir will agree perfectly, totally. "How empty it is" says Lao Tzu "– as empty as the mind of a fool." Emptiness takes nothing seriously, raises no one thing up over another. Worshiping nothing, it celebrates all.

Kabir is a celebrant. He celebrates all – all colors of life, the whole rainbow of it. What he is going to say to you is not philosophy but pure poetry. It is not religion but a hand beckoning, a door half opened, a mirror wiped clean. It is a way back home, a way back to nature.

Nature is God to Kabir – the trees and the rocks and the rivers and the mountains. He does not believe in the temples and the churches and the mosques, he believes in the living reality. God is there, breathing, flowering, flowing. And where are you going? You are going to a temple, man-made, to worship an idol, again manufactured by man, in his own image.

Kabir calls you back from the temples and the mosques: what are you doing there? He calls you back to celebrate life.

When he first entered into this nothingness, Kabir immediately wrote a beautiful poem, in which comes the sentence, "The dewdrop has fallen into the ocean." His own sentences are very beautiful:

Herat herat hey sakhi, rahya Kabir herayi – "O, my friend, my beloved, I had gone to search, to seek myself, but something strange has happened. Rather than finding myself, I have disappeared just like a dewdrop disappearing in the ocean."

Bunda samani samunda men so kat heri jayi – "The dewdrop

has disappeared in the ocean. Now how can you find the dewdrop again?"

That was his first experience. Then he became more and more aware of the ocean, and forgot all about the dewdrop. Before dying he called his son, Kamal. He was certainly rightly named by Kabir. *Kamal* means a miracle – and the son of Kabir was certainly a miracle. He called Kamal and said to him, "I am going to leave my body soon. Before I leave, you have to correct one of my poems. Just a little change …

"I have written that the dewdrop has entered into the ocean. You have to change it. Just reverse it. Say the ocean has disappeared into the dewdrop – because now I know from the other side. My first experience was from this shore; now I am talking from the further shore, the beyond. Now I know the dewdrop has not fallen into the ocean, it is the ocean that has fallen into the dewdrop."

Kamal said to him, "I have always suspected that line. I can show you my copy." And he showed Kabir. He had crossed out that line.

Kabir said, "You are really a *kamal*, you are a miracle. You came to know it before me." The line was crossed out.

Kamal said, "I was suspicious from the very beginning, that this was the statement of a beginner, the first statement when he comes to see the nothingness. But when he becomes nothingness, this statement will be absolutely wrong. So now that you have come to your senses, just before dying, I can rejoice that you are no longer just a beginner, you have become part of the whole." Then he wrote the new line: "the ocean has fallen into the dewdrop."

Kabir was a poor man. As far as the outside world is concerned, he was nobody. But as far as the inner world is concerned, he belongs to the same category as Gautama Buddha, Lao Tzu, Zarathustra.

His statements, of course, cannot be in the language of the learned and the scholarly. And it is not unfortunate in any way; on the contrary, it is very fortunate that he speaks the language of the very ordinary man, but he brings such beauty to language that no scholarship can compete with it. He brings such glamor to the mundane words used in the marketplace ... you could have never thought that this can become a symbol for the ultimate. But he knows no other language.

He has the experience of the ultimate, but his language is that of a weaver; he was a weaver. His whole life he was weaving clothes, going to sell them every Sunday in the marketplace. Even though he became famous far and wide as an awakened, enlightened consciousness and thousands of people started coming to him, even kings, the richest people, he never left his job. He continued weaving.

A thousand and one times Kabir must have been asked by his disciples: "We can take care of all your needs. And your needs are not very many ..." He had only one son, one wife and himself, and they lived in absolute poverty. But he always refused. He said, "God has made me a weaver and I cannot be otherwise. And you never think about those people who get the clothes which I weave. I weave with such love and such joy, such celebration, such consciousness, that nobody else can do it. What will happen to my customers? I am always weaving for my customers, because every customer of mine is a representation of the divine. I am in the service of the divine; please don't distract me."

His language, because he was a weaver, reflects again and again his profession and the language that must have been used by his profession.

In this beautiful statement, which nobody else could have made – Buddha cannot make it, he cannot even think of it – Kabir says: "I leave behind my cloak intact."

This statement was made before his death, just a few moments before. He is saying, I am leaving my cloak intact.

I wore my cloak with great care, then put it aside as I found it, without impairing it in any way. Oh swan, take off on the flight alone.

The moment of departure, the final departure of consciousness from the body … In the Eastern mystic language the swan symbolizes the soul, because the swan is so white and so pure and particularly the swan that comes from the Himalayas has the same purity as the eternal snow of the Himalayas.

Because of the whiteness, the purity … And it lives far away in the Himalayas where very few people have ever reached, the highest lake in the world, Mansarovar. Nine months out of twelve it is frozen; only for three months it melts. The swan for nine months comes down to the plains, but without fail it returns after nine months to Mansarovar.

And a strange mystery is that these months that he is not at Mansarovar are the months when the swan gives birth to children. Even when they leave, their eggs have not opened yet. When the time comes they leave their eggs behind and move away towards Mansarovar. The mystery is that the parents have never met the child, the child has never traveled the path; he knows nothing about Mansarovar, but still when the egg ripens and the child swan is born, it immediately starts flying in the direction of Mansarovar.

Because of this fact it became a tremendously important symbol: you don't know where your home is; there is no guide, no map, you have to go alone. But every child swan reaches Mansarovar, without fail.

Metaphorically, we don't belong to this mundane world. It is not our home. Sooner or later the moment comes: your consciousness opens its wings and flies towards its home.

Kabir is making this statement just before leaving the body. The body is symbolized as the cloak. In Hindi it is called *chadariya*.

"I leave behind my cloak intact." Just as you have given it to me: I have not spoiled it, not even a small scratch, not even a small dark spot. As white and as clean and pure as you had given it to me, I am putting it aside.

"I wore my cloak with great care." This is to be understood. He is not against the body. He is saying, I wore my cloak with great care, I used my body with great care, with love, and then put it aside as I found it. Now the moment has come to put it aside, but I am putting it aside exactly as I had found it.

The words of Kabir are very beautiful. Almost untranslatable is their beauty. They have a certain music that is missing in any translation, but still you should hear those words:

Jyon ki tyon dhari dinhi chadariya
Khoob jatan kar odhi chadariya.

With great effort I have used the cloak you had given to me and I am putting it back – "*Jyon ki tyon*" – just the way you had given it to me, without spoiling it, without impairing it in any way. "Oh swan," and this he addresses to himself, "Oh swan, take off on the flight alone."

Now even this cloak, this *chadariya* that you have been using for your whole life, cannot go with you. Neither your wife nor your son nor your friends nor your disciples – nobody can go with you; you have to go alone. It is a flight of the alone to the alone.

Oh swan, take off on the flight alone.

And Kabir blessed his disciples. Before closing his eyes he said the *chadariya* is simply like a bed cloth, you can wrap it around your body he told his disciples, "Cover me with the *chadariya*, with the cloak."

And one asked, "Why?"

He said, "You will find out later on."

His body was covered with the same cloth that he had used his whole life.

I have been to the place where Kabir died, just near Varanasi, on the other side of the Ganges. On one side is the great city of Varanasi, according to Hindus the most ancient city of the world. And it looks like it. You cannot use cars in the main city, because the roads are so narrow that they were meant to be walked on, not to be used by any vehicles. They must have been made even before bullock carts were invented. Otherwise at least they should have been as broad as a bullock cart.

In the ancient part of Varanasi the roads are so cool the sun almost never reaches there because the buildings are high, and the road is so narrow that only two persons can go side by side. Only for a few seconds, when the sun comes exactly in the middle of the sky, those roads get a few rays and again shadow. They are very cool, almost air-conditioned, and centuries of air-conditioning ...

Just on the other side of the Ganges is the small village of Maghar, where Kabir died. The samadhi, the memorial grave, is divided by a partition. One side belongs to the Mohammedans, the other side belongs to the Hindus. Such is the stupidity of humanity. You worship the same man, you love the same man. You have breathed his philosophy, the same words, but the conditioned mind of man ...

Mohammedans made a grave for the flowers that were their portion, and Hindus burned those flowers that were their portion on a funeral pyre. And they both made the memorial, but with a wall in the middle: half the memorial belongs to the Hindus, half the memorial to the Mohammedans. The Mohammedans will not go to the Hindu side, and the Hindus will not go to the Mohammedan side. And this is the memorial of a single man!

These religions have been spreading such nonsense and stupidity in people. I say unto you, neither Varanasi nor Jerusalem nor Mecca can make any difference. It is your consciousness. If you die consciously you will reach to the ultimate blissfulness; it does not belong to, it is not a monopoly of any religion.

But you will have to go alone. It is not the crowd to which you belong that makes it sure that you will reach to the ultimate truth. The ultimate truth is always individual.

Oh swan, take off on the flight alone.

Krishna

Krishna reached the absolute height and depth of religion, and yet he is not at all serious and sad, not in tears. By and large, the chief characteristic of a religious person has been that he is somber, serious and sad-looking – like one vanquished in the battle of life, like a renegade from life. Krishna comes dancing, singing and laughing.

Religions of the past were all life-denying and masochistic, extolling sorrow and suffering as great virtues. If you set aside Krishna's vision of religion, then every religion of the past presented a sad and sorrowful face. A laughing religion, a religion that accepts life in its totality is yet to be born. And it is good that the old religions are dead, along with them, that the old God, the God of our old concepts is dead too.

It is said of Jesus that he never laughed. It was perhaps his sad look and the picture of his body on the cross that became the focal point of attraction for people, most of whom are themselves unhappy and miserable. In a deep sense Mahavira and Buddha are against life too. They are in favor of some other life in some other world; they support a kind of liberation from this life. Every religion has divided life into two parts, and while they accept one part they deny the other; Krishna accepts the whole of life. That is why India held him to be a perfect incarnation of God, while all other incarnations were assessed as imperfect and incomplete. Even Rama is described as an incomplete incarnation of God, but Krishna is the whole of God.

And there is a reason for saying so. The reason is that Krishna has accepted and absorbed everything that life is.

Albert Schweitzer made a significant remark in criticism of the Indian religion. He said that the religion of India is life-negative. This remark is correct to a large extent, if Krishna is left out. But it is utterly wrong in the context of Krishna. If Schweitzer had tried to understand Krishna he would never have said what he did.

Krishna accepts the body in its totality. And he accepts it not in any selected dimension but in all its dimensions. Apart from Krishna, Zarathustra is another. About him it is said he was born laughing. Every child enters this world crying. Only one child in all of history laughed at the time of his birth, and that was Zarathustra. And this is an index – an index of the fact that a happy and laughing humanity is yet to be born. And only a joyful and laughing humanity can accept Krishna.

The old religions taught suppression as the way to God. Man was asked to suppress everything – his sex, his anger, his greed, his attachments – and then alone would he find his soul, would he attain to God. This war of man against himself has continued long enough. And in the history of thousands of years of this war, barely a handful of people, whose names can be counted on one's fingers, can be said to have found God. So in a sense we lost this war, because down the centuries billions of people died without finding their souls, without meeting God.

Undoubtedly there must be some basic flaw, some fundamental mistake in the very foundation of these religions.

It is as if a gardener has planted 50,000 trees and out of them only one tree flowers – and yet we accept his scripture on gardening on the plea that at least one tree has blossomed. But we fail to take into consideration that this single tree might have been an exception to the rule, that it might have blossomed not because of the gardener, but in spite of him. The rest of the 50,000 trees, those that remained stunted and barren, are enough proof the gardener was not worth his salt.

If a Buddha, a Mahavira or a Christ attains to God in spite of these fragmentary and conflict-ridden religions, it is no testimony to the success of these religions as such. The success of religion, or let us say the success of the gardener, should be acclaimed only when all 50,000 trees of his garden, with the exception of one or two, achieve flowering. Then the blame could be laid at the foot of the one tree for its failure to bloom. Then it could be said that this tree remained stunted and barren in spite of the gardener.

With Freud a new kind of awareness has dawned on man: that suppression is wrong, that suppression brings with it nothing but self-pity and anguish. If a man fights with himself he can only ruin and destroy himself. If I make my left hand fight with my right hand, neither is going to win, but in the end the contest will certainly destroy me. While my two hands fight with themselves, I and I alone will be destroyed in the process. That is how, through denial and suppression of his natural instincts and emotions, man became suicidal and killed himself.

Krishna seems to be relevant to the new awareness, to the new understanding that came to man in the wake of Freud and his findings. Krishna is against repression. He accepts life in all its facets, in all its climates and colors. He does not choose, he accepts life unconditionally. He does not shun love; being a man he does not run away from women. As one who has known and experienced God, he does not turn his face from war. He is full of love and compassion, and yet he has the courage to accept and fight a war. His heart is utterly non-violent, yet he plunges into the fire and fury of violence when it becomes unavoidable. He accepts the nectar, and yet he is not afraid of poison.

In fact, one who knows the deathless should be free of the fear of death. And of what worth is that nectar which is afraid of death? One who knows the secret of non-violence should cease to fear violence. What kind of non-violence is it that is afraid of violence? And how can the spirit, the soul, fear the body and run away from it? Krishna accepts the duality, the dialectics of life altogether and therefore transcends duality. What we call transcendence is not possible so long as you are in conflict, so long as you choose one part and reject the other. Transcendence is only possible when you choicelessly accept both parts together, when you accept the whole.

It is really arduous to understand Krishna. It is easy to understand that a man should run away from the world if he wants to find peace, but it is really difficult to accept that one can find peace in the thick of the marketplace. It is understandable that a man can attain to purity of mind if he breaks away from his attachments, but it is really difficult to realize that one can remain unattached and innocent in the very midst of relationships and attachments, that one can remain calm and still live at the very center of the cyclone. There is no difficulty in accepting that the flame of a candle will remain steady and still in a place well secluded from winds and storms, but how can you believe that a candle can keep burning steadily even in the midst of raging storms and hurricanes? So it is difficult even for those who are close to Krishna to understand him.

Krishna has tested, and tested fully his own strength and intelligence. It has been tested and found that man can remain, like a lotus in water, untouched and unattached while living in the throes of relationship. It has been discovered that man can hold to his love and compassion even on the battlefield, that he can continue to love with his whole being while wielding a sword in his hand.

It is this paradox that makes Krishna difficult to understand. Therefore, people who have loved and worshiped him have done so by dividing him into parts, and they have worshiped his different fragments, those of their liking. No one has accepted and worshiped the whole of Krishna, no one has embraced him in his entirety. The poet Surdas sings hymns of praise to Krishna in his childhood, Bal Krishna. Surdas' Krishna never grows up, because there is a danger with a grown-up Krishna that Surdas cannot ace. There is not much trouble with a boy Krishna flirting with the young women of his village, but it will be too much if a grown-up Krishna does the same. Then it will be difficult to understand him.

After all, we can understand something on our own plane, on our own level. There is no way to understand something on a plane other than ours.

So for their adoration of Krishna, different people have chosen different facets of his life. There is perhaps no one like Krishna, no one who can accept and absorb in himself all the contradictions of life, all the seemingly great contradictions of life. Day and night, summer and winter, peace and war, love and violence, life and death – all walk hand in hand with him. That is why everyone who loves him has chosen a particular aspect of Krishna's life that appealed to him and quietly dropped the rest.

Krishna's life, on the other hand, accepts no limitations. It is not bound by any rules of conduct, it is unlimited and vast. Krishna is free, limitlessly free. There is no ground he cannot tread; no point where his steps can fear and falter, no limits he cannot transcend. And this freedom, this vastness of Krishna, stems from his experience of self-knowledge. It is the ultimate fruit of his enlightenment.

In my view, Krishna's flute is exactly the opposite of the cross. And it is important to know that while it is others who hang Jesus on the cross, they really impose it on him; Krishna chooses the flute for himself. It is necessary to bear in mind that while the flute is intrinsic to Krishna and his life – it symbolizes him – the cross is extrinsic to Christ; it does not represent him. It is others, the Jewish priests and the Roman governor, who force the cross on Christ.

Krishna plays the flute for the love of it. Nobody has forced it on him; he has chosen it for himself. I see Krishna's flute symbolizing life's benediction and man's gratefulness to life for this blessing. Krishna has made his choice for happiness, for bliss. In fact, when life is so good and great, Krishna cannot but choose to be happy, and he says it with the flute.

And just as an unhappy person does not suffer alone, he makes many others unhappy, similarly a happy person becomes the source of happiness for countless numbers of people. So when Krishna plays his flute, its melody, its bliss, does not remain confined to him, it gladdens all those whose hearts come to hear it. And it is as it should be.

If you happen to pass by a cross with Jesus hanging on it, you will immediately be depressed and sad. On the other hand, seeing Krishna dancing in ecstasy on the banks of the river Yamuna will fill your heart with delight and joy. Pleasure and pain, happiness and unhappiness are contagious; they are communicable from one to another; they spread and escalate like wildfire.

So the one who decides to be unhappy is condemning the whole world to be unhappy; he might as well say he has decided to punish the whole earth by choosing to be unhappy. And the person who decides to be happy is going to bless the whole to be happy, he is going to add to the song and music of life all over this planet. Therefore a happy person is a religious person; and an unhappy person is utterly irreligious.

I call the man religious who brings happiness to himself and to others. For me, nothing except happiness, blissfulness, is a religious quality. In this sense Krishna is truly a religious person, whose whole being exudes nothing but happiness and bliss. And such a person can bless the whole of mankind, he is a living blessing to the world.

But why did the great Indian war of the Mahabharat happen in a civilization that had accepted the flute as its symbol? I say, this happened in spite of Krishna's flute. Krishna is not the cause of the Mahabharat. There is no relationship whatsoever between the flute and war. But there exists a logical relationship between the cross and war.

The Mahabharat took place in spite of Krishna and his flute. It simply means we are so attached to sorrow, so steeped in misery that even Krishna's flute fails to bring a ray of hope and joy to our hearts. The flute continued to play, and we plunged into the vortex of war. The flute could not change our sadomasochistic minds; Krishna's flute could not become our flute too.

It is interesting to know how difficult it is for someone to share in another's happiness. It is so easy to share in another's sorrow. You can easily cry with someone crying, but it is so hard to laugh with someone laughing. You can easily sympathize with one whose house has been burned down, but it is arduous to participate in the joys of one who has built himself a beautiful new house. And it is not without some fundamental reasons.

It is easy to come close to Jesus' cross, because it strikes a note of empathy in our hearts, which are already filled with pain and misery. On the other hand Krishna's flute will fill our hearts with envy and we will escape from him. Krishna's bliss will bring up envy in us; it will not find an empathic response from our hearts.

But remember, Krishna is not a warmonger. He is not a hawk, as some pacifists would like to call him. He is a supporter of life, he stands by life, and he will fight for it if need be. If the great values of life – without which life would cease to be life – are in peril, Krishna will not hesitate to defend them with missiles. Not that he relishes violence or war, but if it becomes unavoidable he will not shirk the responsibility.

That is why, from the beginning, he does everything to avoid the Mahabharat. He leaves no stone unturned to avert war and save life and peace. But when all his efforts for peace fail, he realizes that the recalcitrant forces of death and destruction – forces that are against righteousness and religion – are not amenable to an honorable peace. He readies himself to fight on behalf of life and religion.

As I see it, life and religion are not two different things for Krishna. And therefore he can fight as naturally as he can dance. It is remarkable that a man like Krishna, even when he goes to the battle-field, is happy and joyful; he never loses his bliss. And men like Jesus are sad even as they keep a distance from the battlefield. Krishna can be blissful even on the battlefield, because war comes to him as part of life; it cannot be segregated from life.

As I said earlier, Krishna does not divide life into black and white, good and evil, as the moralists and monks do. He does not subscribe to the view that war is purely evil. He says that nothing is good or evil under all circumstances. There are occasions when poison can work like nectar and nectar can work like poison. There are moments when blessings turn into curses and curses into blessings.

Nothing is certain for all time and space, under all circumstances. The same thing can be good in one time and bad in another; it is really determined by the moment at hand. Nothing can be predetermined and prejudged. If someone does so, he is in for troubles in life, because life is a flux where everything changes from moment to moment. So Krishna lives in the moment; nothing is predetermined for him.

For long, Krishna does his best to avert war, but when he finds that it is inescapable he accepts it without hesitation. He does not want that one should go to war with a heavy heart, he does not believe in doing anything reluctantly in fact. If war becomes inescapable he will go to it with all his heart and mind.

With all his heart he tries to avert it, and when he fails, he goes to war wholeheartedly. In the beginning of war, as you know, he has no mind to take any active part in it. He tells Arjuna that he will not use his particular weapon – *sudarshan* – on the battlefield, he will only work as Arjuna's charioteer. But then a moment comes when he takes the *sudarshan* in his hand and becomes an active participant in the war.

J. Krishnamurti

My connection with J. Krishnamurti is a real mystery. I have loved him since I have known him, and he has been very loving towards me. But we have never met; hence the relationship, the connection is something beyond words. We have not seen each other ever, but yet … perhaps we have been the two persons closest to each other in the whole world. We had a tremendous communion that needs no language, that need not be of physical presence.

Once it happened – just a coincidence – he was in Bombay. He used to come to Bombay every year to remain there for a few weeks. He had perhaps more followers in Bombay than anywhere else in the world. I came to Bombay. I was just going to New Delhi and I had to wait a few hours. Some friends who had been deeply connected with J. Krishnamurti and who were also connected with me, came to me and said, "This is a golden opportunity. You are both in the same place. A meeting will be of immense importance, and Krishnamurti wants the meeting."

The man who said this was a very respected revolutionary of India, Ajit Patvardhan. He was one of the closest colleagues of J. Krishnamurti.

I looked into his eyes and said, "Please don't lie. You must have said to J. Krishnamurti, 'Osho wants to meet you.'"

He was taken aback, almost shocked. He said, "But how could you manage to know? That's exactly what we have been conspiring. We knew perfectly well that this would be the only possible way; if we say to you, 'Krishnamurti wants to meet you,' you cannot refuse. If I say to Krishnamurti, 'Osho wants to meet you,' he cannot refuse. And the people who have been connected with Krishnamurti have all become connected with you too. We are all eager to see what transpires when you two both meet."

I simply told Ajit Patvardhan an old story of two great mystics, Kabir and Farid. Kabir had his commune near Varanasi, on the opposite side of the Ganges. Farid was traveling with his disciples; he was a Mohammedan, a Sufi mystic, and he was going to pass the village where Kabir was living.

The disciples of both mystics persuaded them. "It would not be right that Farid passes here and you do not invite him," Kabir's disciples said. "It is simply a matter of love to invite those people to live in our commune for a few days, to rest." Farid's disciples said, "It will not look right to bypass the commune of Kabir. At least we should just go to pay our tribute."

Farid and Kabir both agreed. But the real thing amongst the disciples of both was that they wanted to see what happened when they met, what they would talk about, what would be the things that were important between these two persons.

But they never uttered a word.

The disciples were very much disappointed; this was not what they were waiting for. The moment both the mystics had departed they had to face their disciples, and the disciples were really angry.

The disciples of Kabir said, "You made fools of us. For two days we have been waiting to listen to something – you are always talking – and what happened to you? You became suddenly silent. We do not understand. What is this matter of laughing like madmen, weeping, tears, smiles, hugging – but not saying a single word?"

And the same was the situation with Farid. The disciples were raising the same problem, and the answer that was given was also the same. Farid and Kabir virtually said the same thing to their disciples: "We both know there is nothing to say. He has eyes, I have eyes. We have both experienced, we have both tasted the truth. What is there to say? Whoever would have uttered a single word would have been proved ignorant, that he does not know. We recognized each other; it is impossible not to recognize. Even two blind people recognize each other; do you think two people with eyes will not recognize each other?

"Of course we enjoyed each other. That's why joy, smiles, tears were the only possible language; when it was too much, we hugged each other. We were sitting holding each other's hands for hours and our love was flowing, and there was a communion – two bodies and one soul.

"But forgive us, we completely forgot about you. You cannot understand anything except words, and truth cannot be expressed in words. You have every right to be disappointed, to be angry, but you should consider our position also. We are helpless. When two silences meet, they become one. When two loving hearts beat, they beat in harmony; a music arises which is not mundane, which cannot be heard by the ears – which can be heard only by those who can experience it in their hearts."

So I told Ajit Patvardhan, "It is absolutely useless, wasting Krishnamurti's time. You are not going to hear anything."

And when they went back to Krishnamurti he asked, "What happened? He has not come?"

They told the story, saying, "He simply told us a story."

And he laughed and said, "He did exactly the right thing. In fact I should have told you the story but I don't know the story. I also wanted to explain to you that it is futile, but you would not have understood."

My connection with him was the deepest possible connection – which needs no physical contact, which needs no linguistic communication. Not only that, once in a while I used to criticize him, he used to criticize me, and we enjoyed each other's criticism – knowing perfectly well that the other does not mean it. Now that he is dead, I will miss him because I will not be able to criticize him; it won't be right. It was such a joy to criticize him. He was the most intelligent man of this century, but he was not understood by people.

He has died, and it seems the world goes on its way without even looking back for a single moment now the most intelligent man is no longer there. It will be difficult to find that sharpness and that intelligence again in centuries. But people are such sleepwalkers, they have not taken much note. In newspapers, just in small corners where nobody reads, his death was declared. And it seems that a 90-year-old man who was continuously speaking for almost 70 years, moving around the world, trying to help people to get unconditioned, trying to help people to become free – nobody seems even to pay a tribute to the man who has worked the hardest in the whole of history for man's freedom, for man's dignity.

I don't feel sorry for his death. His death was beautiful; he attained all that life is capable to give. But I certainly feel sorry for the whole world. It goes on missing its greatest flights of consciousnesses, its highest peaks, its brightest stars. It is too concerned with trivia.

I feel such a deep affinity with Krishnamurti that even to talk of connection is not right; connection is possible only between two things that are separate. I feel almost a oneness with him. In spite of all his criticisms, in spite of all my criticisms – which were just joking with the old man, provoking the old man ... and he was very easily provoked. I just had to send my sannyasins to his meetings to sit in the front row, all in red colors, and he would go mad! He could not tolerate the red color. In his past life he must have been a bull; just a red flag and the bull goes crazy. Bulls have their own personality.

But even though he used to become angry – he would forget the subject matter he was going to talk on, and he would start criticizing me and my people – later on he would say about me to the hostess where he was staying, "This guy is something. He disturbs my meetings, sending red-robed people. And the moment I see them, I forget what is the subject I have decided to speak on. It happens every time, and I know that he is simply playing a joke. He is not serious, he is not against me; neither am I against him."

From many of his intimate people I have been informed, "He is not against you. He wants you to know that howsoever angry he becomes, he is not against you."

I said to them, "I know it. I love the man. But to love a man and once in a while to joke with him, do you think it is contradictory? In fact, I am trying to help him to become a little less serious. A little more sense of humor will not do any harm to him. Only on that point I do not agree with him – he is too serious."

Religion needs a certain quality of humor to make it more human. If there is no sense of humor in any religious teaching, it becomes more and more intellectual, mathematical, logical, but it loses the human touch. It becomes more and more a scientific subject. But man cannot be just an object of scientific study. There is something in him which transcends scientific study.

Just look around the world. Trees don't laugh, buffaloes don't laugh. No animal laughs; it is only man who has the sense of humor. There must be something in it because it happens at the highest evolutionary point – man.

Krishnamurti's teaching is beautiful, but too serious. And my experience and feeling is that his 70 years went to waste because he was serious. So only people who were long-faced and miserable and serious types collected around him; he was a collector of corpses, and as he became older, those corpses also became older.

Life needs a little playfulness, a little humor, a little laughter.

Only on that point am I in absolute disagreement with him; otherwise, he was a genius.

Krishnamurti failed because he could not touch the human heart; he could only reach the human head. The heart needs some different approaches. This is where I have differed with him all my life: unless the human heart is reached, you can go on repeating parrot-like, beautiful words – they don't mean anything. Whatever Krishnamurti was saying is true, but he could not manage to relate it to your heart.

In other words, what I am saying is that J. Krishnamurti was a great philosopher but he could not become a master. He could not help people, prepare people for a new life, a new orientation.

But still I love him, because amongst the philosophers he comes the closest to the mystic way of life. He himself avoided the mystic way, bypassed it, and that is the reason for his failure. But he is the only one amongst the modern contemporary thinkers who comes very close, almost on the boundary line of mysticism, and stops there. Perhaps he's afraid that if he talks about mysticism people will start falling into old patterns, old traditions, old philosophies of mysticism. That fear prevents him from entering. But that fear also prevents other people from entering into the mysteries of life.

Why is Krishnamurti so much against masters and disciples? It is a wound that has healed but the scar is still left. He was forced to be a disciple against his will. He was a small child when he was adopted by Annie Besant and the theosophists, only nine years old, completely unaware of what was being done to him. And he was forced to follow a very rigid discipline.

Twenty-four hours a day he was being trained, because one of the theosophist leaders, Leadbeater, had this idea, this vision, that this boy was going to become a world teacher – a *jagatguru*, a master of the whole world – that he was going to become the vehicle of Lord Maitreya, that he had to be prepared so he could receive the new incarnation of Buddha in his body. So he was tortured in many ways.

He was not allowed to eat like other children, he was not allowed to play with other children, as any child would like to. He was guarded. He was not allowed to go to ordinary schools, he was almost completely kept a prisoner. And then getting up early at three o'clock in the morning, and then the ritual bath, and so many, many rituals – Tibetan, Chinese, Indian, Egyptian ... he must have become tired.

And the last wound happened when his brother Nityananda died. There were two brothers, Krishnamurti and Nityananda, and both were being prepared, because there was a little suspicion as to who was really going to be the master. Nityananda died from this rigid discipline, this almost insane imposition. His death was a trauma for Krishnamurti; he had loved his brother tremendously. There was no other outlet for his love. He had been taken away from his family; his mother had died and his father was not able to look after them, he was just a small clerk. Both the children were adopted by Annie

Besant and they had to travel all around the world learning different esoteric disciplines. It was very hard on them. There is every possibility Nityananda died simply because of too much training.

And then those masters whom Krishnamurti had not chosen out of love ... they were like prisoners and the masters were like jailers. He carried a very wrong notion about masters; it was very difficult for him to get free from their trap. Finally he got free from their trap – how long can you hold someone? When he became a young man, and strong enough to get out of the trap, he simply rushed out, and declared, "I am nobody's master, and I am not going to be a world teacher, and this is all nonsense!"

Since then, the scar has remained. Since then he has been talking about things like masters, disciplines, meditations, disciplehood, and he has been against all of them. It is natural. In fact he has never known a master, and he has never known disciplehood – because these are not things that can be imposed on you, these are things which you accept out of joy and love.

Krishnamurti never talks about these things, there is no point in talking about these things, all those old fogies who exploited him are dead. But somewhere there is a scar. Hence his antagonism to masters, to disciplehood, to sannyas, to all kinds of methods. This shows something about his history; it shows nothing about masters and disciples.

What does he know about Buddha and the disciples that Buddha had? What does he know about Atisha and the masters Dharmakirti, Dharmarakshita and Yogin Maitreya – what does he know about these people? Annie Besant and Leadbeater never allowed him to read ancient scriptures because they were afraid he would lose his originality. So he was kept utterly ignorant of all the great traditions of the world.

And if you don't know anything about Atisha and Dharmakirti, you will miss something. Dharmakirti was the master who told Atisha to move to another master, Dharmarakshita, "because what I have known, I have given to you. I can give you the rest too, but that has never been my path. Go to Dharmarakshita, he has followed another route. He will give you something more, something more authentic. I have only heard about it, or only seen it from the mountain top. I give you emptiness. Now, to learn compassion, go to Dharmarakshita."

What beautiful people they must have been! And Dharmarakshita told him, "I know only the feminine kind of compassion, the passive kind. For the active, you must go to another master, Yogin Maitreya; he will teach you."

These are not people who are possessive, who are jealous, who want to dominate. These are people who give freedom! Krishnamurti is utterly unaware of all the great traditions of the world – he only knows the theosophists.

And that was one of the ugliest things that happened in this century. All kinds of fools gathered under the banner of theosophy, it was a hotch-potch. It was an effort to create a synthesis of all that is good out of all the religions. But no such synthesis is possible. And if you make such a synthesis you will only have a corpse on your hands, not an alive body, breathing, pulsating.

It is as if you love many women – one woman has beautiful eyes, you take the eyes out; another woman has a beautiful nose, you cut off the nose – and so on and so forth. Put all the parts together, assemble them, and you will have a corpse. Making the corpse you have killed twenty beautiful women, and the end result is just utter stupidity.

That's what theosophy did. Something is beautiful in Hinduism, something is beautiful in Taoism, something is beautiful in Mohammedanism, something is beautiful in Judaism, and so on and so forth. Collect all that, put it together, put it in a mixer and mix it, and what you will have will be just a corpse.

Krishnamurti unfortunately had to live with these people. But he has tremendous intelligence. Anybody in his place would have been lost, anybody else in his situation would not have been able to come out of the cage. And the cage was so beautiful, so alluring – thousands of followers were available. But he had the courage, he had the guts and intelligence to renounce all that, to simply move out of the whole trap.

It was difficult for him, very difficult; even to survive was difficult. I respect the man, I respect him tremendously. And I can understand why he is against masters, disciples, sannyas.

Krishnamurti's statement that "the observer is the observed" is one of the most significant things ever said by any man on the earth. The statement is as extraordinary as J. Krishnamurti was.

It is difficult to understand it only intellectually, because the way of the intellect is dialectical, dualistic. On the path of intellect the subject can never be the object, the seer can never be the seen. The observer cannot be the observed. As far as intellect is concerned, it is an absurd statement, meaningless – not only meaningless, but insane.

The intellectual approach towards reality is that of division: the knower and the known have to be separate. Only then is there a possibility of knowledge between the two. The scientist cannot become science, the scientist has to remain separate from what he is doing. The experimenter is not allowed to become the experiment itself. As far as intellect is concerned, logic is concerned, it looks absolutely valid.

But there is a knowledge that passeth understanding, there is a knowing that goes beyond science. Only because that kind of knowing which goes beyond science is possible, is mysticism possible, is religiousness possible.

Let us move from a different direction. Science divides the whole of human experience and existence into two parts: the known and the unknown. That which is known today was unknown yesterday, that which is unknown today may become known tomorrow, so the distance is not impossible, unbridgeable. The distance is only because man's knowledge is growing, and as his knowledge grows the area of his ignorance diminishes. In other words, as he knows more, the area of the unknown becomes less and the area of the known becomes bigger.

If we follow this logic, the ultimate result will be that one day there will be nothing left as unknown. Slowly, slowly, the unknown will change into the known, and the moment will come when there is nothing left as unknown. That is the goal of science, to destroy ignorance – but to destroy ignorance means to destroy all possibilities of exploration, all possibilities of the unknown challenging you to move forward.

The destruction of ignorance means the death of all intelligence, because there will be no need for intelligence anymore. It will be simply something which was useful in the past – you can put it in a museum – but it is of no use anymore. This is not a very exciting picture.

Mysticism does not agree with science, it goes beyond it.

According to mysticism, existence and experience is divided into three parts: the known, the unknown, and the unknowable. The known was unknown one day, the unknown will become known one day, but the unknowable will remain unknowable; it will remain mysterious. Whatever you do, the mystery will always surround existence. The mystery will always be there around life, around love, around meditation.

The mystery cannot be destroyed.

Ignorance can be destroyed, but by destroying ignorance you cannot destroy the miraculous, the mysterious.

J. Krishnamurti's statement belongs to the unknowable.

I have been telling you that as you meditate … and by meditation I simply mean as you become more and more aware of your mind process. If the mind process is 100 percent, taking your whole energy, you will be fast asleep inside – there will be no alertness.

One morning Gautama Buddha is talking to his disciples. The king, Prasenjita, has also come to listen to him; he is sitting just in front of Buddha. He is not accustomed to sitting on the floor – he is a king – so he is feeling uncomfortable, fidgety, changing sides, somehow trying not to disturb and not to be noticed by Buddha because he is not sitting silently, peacefully. He is continuously moving the big toe of his foot, for no reason, just to be busy without business. There are people who cannot be without business; they will still be busy.

Gautama Buddha stopped talking and asked Prasenjita, "Can you tell me, why are you moving your big toe?" In fact, Prasenjita himself was not aware of it.

You are doing a thousand and one things you are not aware of. Unless somebody points at them, you may not take any note of it.

The moment Buddha asked him, the toe stopped moving. Buddha said, "Why have you stopped moving the toe?"

He said, "You are putting me in an embarrassing situation. I don't know why that toe was moving. This much I know: that as you asked the question it stopped. I have not done anything – neither was I moving it, nor have I stopped it."

Buddha said to his disciples, "Do you see the point? The toe belongs to the man. It moves, but he is not aware of its movement. And the moment he becomes aware – because I asked the question – the very awareness immediately stops the toe. He does not stop it. The very awareness, that 'It is stupid, why are you moving it?' – just the awareness is enough to stop it."

Your mind is a constant traffic of thoughts, and it is always rush hour, day in, day out.

Meditation means to watch the movement of thoughts in the mind.

Just be an observer, as if you are standing by the side of the road watching the traffic – no judgment, no evaluation, no condemnation, no appreciation – just pure observation.

As you become more and more accustomed to observation, a strange phenomenon starts happening. If you are 10 percent aware, that much energy has moved from the mind process to the observer; now the mind has only 90 percent energy available. A moment comes … you have 50 percent of energy. And your energy goes on growing as mind goes on losing its energy. The traffic becomes less and less and less, and you become more and more and more.

Your witnessing self goes on increasing in integrity, expanding; it becomes stronger and stronger. And the mind goes on becoming weaker and weaker: 90 percent observer and 10 percent mind, 99 percent observer and only 1 percent mind.

One hundred percent observer and the mind disappears, the road is empty; the screen of the mind becomes completely empty, nothing moves. There is only the observer.

This is the state J. Krishnamurti's statement is pointing at. When there is nothing to observe, when there is only the observer left, then the observer itself becomes the observed – because there is nothing else to observe, what else to do? The knower simply knows itself. The seer sees himself. The energy that was going towards objects, thoughts … there are no thoughts, no objects. The energy has no way to go anywhere; it simply becomes a light unto itself. There is nothing that it lights, it lights only itself – a flame surrounded by silence, surrounded by nothingness.

That is Krishnamurti's way of saying it, that the observer becomes the observed. You can call it enlightenment, it is the same thing: the light simply lights itself, there is nothing else to fall upon. You have dissolved the mind. You are alone, fully alert and aware.

Krishnamurti is using a phrase of his own. He was a little fussy about it … not to use anybody else's phrase, anybody else's word – not to use anything that has been used by other masters. So his whole life, he was coining his own phrases.

But you can change only the expression, you cannot change the experience. The experience is eternal. It makes no difference whether somebody calls it enlightenment, somebody calls it nirvana, somebody calls it samadhi, somebody calls it something else. You can give it your own name but remember, the experience should not be changed by your words.

And it is not changed by J. Krishnamurti's words. They are perfectly applicable, although they are not so glamorous as nirvana, Gautama Buddha's word, or samadhi, Patanjali's word, or *il'aham*, Mohammed's word. "The observer is the observed" looks too mundane. It certainly points to the reality, but the words in themselves are not very poetic.

❖

One of my friends met Krishnamurti just three days before he died. He reported to me that Krishnamurti was very sad and the only thing he said was, "I worked hard to reach people, but rather than transforming them I have simply spent my own energy, just like a river getting lost in a desert. The people who have been listening to me have thought it not more than good entertainment. The very word entertainment hurts me – that my whole life has been the life of an entertainer."

And it seems so. He died and there has not been even a small stir anywhere, all over the earth. A man who lived for 90 years and has been serving humanity since he was 25 – and it seems he has been dead for centuries. Nobody thinks about him, nobody is concerned that he needs at least some homage. He was one of the greatest giants of this century, but the Nobel Prize committee never even considered his name – because he was not a politician.

In the beginning he was also trying to reach to the people. But he was opposed by churches, by religions, condemned by all the priests; slowly, slowly he dropped the idea of humanity.

He had a few people, in a few cities of the world. In India he used to visit only New Delhi, Bombay, Varanasi and Rishi Valley, where he has one of his schools – just four places; and the same was true around the world. In these places almost the same people heard him for 30 years, 40 years, 50 years ... Still it is very saddening that people who heard him for 50 years continually have not changed a little bit. He could not manage to find them companions. He tried his best. But humanity is becoming more and more adamant, more and more sleepy, drugged, more and more dead. It is becoming very difficult to wake people up.

Lao Tzu

When I speak on Lao Tzu I speak as if I am speaking on my own self. With him my being is totally one. When I speak on Lao Tzu it is as if I am looking in a mirror – my own face is reflected. When I speak on Lao Tzu, I am absolutely with him. Even to say "absolutely with him" is not true – I am him, he is me. Historians are doubtful about his existence. I cannot doubt his existence because how can I doubt my own existence? The moment I became possible, he became true to me. Even if history proves that he never existed it makes no difference to me; he must have existed because I exist – I am the proof.

Lao Tzu is not mathematical at all, yet he is very, very logical in his madness. He has a mad logic! If you can penetrate into his sayings you will come to feel it; it is not so obvious and apparent. He has a logic of his own – the logic of absurdity, the logic of paradox, the logic of a madman. He hits hard.

To understand Lao Tzu's logic you will have to create eyes. It is very subtle, it is not the ordinary logic of the logicians – it is the logic of a hidden life, a very subtle life. Whatsoever he says is on the surface absurd; deep down there lives a very great consistency. One has to penetrate it; one has to change his own mind to understand Lao Tzu. He zigzags. Sometimes you see him going towards the east and sometimes towards the west, because he says east is west and west is east, they are together, they are one. He believes in the unity of the opposites.

And that is how life is, so Lao Tzu is just a spokesman of life. If life is absurd, Lao Tzu is absurd; if life has an absurd logic to it, Lao Tzu has the same logic. Lao Tzu simply reflects life. He doesn't add anything to it, he doesn't choose out of it; he simply accepts whatsoever it is.

It is simple to see the spirituality of a Buddha, very simple; it is impossible to miss it, he is so extraordinary. But it is difficult to see the spirituality of Lao Tzu. He is so ordinary, just like you. You will have to grow in understanding. A Buddha passes by you – you will immediately recognize that a superior human being has passed you. He carries the glamor of a superior human being around him. It is difficult to miss him, almost impossible to miss him. But Lao Tzu … he may be your neighbor. You may have been missing him because he is so ordinary, he is so extraordinarily ordinary. And that is the beauty of it.

To become extraordinary is simple: just effort is needed, refinement is needed, cultivation is needed. It is a deep inner discipline; you can become very, very refined, something absolutely unearthly. But to be ordinary is really the most extraordinary thing. No effort will help – effortlessness is needed. No practice will help, no methods, no means will be of any help – only understanding. Even meditation will not be of any help. To become a Buddha, meditation will be of help. To become a Lao Tzu, even meditation won't help – just understanding. Just understanding life as it is, and living it with courage; not escaping from it, not hiding from it, facing it with courage, whatsoever it is, good or bad, divine or evil, heaven or hell.

It is very difficult to be a Lao Tzu or to recognize a Lao Tzu. In fact, if you can recognize a Lao Tzu, you are already a Lao Tzu. To recognize a Buddha you need not be a Buddha, but to recognize Lao Tzu you need to be a Lao Tzu – otherwise it is impossible.

It is said that Confucius went to see Lao Tzu. Lao Tzu was an old man, Confucius was younger. Lao Tzu was almost unknown, Confucius was almost universally known. Kings and emperors used to call him to their courts; wise men used to come for his advice. He was the wisest man in China in those days. But by and by he must have felt that his wisdom might be of use to others – but he was not blissful, he had not attained to anything. He had become an expert, maybe helpful to others, but not helpful to himself. So he started a secret search to find someone who could help him.

Ordinary wise men wouldn't do, because they used to come for his advice. Great scholars wouldn't do; they used to come to ask Confucius about their problems. But there must be someone somewhere – life is vast. He went on a secret search. He sent his disciples to find someone who could be of help to him, and they came with the information that there lived a man – nobody knew his name – who was known as "the old guy". Lao Tzu means "the old guy". The word is not his name, nobody knows his name. He was such an unknown man that nobody knows when he was born, nobody knows to whom, who his father was or who his mother was. He had lived for 90 years but only very rare human beings had come across him, very rare, who had different eyes and perspectives with which to understand him. He was only for the rarest – so ordinary a man, but only for the rarest of human minds.

Hearing the news that a man known as "the old guy" existed, Confucius went to see him. When he met Lao Tzu he could feel that here was a man of great understanding, great intellectual integrity, great logical acumen, a genius. He could feel that something was there, but he couldn't catch hold of it. Vaguely, mysteriously, there was something; this man was no ordinary man although he looked absolutely ordinary. Something was hidden; he was carrying a treasure. Confucius asked, "What do you say about morality? What do you say about how to cultivate good character?" – because he was a moralist and he thought that if you cultivate a good character that is the highest attainment.

Lao Tzu laughed out loud, and said, "If you are immoral, only then the question of morality arises. If you don't have any character, only then you think about character. A man of character is absolutely oblivious of the fact that anything like character exists. A man of morality does not know what the word 'moral' means. So don't be foolish! And don't try to cultivate yourself. Just be natural."

The man had such tremendous energy that Confucius started trembling. He couldn't stand him! He escaped. He became afraid – as one becomes afraid near an abyss. When he came back to his disciples, who were waiting outside under a tree, the disciples could not believe it. Confucius had been going to emperors, the greatest emperors, and they had never seen any nervousness in him. But he was trembling, and cold perspiration was pouring out from all over his body. They couldn't believe it – what had happened? What had this man Lao Tzu done to their teacher?

They asked him and he said, "Wait a little. Let me collect myself. This man is dangerous." And about Lao Tzu he said to his disciples: "I have heard about great animals like elephants, and I know how they walk. And I have heard about hidden animals in the sea, and I know how they swim. I have heard about great birds who fly thousands of miles around the earth, and I know how they fly. But this man is a dragon. Nobody knows how he walks, nobody knows how he lives, nobody knows how he flies. Never go near him – he is like an abyss, he is like a death."

And that is the definition of a master: a master is like death. If you come near him, too close, you will feel afraid, a trembling will take over. You will be possessed by an unknown fear, as if you are going to die. It is said that Confucius never came again to see this old man.

Lao Tzu was ordinary in a way, and in another way he was the most extraordinary man. He was not extraordinary like Buddha; he was extraordinary in a totally different way. His extraordinariness was not so obvious – it was a hidden treasure. He was not miraculous like Krishna, he did not do any miracles, but his whole being was a miracle – the way he walked, the way he looked, the way he was. His whole being was a miracle.

He was not sad like Jesus; he could laugh, he could laugh a belly laugh. It is said that he was born laughing. Children are born crying, weeping – it is said about him that he was born laughing. I also feel it must be true; a man like Lao Tzu must be born laughing. He is not sad like Jesus, he can laugh and laugh tremendously, but deep down in his laughter there is a sadness, a compassion – a sadness about you, about the whole existence. His laughter is not superficial.

Zarathustra laughs but his laughter is different, there is no sadness in it. Lao Tzu is sad like Jesus and not sad like Jesus; Lao Tzu laughs like Zarathustra and doesn't laugh like Zarathustra. His sadness has a laughter to it and his laughter has a sadness to it. He is a meeting of opposites. He is a harmony, a symphony.

Remember this … I am not commenting on him. There exists no distance between me and him. He is talking to you through me – a different body, a different name, a different incarnation, but the same spirit.

He says:

The Tao that can be told of is not the absolute Tao.

Let me first tell you the story of how these sutras came to be written, because that will help you to understand them. For 90 years Lao Tzu lived – in fact he did nothing except live. He lived totally. Many times his disciples asked him to write something, but he would always say, "The Tao that can be told is not the real Tao, the truth that can be told becomes untrue immediately." So he would not say anything; he would not write anything.

Then what were the disciples doing with him? They were only being with him. They lived with him, they moved with him, they simply imbibed his being. Being near him they tried to be open to him; being near him they tried not to think about anything; being near him they became more and more silent. In that silence he would reach them, he would come to them and he would knock at their doors.

For 90 years he refused to write anything or to say anything. This was his basic attitude: that truth cannot be taught. The moment you say something about truth, it is no longer true – the very saying falsifies it. You cannot teach it. At the most you can indicate it, and that indication should be your very being, your whole life; it cannot be indicated by words. He was against words; he was against language.

It is said that he used to go for a morning walk every day, and a neighbor used to follow him. Knowing well that he didn't want to talk, that he was a man of absolute silence, the neighbor always kept silent. Even a "hello" was not allowed, even to talk about the weather was not allowed. To say "How beautiful a morning!" would be too much chattering. Lao Tzu would go for a long walk, for miles, and the neighbor would follow him.

For years it went on, but once it happened that a guest was staying with the neighbor and he also wanted to come, so the neighbor brought him. He did not know Lao Tzu or his ways. He started feeling suffocated because his host was not talking, and he couldn't understand why they were so silent – and the silence became heavy on him.

If you don't know how to be silent, it becomes heavy. It is not that by saying things you communicate – no. It is by saying things that you unburden yourself. In fact, through words communication is not possible; just the opposite is possible – you can avoid communication. You can talk, and you can create a screen of words around you so that your real situation cannot be known by others. You clothe yourself through words.

That man started feeling naked and suffocated and awkward; it was embarrassing. So he simply said, when the sun was rising: "Look…! What a beautiful sun is born, is rising! What a beautiful morning!"

That's all he said. But nobody responded because the neighbor, the host, knew that Lao Tzu wouldn't like it. And of course Lao Tzu wouldn't say anything, wouldn't respond. When they came back, Lao Tzu told the neighbor, "From tomorrow, don't bring this man. He is a chatterbox." And he had only said this much: "What a beautiful sun … what a beautiful morning." That much in a two- or three-hour walk. But Lao Tzu said, "Don't bring this chatterbox again with you. He talks too much, and talks uselessly. I also have eyes, I can see that the sun is being born and it is beautiful. What is the need to say it?"

Lao Tzu lived in silence. He always avoided talking about the truth that he had attained and he always rejected the idea that he should write it down for the generations to come.

At the age of 90 he took leave of his disciples. He said goodbye to them, and he said, "Now I am moving towards the hills, towards the Himalayas. I am going there to get ready to die. It is good to live with people, it is good to be in the world while you are living, but when one is getting nearer to death it is good to move into total aloneness, so that you move towards the original source in your absolute purity and loneliness, uncontaminated by the world."

. The disciples felt very, very sad, but what could they do? They followed him for a few miles, but by and by Lao Tzu persuaded them to go back. Then alone he was crossing the border, and the guard on the border imprisoned him. The guard was also a disciple. And the guard said: "Unless you write a book, I am not going to allow you to move beyond the border. This much you must do for humanity. Write a book. That is the debt you have to pay, otherwise I won't allow you to cross." So for three days Lao Tzu was imprisoned by his own disciple.

It is beautiful. It is very loving. He was forced – and that's how the small book, the book of Lao Tzu, Tao Te Ching, was born. He had to write it because the disciple wouldn't allow him to cross. And he was the guard and he had the authority, he could create trouble, so Lao Tzu had to write the book. In three days he finished it.

This is the first sentence of the book:

The Tao that can be told of is not the absolute Tao.

This is the first thing he has to say: that whatsoever can be said cannot be true. This is the introduction for the book. It simply makes you alert: now words will be following, don't become a victim of the words. Remember the wordless. Remember that which cannot be communicated through language, through words. The Tao can be communicated, but it can only be communicated from being to being. It can be communicated when you are with the master, just with the master, doing nothing, not even practicing anything. Just being with the master it can be communicated.

Why can't the truth be said? What is the difficulty? The truth cannot be said for many reasons. The first and the most basic reason is that truth is always realized in silence. When your inner talk has stopped, then it is realized. And that which is realized in silence, how can you say it through sound? It is an experience. It is not a thought. If it were a thought it could be expressed, there would be no trouble in it. Howsoever complicated or complex a thought may be, a way can be found to express it. The most complex theory of Albert Einstein, the theory of relativity, can also be expressed in a symbol. There is no problem about it. The listener may not be able to understand it; that is not the point. It can be expressed.

It was said when Einstein was alive that only 12 persons, a dozen, in the whole world understood him and what he was saying. But even that is enough. If even a single person can understand, it has been expressed. And even if not a single person can understand right now, maybe after many centuries a person will come who can understand it. Then too it has been expressed. The very probability that somebody can understand it, and it has been expressed.

But truth cannot be expressed because the very reaching of it is through silence, soundlessness, thoughtlessness. You reach it through no-mind – the mind drops. And how can you use something which, as a necessary condition, has to drop before truth can be reached? Mind cannot understand, mind cannot realize – how can mind express? Remember it as a rule: if mind can attain it, mind can express it; if mind cannot attain it, mind cannot express it.

All language is futile. Truth cannot be expressed. Then what have all the scriptures been doing? What is Lao Tzu doing? What are the Upanishads doing? They all try to say something that cannot be said in the hope that a desire may arise in you to know about it. Truth cannot be said, but in the very effort to say it a desire can arise in the hearer to know that which cannot be expressed. A thirst can be provoked. The thirst is there, it needs a little provocation. You are already thirsty – how can it be otherwise? You are not blissful, you are not ecstatic – you are thirsty. Your heart is a burning fire. You are seeking something that can quench the thirst. But, not finding the water, not finding the source, by and by you have tried to suppress your thirst itself. That is the only way, otherwise it is too much; it will not allow you to live at all. So you suppress the thirst.

A master like Lao Tzu knows well that truth cannot be said, but the very effort to say it will provoke something, will bring the suppressed thirst in you to the surface. And once the thirst surfaces, a search, an inquiry starts. And he has moved you.

The Tao that can be told of is not the absolute Tao.

At the most it can be relative. For example, we can say something about light to a blind man knowing well that it is impossible to communicate anything about light because he has no experience of it. But something can be said about light – theories about light can be created. Even a blind man can become an expert about the theories of light; there is no problem in it – but he will not understand what light is. He will understand what light consists of. He will understand the physics of light, the chemistry of light, he will understand the poetry of light, but he will not understand the facticity of light, what light is. The experience of light he will not understand. So all that is said to a blind man about light is only relative: it is something about light, not light itself. Light cannot be communicated.

Something can be said about God, but God cannot be said; something can be said about love, but love cannot be said; that "something" remains relative. It remains relative to the listener, his understanding, his intellectual grip, his training, his desire to understand. It depends on, it is relative to, the master and his way of expressing, his devices to communicate. It remains relative – relative to many things – but it can never become the absolute experience. This is the first reason that truth cannot be expressed.

The second reason that truth cannot be expressed is because it is an experience. No experience can be communicated ... leave truth aside. If you have never known love, when somebody says something about love you will hear the word but you will miss the meaning. The word is in the dictionary. Even if you don't understand, you can look in the dictionary and you will know what it means. But the meaning is in you. Meaning comes through experience. If you have loved someone then you know the meaning of the word "love". The literal meaning is in the dictionary, in the language, in the grammar. But the experiential meaning, the existential meaning is in you. If you have known the experience, immediately the word "love" is no longer empty; it contains something. If I say a thing, it is empty unless you bring your experience to it. When your experience comes to it, it becomes significant; otherwise it remains empty – words and words and words.

How can truth be expressed when you have not experienced it? Even in ordinary life an unexperienced thing cannot be told. Only words will be conveyed. The container will reach you but the content will be lost. An empty word will travel towards you; you will hear it and you will think you understand it because you know the literal meaning of it, but you will miss. The real, authentic meaning comes through existential experience. You have to know it, there is no other way.

Lao Tzu does not seem to be ordinarily religious. He is more like a poet, a musician, an artist, a creator, rather than like a theologian, a priest, a preacher, philosopher. He is so ordinary that you cannot think that he is religious. But really to be religious is to be so extraordinarily ordinary in life that the part is not against the whole, but the part is flowing with the whole.

To be religious is not to be separate from the flow. To be irreligious is to have your own mind, in an effort to win, to conquer, to reach somewhere. If you have a goal you are irreligious. If you are thinking of tomorrow you have already missed religion. Religion has no tomorrow to it. That's why Jesus says: think not of the morrow; look at the lilies in the field, they are blossoming now. Everything that is, is now; everything that is alive is now alive. Now is the only time, the only eternity.

Two possibilities are there. You can fight with life, you can have your private goals against life – and all goals are private, all goals are personal, you are trying to impose a pattern on life, something of your own; you are trying to drag the life to follow you, and you are just a tiny part, infinitesimal, so small, so atomic, and you are trying to drag the whole universe with you. Of course you are bound to be defeated. You are bound to lose your grace, you are bound to become hard. Fighting creates hardness. Just think of fight, and a subtle hardness comes around you; just think of resisting, and a crust arises around you that covers you like a cocoon.

The very idea that you have a certain goal makes you an island, you are no longer part of the vast continent of life. And when you are separated from life you are like a tree which is separated from the earth. It may live a little on past nourishment, but really it is dying. The tree needs roots, the tree needs to be in the earth, joined together, part of it.

You need to be joined with the continent of life, part of it, rooted in it. When you are rooted in life you are soft – because you are not afraid.

Fear creates hardness. Fear creates the idea of security, fear creates the idea to protect yourself. And nothing kills like fear because in the very idea of fear you are separated from the earth, uprooted. Then you live on the past – that is why you think so much of the past. It is not coincidental. The mind continuously thinks either of past or of the future. Why think so much of the past? The gone is gone! It cannot be recovered. The past is dead! Why do you go on thinking about the past which is no more and about which nothing can be done? You cannot live it, you cannot be in it. But it can destroy your present moment. There must be some deep-rooted cause for it – the deep-rooted cause is that you are fighting the whole. Fighting the whole, fighting the river of life, you are uprooted. You have become tiny, a capsule-like phenomenon, closed in yourself. You have become an individual, you are no longer part of existence, the expanding universe, the vast. No, you are no longer part of it, you have to live like a miser on your past nourishment. That's why mind goes on thinking about the past.

And you have to pull yourself somehow to be ready to fight – that's why you go on thinking about the future. The future gives you hope, the past gives you nourishment, and just between the two is eternity, the very life which you are missing. Between the past and the future you are dying, not living.

There is another way to be – really, the only way to be because this way is not the way to be. The way of fight is not the way to be.

The other way is to flow with the river, flow so together with it that you don't feel even the separation – that you are separate and flowing with it. No you become part, not only part, you are immersed in it, you have become the river, there exists no separation. When you are not fighting, you become life. When you are not fighting you have become the vast, the infinite. When you are not fighting, that state in the East has been known as surrender; trust, what we have called *shraddha* – trusting life. Not trusting your individual mind, but trusting the whole. Not trusting the part, but the whole. Not trusting the mind, but trusting existence.

Surrendered, suddenly you become soft, because then there is no need to be hard. You are not fighting, there is no enmity, there is no need to protect, there is no urge to be secure; you are already merged with life.

And life is secure, only individual egos are insecure; they need protection, they need safety, they need armor around them. Afraid, continuously trembling – then how can you live? You live in anguish and anxiety, you don't live. You lose all delight, the sheer joy of being here – and it is a sheer joy. It has no cause to it. It simply arises because you are. It simply bubbles up within you just because you are. Once you are open, flowing with life, you are bubbling with joy continuously. For no reason at all! You simply start feeling that to be is to be happy.

There is no other way of being. If you are miserable that only shows that you have lost contact with being. To be miserable means somehow you are uprooted from the earth, you have become separate from the river, you have become a frozen block, an ice cube, floating in the river, but not with it; fighting, even trying to go upstream – the ego always wants to go upstream, because wherever there is challenge the ego feels good. The ego is always in search of fight. If you cannot find anybody to fight you will feel very miserable. Somebody is needed to fight. In fighting you feel good, you are. But that is a very ill way to be, a pathological way, a neurotic way to be. Neurosis is fighting with the river. If you fight, you become hard. If you fight, you surround yourself with a dead wall. Of course, your own being is dead. You lose softness, lucidity, grace, gentleness. Then you are just dragging, not alive.

Lao Tzu is for surrender. He says: surrender to life. Allow life to lead you, don't try to lead life. Don't try to manipulate and control life, let life manipulate and control you. Let life possess you. You simply surrender! You simply say, "I am not." You give total power to life, and be with it.

Difficult, because the ego says, "Then what am I? Surrendered, I am no more." But when the ego is not, in fact for the first time you are. For the first time you are not the finite, you are the infinite. For the first time you are not the body, the embodied, you are the unembodied, the vast, which goes on expanding, beginningless, endless. But the ego does not know about it. The ego is afraid. It says, "What are you doing, losing yourself? Then you will be lost, you will be a nobody!" If you listen to the ego, the ego will put you again and again on a neurotic path, the path of "being somebody". And the more you become somebody the more life has disappeared from you.

Look at people who have succeeded in the world, who have become somebody, whose names are found in *Who's Who*. Look at them, watch them, you will find that they are living a fake life! They are only masks, nothing inside, hollow men, stuffed maybe, but not alive. Empty. Watch people who have become successful in the world, and have become somebodies: presidents, prime ministers, rich people, the very rich, who have attained all that can be attained in the world. Watch them, touch them, look at them – you will feel death. You will not find throbbing hearts there. Maybe the heart is still beating but the beat is mechanical. The beat has lost the poetry. They look at you, but their eyes are dull. The lustre of being alive is not there. They will shake hands with you but in their hands you will not feel anything flowing, you will not feel any exchange of energy, you will not see warmth welcoming you. A dead hand, weight you will find there, love you will not find. Look around them: they live in hell. They have succeeded, they have become somebodies, and now only hell surrounds them. You are on the same way if you are trying to be somebody.

Lao Tzu says: be a nobody, and then you will have infinite life flowing in you. For the flow of life, to be a somebody becomes a block. To be a nobody, vast emptiness, allows all. Clouds can move, stars can move in it, and nothing disturbs it. And you have nothing to lose, because all that can be lost you have surrendered already.

In such a state of being one is ever young. The body of course will become old, but the innermost core of your being remains young, fresh. It never becomes old, it is never dead.

And Lao Tzu says: this is the way to be really religious. Float with Tao, move with Tao, don't create any private goals and ends, the whole knows better, you be simply with it. The whole has created you, the whole breathes within you, the whole lives in you, why do you bother? Let the responsibility be with the whole. You simply go wherever it leads. You don't try to force and plan, and you don't ask for any certain goals because then there will be frustration, and you will become hard, and you will miss an opportunity of being alive. And this is the point – that if you allow life, more life happens, then if you allow yourself to be alive still more life happens.

Lao Tzu insists also that life does not believe in strength. Weakness has a beauty in it, because it is tender and soft. A storm comes, big trees will fall – strong; and small plants – they will simply bend; and then the storm goes by and they are again smiling and flowering. In fact the storm has made them just fresh, it has taken their dust, that's all. They are more alive, younger, fresher, and, the storm has given them a good bath. And the old trees – very strong – they have fallen because they resisted, they would not bend; they were very egoistic.

Lao Tzu says: life loves the weak. And that is the meaning of Jesus' sayings: "Blessed are the meek, because they shall inherit the earth. Blessed are the poor, the poor in spirit. Blessed are those who weep, because they shall be comforted." Christianity goes on missing the meaning of Jesus' sayings, because those sayings are Lao Tzuan. Unless they are related to Lao Tzu they cannot be interpreted rightly. The whole teaching of Jesus is: be alive and be weak. That's why he says if somebody hits you on the face give him the other side also. If somebody takes your coat, give him your shirt also. And if somebody forces you to walk with him for one mile, go for two miles. He is saying be weak – blessed are the meek.

What is there in weakness which is blessed? Because ordinarily the so-called leaders of the world, teachers of the world, they go on saying: be strong. And this Lao Tzu and Jesus, they say: be weak. Weakness has something in it – because it is not hard. To be strong one needs to be hard. To be hard one needs to flow against life. If you want to be strong, you will have to fight the flow, only then will you become strong; there is no other way to become strong. If you want to become strong, move up-current. The more the river forces you against it, the stronger you become.

To be weak, flow with the river; wherever it is going, go with it. To flow with the river … if the river says go with me for one mile, go for two miles, if the river takes your coat give your shirt also, and if the river slaps you on one cheek, give the other. Weakness has a certain beauty in it. That beauty is of grace, the beauty is of non-violence, that beauty is of love, forgiveness. The beauty is of no conflict. And unless Lao Tzu is understood well, and humanity starts feeling for Lao Tzu, humanity cannot live in peace.

If you are taught to be strong you are bound to fight, wars will continue. All political leaders in the world go on saying that they love peace – and they all prepare for war. They say they stand for peace and they all go on accumulating armaments. They talk about peace and they prepare for war. And they all say they have to prepare for war because they are afraid of the other; and the other says the same thing. The whole thing looks so foolish and stupid. China is afraid of India, India is afraid of China. Why can't you see the point! Russia is afraid of America, America is afraid of Russia. They both talk about peace and they both go on preparing for war. And of course, that which you prepare for happens. Your talk about peace looks just rubbish. Your talk about peace is nothing but cold war. In fact politicians need time to prepare: in that time they talk about peace so that they can have enough time to prepare. Humanity for centuries has lived in only two periods: the war, the period of war, and the period of preparation for war – these are the only two periods; the whole history seems to be just neurotic. But this is going to be so because strength is praised, ego praised. If two persons are fighting on the road, one is stronger, another is weak, the weaker has fallen and the stronger is sitting on his chest, whom do you appreciate? Do you appreciate the one who has become a conqueror? Then you are violent, then you are for war; then you are a warmonger. Then you are very dangerous and neurotic.

Or do you appreciate the one who is weak? But nobody appreciates the weak, nobody wants to be associated with the weak because deep down you would also like to be strong. When you appreciate the strong you say, "Yes, this is my ideal, I would also like to be like him."

If strength is praised, then violence is praised. If strength is praised, then death is praised, because all strength kills – kills the other and kills you also. Strength is murderous and suicidal both.

Weakness, the very word seems to be condemnatory. But what is weakness? A flower is weak. A rock by the side of the flower is very strong. Would you like to be like a rock, or would you like to be like a flower? A flower is weak, remember, very weak. Just a small strong wind, and the flower will be gone. The petals will fall to the earth. A flower is a miracle; it is a miracle how the flower exists – so weak, so soft! Seems to be impossible.

How is it possible? Rocks seem to be okay, they exist, they have their arithmetic to exist, but the flower? It seems to be completely unsupported, but still a flower exists. That's the miracle. Would you like to be like a flower? If you ask deep down your ego will say, "Be like a rock." And even if you insist, because a rock looks ugly, then the ego will say, "Even if you want to be a flower, be a plastic flower. Be at least strong! Winds won't disturb you, rains won't destroy you, and you can remain for ever and ever."

A real flower comes in the morning, laughs for a moment, spreads its fragrance – and is gone. An unreal flower, a plastic flower, can remain forever and ever. But it is unreal, and it is strong because it is unreal. Reality is soft and weak. And the higher the reality is, the softer.

The emperor of China wanted the wisest man to be the chief justice of the supreme court of China. People suggested Lao Tzu's name. It was absolutely right, there was no disagreement about it in his court, and Lao Tzu was called.

Lao Tzu came in his own way. He used to ride on a buffalo – which is a very rare thing. People ride on horses, and people ride on elephants, but a buffalo …? But he loved his buffalo; it carried him from one place to another, and it gave him nourishment. No horse can do that. And buffalos are so silent – Lao Tzu was in immense love with silence – they don't chatter. They are so contented, they don't have any grudge against existence.

He came into the court riding on his buffalo. The emperor was shocked, but they had invited him, and they were well-mannered, well-educated people, so they ignored the buffalo. The emperor asked Lao Tzu, "I want you to be the chief justice of the supreme court of China."

Lao Tzu said, "You are choosing the wrong person."

The emperor said, "Why?"

"Because," Lao Tzu said, "I will be really just."

The emperor said, "That is the very function. Don't say no to your own emperor."

Lao Tzu said, "Okay, but it won't last long – perhaps one day."

And it lasted only one day. The first case was about a thief who had stolen money from the richest man in China. The man was so rich that even the emperor used to borrow money from him. Lao Tzu listened to the whole case and gave his judgment: "Six months' jail for both the rich man and the thief."

The rich man said, "What?! My money is stolen and you are sending me to jail?"

Lao Tzu said, "I am looking at the whole thing as deeply as possible. This thief is a secondary criminal, you are the primary criminal. You have collected all the money of the capital, you have deprived millions of people of money. Even if he had not stolen from you, you needed punishment. And I will not call this poor man a thief; he was simply distributing wealth to those to whom it belongs. You are a bloodsucker, a parasite!"

The rich man said, "I want to see the emperor before you send me to jail."

He went to the emperor and he said, "Listen, this man is absolutely absurd and dangerous. He is sending me to jail for six months."

The emperor said, "You are being judged? You have not done anything wrong."

He said, "I told that man, but he is telling me that 'You have been exploiting the money of the poor. Where will they get money? Except by stealing there seems to be no way!' So he calls me a primary criminal, and the thief only a by-product. I warn you, if I go to jail, it will not be long before you will be coming to jail too, because you have been committing murders, you have been raping women, you have been collecting all the beautiful women of the country into your palace. This man has to be immediately removed from his post."

The emperor understood. He said, "He was saying himself that he would not last more than one day. Even the full day is not ended, this is just the first case!"

Lao Tzu was given his freedom and told, "You are right. You go on your buffalo wherever you want to go."

He was a man of tremendous consideration, of in-depth exploration of everything.

❖

Lao Tzu is impractical. Lao Tzu in fact praises impracticalness.

There is a story:

Lao Tzu was passing with his disciples and they came to a forest where hundreds of carpenters were cutting trees, because a great palace was being built. So the whole forest had been almost cut, but only one tree was standing there, a big tree with thousands of branches – so big that 10,000 persons could sit under its shade. Lao Tzu asked his disciples to go and inquire why this tree had not been cut yet when the whole forest had been cut and was deserted.

The disciples went and they asked the carpenters, "Why have you not cut this tree?"

The carpenters said, "This tree is absolutely useless. You cannot make anything out of it because every branch has so many knots in it. Nothing is straight. You cannot make pillars out of it. You cannot make furniture out of it. You cannot use it as fuel because the smoke is so dangerous to the eyes – you almost go blind. This tree is absolutely useless. That's why."

They came back. Lao Tzu laughed and he said, "Be like this tree. If you want to survive in this world be like this tree – absolutely useless. Then nobody will harm you. If you are straight you will be cut, you will become furniture in somebody's house. If you are beautiful you will be sold in the market, you will become a commodity. Be like this tree, absolutely useless. Then nobody can harm you. And you will grow big and vast, and thousands of people can find shade under you."

Lao Tzu has a logic altogether different from your mind. He says: be the last. Move in the world as if you are not. Remain unknown. Don't try to be the first, otherwise you will be known. Don't be competitive, don't try to prove your worth. There is no need. Remain useless and enjoy. Of course he is impractical. But if you understand him you will find that he is the most practical on a deeper layer, in the depth – because life is to enjoy and celebrate, life is not to become a utility. Life is more like poetry than like a commodity in the market; it should be like poetry, a song, a dance, a flower by the side of the road, flowering for nobody in particular, sending its fragrance to the winds, without any address, being nobody in particular, just enjoying itself, being itself.

Lao Tzu says: if you try to be very clever, if you try to be very useful, you will be used. If you try to be very practical, somewhere or other you will be harnessed, because the world cannot leave the practical man alone. Lao Tzu says: drop all these ideas. If you want to be a poem, an ecstasy, then forget about utility. You remain true to yourself. Be yourself. The hippies had a saying: "Do your own thing." Lao Tzu was the first hippie in the world. He says: be yourself and do your thing and don't bother about anything else. You are not here to be sold. So don't think of utility, just think of your bliss. Be blissful, and if something flows out of your bliss it is okay – share it. But don't force yourself just to be a utility because that is how suicide happens. One kills oneself. Don't be suicidal.

All the teachers of the world will be more practical than Lao Tzu, that's why they have much appeal. That's why they have great organizations. Christians – almost half the world has become Christian – Mohammedans, Hindus, Jains, Sikhs. They are all utilitarians. Lao Tzu stands alone, aloof. Lao Tzu stands in a solo existence.

But Lao Tzu is rare and unique. If you can understand him you can also become rare and unique. And the way is to be ordinary – then you become extraordinary; the way is to be just the last, and then suddenly you find you are the first; the way is not to claim, not to claim the credit, and then nobody can take it from you; the way is to exist as a non-being, as a nobody, and then, in a subtle and mysterious way, you and only you become somebody – somebody the whole existence feels blessed with, feels blessed by, somebody with whom the whole existence celebrates.

Meera

Meera's love for Krishna did not begin with Meera. Such a rare expression of love cannot begin just like that. The story goes back. This Meera is one of the *gopis* – devotees – who was with Krishna. Meera herself declared it, but the scholars can't accept it, as there is no historical proof for it.

I accept what Meera says. I am not interested in measuring true and false. To me it is pointless whether it is history or not. Meera's statement – my agreement; when Meera herself says it, the matter is finished. The question does not arise of someone else raising further doubts about it. And those who raise doubts like this, they won't ever be able to understand Meera.

Meera says, "I was Lalita. I danced with Krishna in Vrindavan, I sang with Krishna. This love is ancient." Meera insists, "This love is not new." And it entered Meera's life in such a way that it is clear from the very beginning that the pundits were wrong and Meera was right.

Meera was little, some four or five years old, when a sadhu was a guest at her house. When this monk got up in the morning, taking out his idol – a statue of Krishna hidden away in his bag – to set it up to worship, Meera went completely mad.

Déjà vu happened, a memory from a previous existence came. That statue was such that picture after picture began opening. That statue became a catalyst – and once again the story began. It shocked her. Krishna's form returned to her memory. Again that dark face, those wide eyes, that crown of peacock feathers, the flute-playing Krishna – Meera went back thousands of years in her memory.

She started to cry. She began begging the sadhu for the statue. But the sadhu also had great affection for his idol. He refused to give it; he traveled on.

A whole day passed. She ate no food, and drank no water. From her eyes tears flowed – on and on she cried. Her family was alarmed, now what can be done? The sadhu has gone, where can he be found? And will he give it up? Very unlikely.

And this statue of Krishna was certainly very lovely – the rest of the family felt it too. They had seen many idols, but in this one there was something alive, there was something alert, the aura of this statue was something more. Certainly someone had carved it with love, not just for trade. Someone had carved it with feeling. Someone had put his total prayer, his full worship into it; or someone who had once seen Krishna had carved it. But the statue was such that Meera was gone, she simply forgot this world. For her the idol must be brought back to stay, if not she will die. This is the beginning of a deep longing for God – at the age of four.

That night the sadhu saw a dream. Far away in the next village he slept. A dream in the night – and Krishna was standing there. He said, "Return the statue to whom it belongs. You have kept it for many years, this was a guardianship, but it is not yours. Now don't carry it on unnecessarily. You go back and give the statue to that girl. It is hers, give it back. It is hers, your caretaking is over now. You have arrived where you were to deliver it, now the matter is finished." The idol is for the one whose heart contains love for it. Who else?

The sadhu was scared. Krishna had never shown himself to him before. For years he had been praying to and worshiping this same idol – flowers were offered, bells were rung. Krishna had never appeared. He became very frightened. He fled back in the middle of the night. Arriving at midnight he woke everyone up and said, "You must forgive me, I have committed a great wrong." He fell at the feet of that little girl, gave her the statue and went back.

This event, happening at the age of four or five, reopened her vision. Again the love flowed, again the journey began. Thus a deep relationship with Krishna was started again by this Meera in this lifetime.

This small, accidental event, happening when she was four or five years old … and a revolution happened. Meera remained ecstatic, as if she'd drunk liquor. By the time Meera was 32 or 33 years old, all those who had been important in her life until then had died. Everyone that her affection went out to, that she had loved, they all died.

Those who have written books about Meera, they all say, "unfortunately". I can't say that. I will say, "most fortunately", because death is not necessarily some kind of curse. It all depends on you. Meera used it rightly. Wherever love was torn out, each and every vessel of love gone, she offered this love of hers up to God.

The last stage was staying with her father. Her mother died, her husband died, her father died. There were five deaths passing in a continuum. All her attachments in the world were broken.

She made good use of it. She turned broken worldly attachments into detachment towards the world. And the love that became freed from the world, she offered up to the feet of God. She submerged herself in the passion-song for Krishna.

And these deaths did one more fortunate task – she was shown one thing, that everything in this universe is momentary. If the beloved is to be sought, seek in the eternal. Here nothing is yours. Don't go astray here, don't lead yourself astray. Here everything touched will go away. Here death, and death only, increases. This is a graveyard. Don't get any idea of dwelling here. No one has ever remained here.

All that she'd seen with her own eyes …

Thirty-three years old is not very old. She was young. So many deaths happened in her youth that the thorn of death showed her totally, clearly, that life is momentary. And then her mind turned away from all this. Turning away from this one can turn towards the divine.

First Meera danced only at home, before her Krishna statue. Then love began to rise like a flood, and the house could not contain it. Then she danced in the village temples, in the sadhus' gatherings. Then love started rushing in such a flood that she was no longer conscious. She drowned, she became absorbed, she became filled with Krishna.

Naturally, because she was a lady of the royal household, of a respected family, trouble came to the family. A thousand kinds of rumor began to spread in the community, because all this went beyond the tradition.

In Rajasthan of 500 years ago, women didn't come out from behind their veils; their faces were never seen in public. In the royal household, it was even more difficult. And Meera began dancing in the streets, she began dancing in the midst of the common people. Even though the dance was for God, to her relatives dance was still dance – there was no difference for them. And those who had been the closest to her were all gone.

Her brother-in-law was on the throne. Wherever Meera sings that the king sent poison, that the king sent a snake in a basket, that the king had thorns scattered in her bed, it indicates her husband's younger brother. Her husband had passed away.

Her brother-in-law was Vikramajit Singh. He was an angry youth, bitter. And this was too much to hear ... Meera's fame was insufferable to him. Meera was so famous, people began coming from far away. Ordinary people came for her blessings; saints, monks, respectable people came too. Hearing the news of Meera they came from afar. The fragrance began to spread.

From every part of the country people came, but the blind family members couldn't see. Those people coming became the cause of more difficulty for the family because Meera's fame was a shock to their egos. The king on his throne thought, "Someone in my own family higher than me? This is unbearable." Then he found a thousand excuses, and all the excuses logical – fault can never be found in them: "She is mixing with the commonfolk, with her veil aside. She is dancing in the streets; sometimes while dancing she doesn't pay attention to her clothes. This is unbecoming. It is not proper for a lady of the royal household."

But consider the stories: poison was sent and in Krishna's name Meera drank it; and it is said that the poison became nectar. It must have become! It's bound to. With so much love, so much welcoming

– if someone drinks even poison it must turn into divine nectar. And if in anger, in violence, in hate, in enmity you drink ambrosia it too will become poison.

In these events that have taken place in the lives of enlightened ones, I look for demonstration of this psychological truth. Meera receives the poison as nectar; then it becomes nectar. How you accept the world is how the world becomes. This world is created from your acceptance. This world is the extension of your vision.

It became difficult for Meera to remain in her village, so she left Rajasthan. She went to Vrindavan. "I'll go to my beloved's town," she thought. She went to Krishna's village, but the same troubles started up. Because he was not there now, Krishna's village was under the yoke of Brahmin scholar-priests.

There is a lovely story. When Meera arrived at Vrindavan's most famous temple, an attempt was made to stop her at the door, because entry to the temple was forbidden to women. The high priest of the temple had never seen women. Meera was a woman, so arrangements were made to stop her.

But those people who were standing by the door to stop her, they were struck dumb. When Meera came dancing, playing music, with a crowd of devotees behind her spreading wine in all directions, and all drunk – in that drunkenness those who stood guard were also stunned. They forgot they were meant to stop her until Meera had entered inside.

The breeze was as one wave – it went right in and reached the inner sanctum. The priest freaked out. He had been worshiping Krishna; the tray fell from his hands. He had not seen a woman for years. Women were not admitted to that temple. How had this woman come inside here?

Now think a little … the guards at the door became immersed in feeling, but the priest could not dive in! No, the priests are the most blind people in the world. And to find a more unintelligent person than a scholar is difficult. The guards too were drowned in this juice. This drunken woman, this ecstatic Meera came, came as a wave – they too forgot for a moment, forgot completely what their job was. They remembered only when Meera had gone past.

It was a thunderbolt. Once the music was playing inside and the crowd had gone in, then they became alert to what had happened. But the pundit was not affected. Meera came dancing in front of Krishna, but the pundit was not immersed in what was happening. He said, "Hey woman, do you understand that women are not permitted in this temple?"

Meera listened. Meera spoke, "I had thought that besides Krishna no other man existed. Are you also a man? I had understood Krishna was the only man and the rest of the world were his beloveds, that all were celebrating with him. So you, too, are a man? I hadn't thought that there were two. So you are in competition?"

He was shaken. The pundit didn't understand how to answer now. Scholars have answers to fixed questions, but this question had never been raised before. No one had asked it before Meera, no one had ever asked, "Does there exist some other man? I have never heard of this. You are saying very strange things. Where did you get such arrogance? Krishna is the one man, the rest are all his beloveds."

But troubles were beginning, after this event. Meera was unable to stay in Vrindavan. We have always given ill treatment to enlightened people. After death we worship them; living we misuse them. Meera had to leave Vrindavan. She went to Dvarika.

Years later the political situation changed in Rajasthan; the kingship changed and the youngest son of King Sanga ascended the throne, Udaysingh Mevar. He was King Sanga's son and the father of King Pratap. Udaysingh had great feeling for Meera. He sent innumerable messengers to Meera to bring her back: "This is our disgrace. This is Rajasthan's disgrace that Meera wanders from village to village, moving here and there. This stain will always remain on us. Let her come back. Bring her back. We ask forgiveness for our mistakes. That which has happened in the past is gone."

People went, pundits were sent, priests were sent to explain and convince, but Meera always gave the explanation, "Now where to come or go? Where should I go now, giving up this temple of my life's love?" She was ecstatic in the Ranchhordasji temple.

Still Udaysingh tried very hard. He sent a group of 100 men and said, "Bring her back no matter what. If she doesn't come, give her a threat. Tell her you'll fast sitting at the door of the same temple." And they gave the threat. They insisted, "You must come, if not then we'll die right here."

Then Meera said, "This again; if I am to go, then I will go and ask my love. Without his giving permission, I cannot go. So I'll ask Ranchhordasji." She went inside and the story is very lovely, very surprising, very significant. She went inside and it is said she never came out again. She disappeared into Krishna's statue.

This too couldn't be historical, but it should be, because if Meera cannot merge into Krishna's statue, then who can? And she had dissolved Krishna so deeply into herself, couldn't Krishna at least let her be merged into himself? If not then the whole foundation of devotion will be broken. Then the trust of the devotee will be broken. Meera has dissolved Krishna so deeply into herself, then Krishna too has a responsibility.

Be aware, don't take this as a fact and sit thinking over it. This is truth and truth is very different from fact. Truth is far above facts. Just what is there in facts? Not worth two cents. Fact is not the limit of truth. Fact is that which man's small intelligence can understand. It is a fragment of truth; truth is vast.

If you ask me, I say it is so. It has to be.

Meera must have said, "Now what's your feeling, shall I go now? Where will I go? Either come with me or take me into you." Ultimately that which you love, you become.

Love with care and understanding. Make your friendships with awareness. Because this friendship is no ordinary matter. Meera's friendship was with Krishna, and if finally she merged into his image then to me this seems to be completely right. It must be so. It is just so.

Friedrich Nietzsche

Friedrich Nietzsche is perhaps the greatest philosopher the world has known. He is also great in another dimension which many philosophers are simply unaware of: he is a born mystic.

His philosophy is not only of the mind but is rooted deep in the heart, and some roots even reach to his very being. The only thing unfortunate about him is that he was born in the West; hence, he could never come across any mystery school. He contemplated deeply, but he was absolutely unaware about meditation. His thoughts sometimes have the depth of a meditator, sometimes the flight of a Gautama Buddha; but these things seem to have happened spontaneously to him.

He knew nothing about the ways of enlightenment, about the path that reaches to one's own being. This created a tremendous turmoil in his being. His dreams go as high as the stars but his life remained very ordinary – it does not have the aura that meditation creates. His thoughts are not his blood, his bones, his marrow. They are beautiful, immensely beautiful, but something is missing; and what is missing is life itself. They are dead words; they don't breathe – there is no heartbeat.

But I have spoken on him for a special reason: he is the only philosopher, from East or West, who has at least thought of the heights of human consciousness. He may not have experienced them; he certainly has not experienced them. He also thought of becoming a man again. That idea, of descending from your heights into the marketplace, descending from the stars to the earth, has never happened to anybody else.

He has something of Gautama Buddha, perhaps unconsciously carried over from his past lives, and he has something of the Zorba.

Both are incomplete. But he is the only proof that Buddha and Zorba can meet; that those who have reached to the highest peaks need not remain there.

In fact, they should not remain there. They owe something to humanity; they owe something to the earth. They have been born amongst human beings; they have lived in the same darkness and in the same misery. And now that they have seen the light, it becomes obligatory that they should come back to wake up those who are fast asleep; to bring the good news – that darkness is not all, that unconsciousness is our choice.

If we choose to be conscious, all unconsciousness and all darkness can disappear. It is our choice that we are living in the dark valleys. If we decide to live on the sunlit peaks, nobody can prevent us because that is also our potential.

It is the destiny of the genius to be misunderstood. If a genius is not misunderstood, he is not a genius at all. If the common masses can understand, that means the person is speaking at the same level where ordinary intelligence is.

Friedrich Nietzsche is misunderstood, and out of this misunderstanding there has been tremendous disaster. But perhaps it was unavoidable. To understand a man like Nietzsche you have to have at least the same standard of consciousness, if not higher.

Adolf Hitler is so retarded that it is impossible to think that he can understand the meaning of Nietzsche; but he became the prophet of Nietzsche's philosophy. And according to his retarded mind he interpreted – not only interpreted, but acted according to those interpretations – and the second world war was the result.

When Nietzsche is talking about "will to power", it has nothing to do with will to dominate. But that is the meaning the Nazis had given to it.

"The will to power" is diametrically opposite to the will to dominate. The will to dominate comes out of an inferiority complex.

One wants to dominate others, just to prove to himself that he is not inferior – he is superior. But he needs to prove it. Without any proof he knows he is inferior; he has to cover it up by many, many proofs.

The really superior man needs no proof, he simply is superior. Does a rose flower argue about its beauty? Does the full moon bother about proving its gloriousness? The superior man simply knows it, there is no need for any proof; hence he has no will to dominate. He certainly has a "will to power," but then you have to make a very fine distinction. His will to power means: he wants to grow to his fullest expression.

It has nothing to do with anybody else, its whole concern is the individual himself. He wants to blossom, to bring all the flowers that are hidden in his potential, to rise as high as possible in the sky. It is not even comparative, it is not trying to rise higher than others – it is simply trying to rise to its fullest potential.

"Will to power" is absolutely individual. It wants to dance to the highest in the sky, it wants to have a dialogue with the stars, but it is not concerned with proving anybody inferior. It is not competitive, it is not comparative.

Adolf Hitler and his followers, the Nazis, have done so much harm to the world because they prevented the world from understanding Friedrich Nietzsche and his true meaning. And it was not only one thing; about every other concept too, they have the same kind of misunderstanding.

It is such a sad fate, one which has never befallen any great mystic or any great poet before Nietzsche. The crucifixion of Jesus or poisoning of Socrates are not as bad a fate as that which has befallen Friedrich Nietzsche – to be misunderstood on such a grand scale that Adolf Hitler managed to kill more than 8 million people in the name of Friedrich Nietzsche and his philosophy. It will take a little time … When Adolf Hitler and the Nazis and the second world war are forgotten, Nietzsche will come back to his true light. He is coming back.

Just the other day, sannyasins from Japan informed me that my books are selling in their language at the highest rate and next to them are Friedrich Nietzsche's – his books are also selling. And just a few days earlier the same information came from Korea. Perhaps people may be finding something similar in them.

But Friedrich Nietzsche has to be interpreted again, so that all the nonsense that has been put, by the Nazis, over his beautiful philosophy can be thrown away. He has to be purified, he needs a baptism.

❖

Little Sammy tells his grandfather about the great scientist, Albert Einstein, and his theory of relativity.

"Ah yes," says the grandfather, "and what does the theory have to say?"

"Our teacher says that only a few people in the whole world can understand it," the boy explains, "but then she told us what it means. Relativity is like this: if a man sits for an hour with a pretty girl, it feels like a minute; but if he sits on a hot stove for a minute, it feels like an hour – and that's the theory of relativity."

Grandpa is silent and slowly shakes his head. "Sammy," he says softly, "from this your Einstein makes a living?"

People understand according to their own level of consciousness.

It was just a coincidence that Nietzsche fell into the hands of the Nazis. They needed a philosophy for war, and Nietzsche appreciates the beauty of the warrior. They wanted some idea for which to fight, and Nietzsche gave them a good excuse – for the superman.

Of course, they immediately got hold of the idea of superman. The Nordic German Aryans were going to be Nietzsche's new race of man, the superman. They wanted to dominate the world, and Nietzsche was very helpful, because he was saying that man's deepest longing is "will to power". They changed it into will to dominate.

Now they had the whole philosophy: the Nordic German Aryans are the superior race because they are going to give birth to the superman. They have the will to power and they will dominate the whole world. That is their destiny – to dominate the inferior human beings. Obviously, the arithmetic is simple: the superior should dominate the inferior.

These beautiful concepts ... Nietzsche could not ever have imagined they would become so dangerous and such a nightmare to the whole of humanity. But you cannot avoid being misunderstood, you cannot do anything about it.

A drunk who smelt of whiskey, cigars, and a cheap perfume staggered up the steps into the bus, reeled down the aisle, then plopped himself down on a seat next to a Catholic priest.

The drunk took a long look at his offended seat partner and said, "Hey Father, I have got a question for you. What causes arthritis?"

The priest's reply was cold and curt. "Amoral living," he said, "too much liquor, smoking and consorting with loose women."

"Well, I'll be damned!" said the drunk.

They rode in silence for a moment. The priest began to feel guilty, that he had reacted so strongly to a man who obviously needed Christian compassion. He turned to the drunk and said, "I am sorry, my son. I did not mean to be harsh. How long have you suffered from this terrible affliction of arthritis?"

"My affliction?" the drunk said. "I don't have arthritis. I was just reading in the paper that the Pope had it."

Now, what can you do? Once you have said something, then it all depends on the other person, what he is going to make of it.

But Nietzsche is so immensely important that he has to be cleaned of all the garbage that the Nazis have put on his ideas. And the strangest thing is that not only the Nazis but other philosophers around the world have also misunderstood him. Perhaps he was such a great genius that your so-called great men also were not able to understand him.

He was bringing so many new insights into the world of thinking, that even just a single insight would have made him one of the great philosophers of the world – and he has dozens of insights which are absolutely original, which man has never thought about. If rightly understood, Nietzsche certainly could create the atmosphere and the right soil for the superman to be born. He can help humanity to be transformed.

I have tremendous respect for the man, and also a great sadness that he was misunderstood – not only misunderstood, but forced into a madhouse. The doctors declared that he was mad. His insights were so far away from the ordinary mind that the ordinary mind felt very happy in declaring him mad: "If he is not mad, then we are too ordinary." He has to be mad, he has to be forced into a madhouse.

My own feeling is, he was never mad. He was just too much ahead of his time, and he was too sincere and too truthful. He said exactly what he experienced without bothering about politicians, priests and other pygmies. But these pygmies are so many and this man was so alone, that they would not hear that he was not mad. And the proof that he was not mad is his last book, which he wrote in the madhouse.

But I am the first man who is saying that he was not mad. It seems that this whole world is so cunning, so politically minded, that people say only things that bring reputation to them, which bring applause from the crowd. Even your great thinkers are not very great.

The book that he wrote in the madhouse is his greatest work, and is an absolute proof because a mad man could not write it. His last book is *The Will to Power*. He did not see it printed, because who is going to print a madman's book? He knocked on many publishers' doors, but was refused – and now everybody agrees that that is his greatest work. After his death, his sister sold the house and other things to publish the book, because that was his last desire, but he did not see it in print.

Was he mad? Or are we living in a mad world? If a madman can write a book like *The Will to Power*, then it is better to be mad than to be sane like Ronald Reagan, piling up nuclear weapons – there are thousands of people employed in creating nuclear weapons 24 hours a day. You call these people sane, and you call Friedrich Nietzsche mad?

❖

Friedrich Nietzsche declared that God is dead. He had to declare it, because God WAS dead. The God that had been worshiped for thousands of years was dead; not the real God, but the God that the human mind had created – the God that was in the temples and the mosques and the churches and the synagogues, the God of the Old Testament, the God of the Vedas. Man has outgrown those concepts.

Nietzsche simply declared a fact. Of course, he was as shocked by it as everybody else was. He himself was not ready to accept it. In fact, for his whole life he struggled to accept it. He tried to convince himself by arguing that God is REALLY dead, but it was difficult for the poor man. It would have been difficult for anybody. And he was a man of steel; he was no ordinary man, he was really a strong man, but still it was too much. He had to suffer tremendously because he was the first to declare it, and to be a pioneer is always dangerous. He went through a nervous breakdown. The last part of his life was a state of madness. He risked much for this declaration.

"God is dead" is now almost a cliché. But when Nietzsche used that phrase it was like an earthquake, a thunderbolt from the skies – it shattered man's illusions. But it is only half of his message, remember; the other half has been almost forgotten. He declared "God is dead" because he wanted to declare the coming of a new man. He called that new man "overman" or "superman". He said: if God continues to live the old way, man cannot assert himself in total freedom. Man cannot grow, man cannot mature. He will always remain dependent on the father-figure. God as the great father is dead: this is half of the message.

The other half is: now be on your own, stand on your own. Now become mature. Enough of this dependence! Enough of this stupid praying! Enough of your rituals! Stop these games!

Man has been playing many, many games in the name of God, and priests have been exploiting man in the name of God. Nietzsche put an end to all that; the world has never been the same again. Although

Nietzsche suffered much for his declaration, he has served humanity in a tremendous way: he heralded a new age.

The OLD God is dead – that is a very basic requirement for the new God to appear, a new vision of God, more in harmony with the modern, contemporary consciousness. The God of the Old Testament was perfectly right for the people who invented it. It was perfectly right for the people Moses was talking to; it was a language that they understood. Now thousands of years have passed; God needs new garments, and you go on and on putting the old, rotten garments on Him.

God is not dead. God cannot be dead! But the old concept is dead.

Man has to be loved, because it is only through the nourishment of love that man can grow. Man has to know that he is alone, and he has to know that he has to depend on his own resources and not on some heavenly father. Once man takes responsibility, total responsibility on his own shoulders, a great revolution is bound to happen, because man has infinite potential to grow. Remaining dependent on some God, he has completely become oblivious to his potential, to his future, to his growth.

It is good that God has been discarded. Now man has to take his life in his own hands. And the beauty is, if you become responsible, responsible for yourself, if you declare your freedom – you have to declare it because God is dead; there is nobody higher than you – if you accept that now you have to seek and search your way, you have to grope for it on your own, life will take a new plunge into the depths of the unknown. Life will become again an adventure. Life will again be an ecstatic discovery of new facts, new truths, of new territories, of new peaks of joy.

And it is only by becoming an adventurer that you will come upon the new face of God – which will be far more true than the old, because it will be far more mature than the old.

If Nietzsche had met Buddha, Buddha would have perfectly agreed, and yet disagreed. He would have said, "You are right: God is dead, the God of the crowds. But there is another vision, the vision

189

of the enlightened ones. Their God is not a person, their God is life in its essence. And how can life be dead? Trees are still green, birds are still singing, the sun is still there, the night still becomes poetry, love still happens. How can God be dead?"

God AS EXISTENCE can never be dead; God as a concept has to die many times. Each time man grows, the old concept has to be dropped.

❖

Nietzsche has so much to say that he cannot go into details of the arguments and procedures of how he has arrived – he simply writes the conclusion, and that conclusion is aphoristic. He then moves to another subject; and he goes on moving that way.

But I love the way he writes. That should be ultimately the way of writing. If people are intelligent you need not go through all the arguments before you give the conclusion; just the conclusion should be enough. If they are sharp and intelligent they will immediately get all the preceding arguments that are not given to them; there is no need …

He was not writing for children, he thought he was writing for philosophers. But he misunderstood: those philosophers were also not mature enough. They wanted the whole procedure. They could not immediately see the whole procedure in the conclusion; and he had to say so much that it was impossible for him to go into the whole procedure. In every direction and dimension he was touching the foundations.

But whatever he has said is just in seed form. So it is natural that it took almost 100 years … and now people can reconsider this man.

I have a tremendous love for Friedrich Nietzsche, and a deep compassion, because the man suffered his whole life for the simple reason that he remained a thinker and he never went beyond thoughts; otherwise there would be no question of suffering.

He should have been in the East, because in the East it is very difficult to avoid meditation. Sooner or later you are bound to stumble upon it, and particularly a great thinker like Nietzsche. If he had meditated too, he would have been in the same state as Gautama the Buddha – not less than that. As far as intelligence is concerned, perhaps he is more intelligent than Gautama the Buddha.

If he had just had the meditative quality also, he would have given many more treasures to the world, and he would not have suffered through it. And he would not have given the chance to the people to say that whatever he has written is all insane. His madness became a proof for them that he was insane from the very beginning; it was just growing and growing and growing, and finally it exploded.

From Friedrich Nietzsche much has to be learned.

What I would like the people who are interested in Nietzsche to understand, is that they should not miss meditation the way Nietzsche missed it; otherwise they will become great intellectuals, but empty within, with no roots, with no great solidity.

And the danger of madness is always there, because the mind's full growth can only lead to madness – there is no other way. If the mind is developed fully, the person is going to be mad, unless, side by side, he is also developing no-mind, and no-mind becomes his base. Then he can use the mind as much as he wants; it leaves no trace behind.

So this is my message to the lovers of Nietzsche: they should not become just intellectuals. Before Nietzsche, they need a good centering in meditation; then Nietzsche can be a great joy. His every insight can give you immense clarity about things which are always clouded.

The traditionalists don't want the clouds to be removed, because those clouds are helping them – so they can go on telling people whatever they want to, and they can go on exploiting people and enslaving people.

Nietzsche can be a great freedom. But – without meditation – a great danger.

Pythagoras

Pythagoras is a seeker of truth par excellence. He staked all that he had for the search. He traveled far and wide, almost the whole known world of those days, in search of the masters, of the mystery schools, of any hidden secrets. From Greece he went to Egypt – in search of the lost Atlantis and its secrets.

In Egypt, the great library of Alexandria was still intact. It had all the secrets of the past preserved. It was the greatest library that has ever existed on the earth; later on it was destroyed by a Mohammedan fanatic. The library was so big that when it was burnt, for six months the fire continued.

Just 25 centuries before Pythagoras, a great continent, Atlantis, had disappeared into the ocean. The ocean that is called "Atlantic" is so called because of that continent, Atlantis.

Atlantis was the ancientmost continent of the earth, and civilization had reached the highest possible peaks. But whenever a civilization reaches a great peak there is a danger: the danger of falling apart, the danger of committing suicide.

Humanity is facing that same danger again. When man becomes powerful, he does not know what to do with that power. When the power is too much and the understanding is too little, power has always proved dangerous. Atlantis was not drowned in the ocean by any natural calamity. It was actually the same thing that is happening today: it was man's own power over nature. It was through atomic energy that Atlantis was drowned – it was man's own suicide. But all the scriptures and all the secrets of Atlantis were still preserved in Alexandria.

All over the world there are parables, stories, about the great flood. Those stories have come from the drowning of Atlantis. All those stories – Christian, Jewish, Hindu – they all talk about a great flood that had come once in the past and had destroyed almost the whole civilization. Just a few initiates, adepts, had survived. Noah is an adept; a great master, and Noah's ark is just a symbol.

A few people escaped the calamity. With them, all the secrets that the civilization had attained survived. They were preserved in Alexandria.

Pythagoras lived in Alexandria for years. He studied, he was initiated into the mystery schools of Egypt – particularly the mysteries of Hermes. Then he came to India, was initiated into all that the Brahmins of this ancient land had discovered, all that India had known in the inner world of man.

For years he was in India, then he travelled to Tibet and then to China. That was the whole known world. His whole life he was a seeker, a pilgrim, in search of a philosophy – philosophy in the true sense of the word: love for wisdom. He was a lover, a philosopher – not in the modern sense of the word but in the old, ancient sense of the word. Because a lover cannot only speculate, a lover cannot only think about truth: a lover has to search, risk, adventure.

Truth is the beloved. How can you go on only thinking about it? You have to be connected with the beloved through the heart. The search cannot be only intellectual; it has to be deep-down intuitive. Maybe the beginning has to be intellectual, but only the beginning. Just the starting point has to be intellectual, but finally it has to reach the very core of your being.

He was one of the most generous of men, most liberal, democratic, unprejudiced, open. He was respected all over the world. From Greece to China he was revered. He was accepted in every mystic school; with great joy he was welcomed everywhere. His name was known in all the lands. Wherever he went he was received with great rejoicing.

Even though he had become enlightened, he still continued to reach into hidden secrets, he still continued to ask to be initiated into new schools. He was trying to create a synthesis; he was trying to know the truth through as many possibilities as is humanly possible. He wanted to know truth in all its aspects, in all its dimensions. His search was such that he was ready to learn from anybody. He was an absolute disciple. He was ready to learn from the whole existence. He remained open, and he remained a learner to the very end.

The whole effort was ... and it was a great effort in those days, to travel from Greece to China. It was full of dangers. The journey was hazardous; it was not easy as it is today. Today things are so easy that you can take your breakfast in New York and your lunch in London, and you can suffer indigestion in Pune. Things are very simple. In those days it was not so simple. It was really a risk; to move from one country to another country took years.

By the time Pythagoras came back, he was a very old man. But seekers gathered around him; a great school was born. And, as it always happens, the society started persecuting him and his school and his disciples. His whole life he searched for the perennial philosophy, and he had found it! He had gathered all the fragments into a tremendous harmony, into a great unity. But he was not allowed to work it out in detail; to teach people he was not allowed.

He was persecuted from one place to another. Many attempts were made on his life. It was almost impossible for him to teach all that he had gathered. And his treasure was immense – in fact, nobody else has ever had such a treasure as he had. But this is how foolish humanity is, and has always been.

This man had done something impossible: he had bridged East and West. He was the first bridge. He had come to know the Eastern mind as deeply as the Western mind.

He was a Greek. He was brought up with the Greek logic, with the Greek scientific approach, and then he moved to the East. And then he learnt the ways of intuition. Then he learnt how to be a mystic. He himself was a great mathematician in his own right. And a mathematician becoming a mystic is a revolution, because these are poles apart.

Pythagoras was the first man to try the impossible, and he

succeeded! In him, East and West became one. In him, yin and yang became one. In him, male and female became one. He was a total unity of the polar opposites. Intellect of the highest caliber and intuition of the deepest caliber. Pythagoras is a peak, a sunlit peak, and a deep, dark valley too. It is a very rare combination.

But his whole life's effort was destroyed by the stupid people, by the mediocre masses. Just a few verses are the only contribution left. These verses can be written on one postcard. This is all that is left of that great man's effort, endeavour. And this too is not written by his own hand; it seems all that he had written was destroyed.

The day Pythagoras died, thousands of his disciples were massacred and burnt. Only one disciple escaped the school; his name was Lysis. And he escaped, not to save his life – he escaped just to save something of the Master's teachings. *The Golden Verses of Pythagoras* were written by Lysis, the only disciple who survived.

The whole school was burnt, and thousands of disciples were simply murdered and butchered. And all that Pythagoras had accumulated on his journeys – great treasures, great scriptures from China, India, Tibet, Egypt, years and years of work – all was burnt.

Lysis wrote a few verses. And, as it has been the ancient tradition that a real disciple knows no other name than his Master's, these verses are not called *Lysis' Verses* – they are called *The Golden Verses of Pythagoras*. He has not written his name on them.

Pythagoras is the first experiment in creating a synthesis. Twenty-five centuries have passed since then and nobody else has tried it again. Nobody else before had done it, and nobody else has done it afterwards either. It needs a mind which is both scientific and mystic. It is a rare phenomenon. It happens once in a while.

There have been great mystics – Buddha, Lao Tzu, Zarathustra. And there have been great scientists – Newton, Edison, Einstein. But to find a man who is at home with both worlds, easily at home, is very difficult. Pythagoras is that kind of man – a class unto himself. He cannot be categorized by anybody else.

❖

Pythagoras' sutras are divided into three parts; they are known as the three famous Ps of Pythagoras: preparation, purification, perfection.

Preparation means getting ready, into a receptive mood, becoming available, opening up. Preparation means creating a thirst, a longing for truth. Preparation means, not only curious, not only intellectually interested in what truth is, but committed to the search. Not just as a speculator standing outside but as a participant.

Preparation is the introductory part – to create a great thirst in you. Whenever you come close to a master, the first thing that he is going to give you is a fiery thirst. A great longing he will give to you; he will sow the seeds of great longing. In fact, he will make you very discontented.

You may have come to him in search of contentment, you may have come to him to be consoled, but he will make you aflame, afire, with a new desire that you have not even dreamt about, of which you have never been aware. Maybe it was lurking there somewhere in the dark nooks and corners of your being, or hiding in some recesses underground – he will bring it forth into light, he will provoke it into a great fire. He will pour all his energy into you, to make you so thirsty, so discontented, that you start the search and you become ready to risk all; that you forget all about other desires, that you pour all your desires into one stream, that your only desire, day and night, becomes truth – or God, or nirvana. Those are just names for the same phenomenon.

Preparation means the disciple is being awakened – awakened to the truth that we are existing in darkness and light has to be searched for and sought, awakened to the fact that we have been wasting our lives, that this is not the right way to live. Unless one starts moving towards God, life remains empty, impotent. The disciple has to be shocked, shaken, out of his dreams – dreams of money and power politics and prestige – and he has to be given a new dream, the ultimate dream, in which ALL dreams will be consumed. The ultimate dream is to know truth, to know that which is, to know that from which we come, to know that source and to know that goal to which we are going.

Then the second part is purification. When the desire has arisen then you have to be purified, because to reach the ultimate truth you will have to drop much unnecessary weight, much luggage that you have always carried. You have carried it because you have been thinking it is very valuable. Your system has to be purified of all the toxic things that you have absorbed on the way. And we have been drinking poison, many kinds of poison. One is a Hindu, another is a Mohammedan, another is a Christian – these are all poisons, prejudices. They keep you tethered to the society, to the conditionings of the society.

Purification means one has to drop all conditionings, all ideologies, all prejudices, all concepts, all philosophies ... all that you have been taught by others. One has to become a clean slate – a *tabula rasa* – one has to become utterly clean. Only when you are utterly clean, when nothing is written on you, can God write something. Only when you are utterly silent and all words given by the society have disappeared can God speak to you. Truth can whisper its mysteries into your ears only when you are absolutely empty – emptiness is purity.

Purification is a purgative part. Man has to drop many things. In fact, truth is not far away – you have just accumulated many things around yourself. You have grown many layers around yourself, many personalities around yourself, many masks you are wearing. Hence you cannot see your original face. All those masks have to be dropped. You have to become authentic, truly as you are, utterly naked as you are.

Purification means: stop hiding! Stop lying! Stop being phony!

And third is perfection. When you have stopped being phony, when you have dropped all the poisons that you had gathered on the way, when the dust is cleaned off the mirror, then perfection starts happening of its own accord.

❖

Pythagoras was the first to coin and use the words "philosophy" and "philosopher". "Philosophy" means love of wisdom, and "philosopher" means a friend of wisdom. Before Pythagoras, other words were used for the same purpose. For philosophy, the word *sophia* was used – *sophia* means wisdom; and for the philosopher, *sophos* – *sophos* means the wise man, the sage. They were beautiful words, but they had fallen, they had become associated with wrong people. They had fallen on bad times. Words also have good times and bad times, days of glory and days of humiliation.

Sophos is a beautiful word – the sage. Remember, the sage does not mean the saint. The saint is against the sinner; it has a polar opposite to it. The saint is one who is not a sinner; he has chosen to be virtuous, against vice. The sinner is one who has chosen vice against virtue. They are polarities like negative and positive. The saint cannot exist without the sinner; the sinner cannot exist without the saint – they are partners, they can only co-exist. A world without saints will be a world without sinners too. If you really want sinners to disappear from the world, let the saints disappear first – and immediately there will be no sinner.

The existence of the saint creates the sinner. And the more you respect the saint, the more you condemn the sinner, and the rift goes on becoming bigger and bigger. And the irony is that they exist together, two sides of the same coin. They are not different, their logic is not different – just their choice is different. One has chosen the night part of life, the other has chosen the day part. But life consists of both day and night; it is neither day alone nor night alone. Both are halves of one whole – hence both remain in misery.

Your sinners are miserable because they go on missing the beauties of virtue, the beauties of the other part that they have chosen not to choose. And your saints are miserable because they have repressed something which cannot be destroyed, which is an absolutely essential part of their being.

If you look deep into your saint, you will find a sinner hiding somewhere in his unconscious. And the same is the case with the sinner: look deep, and you will find a saint hiding somewhere in his unconscious. The conscious of the saint is the unconscious of the sinner, and the conscious of the sinner is the unconscious of the saint.

The sage is neither this nor that. He is *neti, neti* – neither this nor that – he has not chosen. He has accepted his wholeness; he is total, as much day, as much night. He has dropped the constantly choosing ego. He has simply accepted whatsoever is the case. He lives the truth in its utter nakedness, whatsoever it is – he has no business to interfere in the stream of life.

The sage is a tremendously beautiful phenomenon, because of his wholeness. The sage is a perfect circle. He contains all, he rejects nothing. That was the idea of *sophos*; it was a beautiful word. But it fell from its reputation.

It fell because it is a dangerous word too: it can easily be used by the cunning people. Because the sage is whole, he is both, now the sinner can use it. He can say, "I am both. I don't choose – whatsoever is the case …" Now the sinner can pretend to be a sage. He can say, "Because it is so, this moment I am like this. This is happening – what can I do? I have dropped choosing. I have accepted life in its totality."

Now, the sage is a totally different phenomenon from this cunning person. This cunning person used the word and the word became associated with this cunning mind. It became a camouflage for doing whatsoever you want to do. Deep down there is choice, but you can pretend on the surface that you are not a chooser, and you live in choiceless awareness. It is a very subtle cunningness.

So the word *sophos* fell from its pedestal and became "sophist". The word "sophist" is ugly – it means a pretender. It means one who is pretending to be a sage and is not, one who is pretending to be a sage and is not even a saint. He is simply a sinner but has found a beautiful rationalization for remaining a sinner.

The murderer can say, "What can I do? – God intended to murder through me." The thief can say, "What can I do? – that's how God commanded me. I simply followed." And it will be very difficult to argue with him; he has a beautiful rationalization there.

So the *sophos* fell and became a sophist. And the same happened with *sophia*: wisdom is not knowledge, but they look alike. Knowledge only pretends to be wisdom; it is just the opposite of wisdom. Knowledge is always borrowed, and because it is borrowed it is basically untrue.

Wisdom arises in you – it is your flowering, it is your fragrance. It is self-understanding, self-knowing. You become luminous; you attain to a solid presence. You have a center, you feel rooted, integrated; you are no more fragmentary, you are one piece.

Wisdom is a revolution in your being: knowledge is just rubbish. You can gather it from others; it does not change you, you remain the same. Of course you become very decorated, you gain many beautiful masks, but your own face remains the same. You go on accumulating knowledge, your memory becomes richer and richer, but your being remains as poor as ever. But knowledge can pretend to be wisdom; they both use the same language.

Sophia is wisdom. Wisdom happens in the innermost shrine of your being. It is never borrowed, it has nothing to do with knowledge, information, nothing to do with scriptures, doctrines, systems of thought. It is your own experience, individual, authentic. You have known. You have arrived. Then it is *sophos* – it is wisdom.

If you are simply repeating from other people's experiences it is sophistry, it is knowledge – dead, meaningless, nothing but gibberish. You can decorate yourself with it, you can strengthen your ego through it, but you will not know the truth.

Sophos fell and there was that ugly phenomenon, the sophist. *Sophia* fell and what came into existence was sophistry. Sophistry is pure argument for argument's sake, with no concern for truth. It is just linguistic analysis, logical, rational, of course, but not intuitive, not experiential.

And one can go on arguing and guessing, and yet, even if you argue for millennia you will not arrive at truth – because truth is never a conclusion, not a conclusion of any logical process. Truth has not to be invented by logic; truth has to be discovered by love. The way to truth is not logic but love. Wisdom is love; knowledge is logic.

And whenever logic starts pretending that "I am the door, I am the way to truth," truth disappears from the world.

Pythagoras had to coin new words, and he coined beautiful words. "Philosophy" means love of wisdom – not love of knowledge, remember, love of wisdom. Knowledge is intellectual, wisdom is intuitive. Knowledge is of the head, wisdom is of the heart. Hence love – not logic but love, not calculation but innocence, not cunningness but intelligence, not intellectuality but intelligence.

And he also coined the word "philosopher" – a friend of wisdom. Have you ever observed? – whenever you start arguing with somebody you are more concerned with your ego than for the truth. Sometimes you even see the falsity of your argument, but you cannot accept it because it hurts the ego. You argue because it is your opinion, not because it is true. You argue against the other's opinion because it is HIS opinion, not because it is untrue.

Argument arises not for truth but for egoistic trips – then it is sophistry, then it is a very ugly phenomenon.

You love a woman – it is a beautiful experience. A love between a man and a woman has tremendous truth, a fragrance of its own, a benediction. It is one of the most incredible mysteries of life. But to go to a prostitute is not the same – physically it is the same, spiritually it is totally different. The prostitute is an ugly phenomenon; the beloved is something divine.

Philosophy is like your beloved; sophistry is a prostitute.

Pythagoras also introduced the word "cosmos".

"Cosmos" means order, rhythm, harmony. Existence is not a chaos but a cosmos. Pythagoras has contributed much to human thought, to human evolution. His vision of a cosmos became the very foundation of scientific investigation.

Science can exist only if existence is a cosmos. If it is a chaos, there is no possibility of any science. If laws change every day, every moment – one day the water evaporates at 100 degrees, another day at 500 degrees – if water functions in a whimsical way and follows no order, how can there be a science?

Science presupposes that existence functions in a consistent way, in a rational way, that existence is not mad, that if we search deep into existence, we are bound to find laws – and those laws are the keys to all the mysteries.

Just as it is true for science so it is true for religion too – because religion is nothing but the science of the inner. The outer science is called science; the inner science is called religion – but both can exist only in a cosmos.

There are laws of the inner world. Those laws have been discovered just as much as scientific laws have been discovered. Neither have scientific laws been invented, nor have religious laws been invented. Truth is – you need not invent it. And whatsoever you invent will be untrue – all inventions are lies.

Truth has to be discovered, not invented. Einstein discovers a certain law, Patanjali also discovers a certain law; Newton discovers gravitation, Krishna discovers grace – both are laws. One belongs to the earth, the other belongs to the sky; one belongs to the world of necessity, the other belongs to the world of power. One belongs to the visible and the other belongs to the invisible.

It is in the vision of a cosmos that Pythagoras became the originator of a scientific concept of the world. He was the first scientist because he provided the very foundation. His idea of cosmos has to be understood, because without understanding it you will not be able to understand what he is talking about.

The inner world, the world of the spirit, follows certain laws, and those laws are unchangeable, they are perennial. Those laws are not time-bound, they are beyond time. Time itself functions within those laws. If you want to do something in the outside world, you will need to know how the outer existence functions, because unless you know how it functions you are bound to fail.

Nature has no obligation to adjust to you – you will have to adjust to nature. You can win nature only by adjusting yourself to nature. You can become a conqueror too, but not against nature – with nature, in tune with nature. You can become a master of the inner kingdom too – not against the laws but in tune with those laws.

It is because of this mystic vision – that the world is not accidental, not anarchic, but an absolutely harmonious, cosmic, orderly world – that Pythagoras was able to discover many things for seekers.

For Pythagoras, science is a search for truth in the objective world and religion is a search for truth in the subjective world – and philosophy is a search for the truth. So science and religion are like two hands or two wings. They are not opposites but complementaries. And the world would be better if we were reminded of it again.

The church, the temple and the lab need not be enemies. They should exist in a kind of friendship. Man will be far richer then. Now, if he chooses science he becomes rich outside and goes on becoming poorer and poorer inside. If he chooses religion, he becomes rich inside, but goes on becoming poorer and poorer on the outside. And both are ugly scenes.

The West has chosen science; it has all the riches of the world, but the man is completely lost, feeling meaningless, suicidal. The man, when he looks inside, finds nothing but hollowness, emptiness. The inner world has become very poor in the West.

In the East, just the opposite has happened: people have chosen religion against science. Their inner world is calmer, quieter, richer; but on the outside they are starving, dying – no food, no medicine, no facilities to live a human life, living almost like animals or even worse.

This is the consequence of not listening to Pythagoras. The whole history of humanity would have been totally different if Pythagoras had been listened to, understood. There is no need for the East to be East and the West to be West. There is no need for anybody to be just a materialist or just a spiritualist. If body and soul can exist together – they ARE existing together in you, in everybody – then why can't materialism and spiritualism exist together? They should!

A man must be materialist and spiritualist. To choose is fatal. There is no need to choose; you can have both the worlds – you should have both the worlds; that is your birthright.

Rabiya al-Adabiya

Rabiya al-Adabiya was a Sufi woman who was known for her very eccentric behavior. But in all her eccentric behavior there was a great insight.

Once, another Sufi mystic, Hasan, was staying with Rabiya. Because he was going to stay with Rabiya, he had not brought his own Koran, which he used to read every morning as part of his discipline. He thought he could borrow Rabiya's Koran, so he had not brought his own copy with him.

In the morning he asked Rabiya, and she gave him her copy. He could not believe his eyes. When he opened the Koran he saw something which no Mohammedan could believe: in many places Rabiya had corrected it. It is the greatest sin as far as Mohammedans are concerned; the Koran is the word of God according to them. How can you change it? How can you even think that you can make something better? Not only has she changed it, she has simply cut out a few words, a few lines – removed them.

Hasan said to her, "Rabiya, somebody has destroyed your Koran!"

Rabiya said, "Don't be stupid, nobody can touch my Koran. What you are looking at is my doing."

Hasan said, "But how could you do such a thing?"

She said, "I had to do it, there was no way out. For example, look here: the Koran says, 'When you see the Devil, hate him.' Since I have become awakened I cannot find any hate within me. Even if the Devil stands in front of me I can only shower him with my love, because I don't have anything else left. It does not matter whether God stands in front of me, or the Devil; both will receive the same love. All that I have is love; hate has disappeared. The moment hate disappeared from me I had to make changes in my book of the holy Koran. If you have not changed it, that simply means you have not arrived to the space where only love remains."

Rabiya was passing along the street – she was not much known; it is a man's world. Who cares about a woman, even if she is enlightened? She saw Hasan in front of a mosque with his hands stretched towards the sky, praying to God, "Give me this, give me that."

Rabiya was a rare woman in the history of men. She went, stood behind Hasan, and hit him on his head. He certainly could not believe that he was asking God for beautiful things, and a hit comes! He looked back, and he found Rabiya. Hasan said, "This is not right, disturbing somebody in his prayer time."

Rabiya said, "You idiot! You were asking, 'Please open the doors' – and I tell you the doors have never been closed! So who is going to open them? There is nobody to close them, there is nobody to open them. Just enter!"

Jesus says, "Knock, and the doors shall be opened unto you." There are no doors. If you knock you will be knocking on a wall. Then you can knock with your head, still the doors will not open.

As far as existence is concerned there are no doors. It is all open, from all sides. Just enter from anywhere, and the closest place to enter it is within you. Any other place will be distant. Why not start from the point where you are? So first, get there where you are – grounded, centered in your own interiority – and the miracle is, there will be no need for you to go anywhere. No need to knock – the doors are open. Your interiority is the door, the open door for the whole cosmos.

One evening when the sun was setting, Rabiya was found searching for something just in front of her door on the road. A few people gathered and they said, "Rabiya, what have you lost? We can help you."

She was an old woman by this time, and loved by the people, loved because she was beautifully crazy. Rabiya said, "I have lost my needle. I was sewing and I lost my needle. I am searching for it, and there is not much time because the sun is setting. If you want to help me, help quickly, because once the sun has set and darkness has descended, it will be impossible to find the needle."

So they all started a hectic search for the needle. One of them suddenly thought, "The needle is such a small thing and the road is so big, and the sun is going down every moment, the light is disappearing – unless we know the exact spot where it has fallen it will be impossible to find it." So he asked Rabiya, "Will you please tell us where the needle has fallen exactly? Then it will be possible to find it. Otherwise soon there will be darkness, and the road is very big and the needle is very small."

Rabiya started laughing. She said, "Please don't ask that, because I feel embarrassed by the question!"

They all stopped searching. They said, "What is the matter? Why should you feel embarrassed?"

She said, "I feel embarrassed because I lost the needle inside the house, but because there is no light there, how can I find it? Outside on the road there is just a little light from the setting sun."

They all said, "Now you have gone completely crazy! We had always suspected that you were not sane, but this is an absolute proof!"

Rabiya said, "You think me insane, yet you have been doing the same for lives together – and you are sane? Where have you lost yourself, and where are you trying to find it? Where have you lost your bliss, and where are you trying to find it? It is lost in your inner world, and you are searching on the outside!"

Another story …

One day Hasan went to Rabiya. He had just learned how to walk on water, so he told Rabiya, "Let us go and walk on water and have a little spiritual discourse, discussion." That spiritual discussion was just an excuse; he wanted to show Rabiya that he could walk on the water.

Rabiya said, "On the water? That does not appeal to me. Let us go to the clouds! We will sit on the clouds and have spiritual discourse."

Hassan said, "But I don't know how to go to the clouds and sit on the clouds."

Rabiya said, "Neither do I! But what is the point? Why can't we have a religious discourse here?

Why go to the water or to the clouds?"

All great mystics have been against miracles, and all fools are interested in miracles.

Jalaluddin Rumi

Rumi says: "Move within, but don't move the way fear makes you move."

The words of Mevlana Rumi are immensely significant. There have been very few people who have moved and transformed as many hearts as Jalaluddin Rumi.

In the world of the Sufis, Mevlana Rumi is the emperor. His words have to be understood not as mere words, but sources of deep silences, echoes of inner and the innermost songs. He is the greatest dancer the world has known. Twelve hundred years have passed since he was alive.

His dance is a special kind of dance. It is a kind of whirling, just the way small children whirl; standing on one spot they go on round and round. And perhaps everywhere in the world small children do that and their elders stop them saying, "You will become dizzy, you will fall, you will hurt yourself," and, "What is the point of doing it?"

Jalaluddin Rumi made a meditation of whirling. The meditator goes on whirling for hours – as long as the body allows him; he does not stop on his own. When whirling a moment comes that he sees himself utterly still and silent, a center of the cyclone. Around the center the body is moving, but there is a space which remains unmoved; that is his being.

Rumi himself whirled for 36 hours continuously and fell, because the body could not whirl anymore. But when he opened his eyes he was another man. Hundreds of people had gathered to see. Many thought he was mad: "What is the point of whirling? Nobody can say this is a prayer; nobody can say this is great dance; nobody can say in any way that this has something to do with religion, spirituality …"

But after 36 hours when they saw Rumi so luminous, so radiant, so new, so fresh – reborn, in a new consciousness, they could not believe their eyes. Hundreds wept in repentance, because they had thought that he was mad. In fact he was sane and they were mad.

And down these 12 centuries the stream has continued to be alive. There are very few movements of spiritual growth which have lived so long continuously. There are still hundreds of dervishes. "Dervish" is the Sufi word for sannyas. You cannot believe it unless you experience, that just by whirling you can know yourself. No austerity is needed, no self-torture is needed, but just an experience of your innermost being and you are transported into another plane of existence from the mortal to the immortal. The darkness disappears and there is just eternal light.

His words have to be understood very carefully because he has not spoken much – just a few small poems. His statement, "Move within, but don't move the way fear makes you move" – it is so beautiful.

Don't move the way fear makes you move.
Move the way love makes you move.

Move the way joy makes you move – not out of fear, because all so-called religions are based on fear. Their God is nothing but fear, and their heaven and hell are nothing but projections of fear and greed.

Rumi's statement is very revolutionary: do not move because of fear. All the religions say to people, "Fear God!"

Mahatma Gandhi used to say, "I do not fear anybody but God." When I heard this I said this is the most stupid statement anybody can make. You can fear everybody, but don't fear God because God can only be approached through love. God is not a person but the universal heartbeat. If you can sing with love and dance with love … an ordinary activity like whirling out of love … Joy and celebration are enough to reach to the innermost sanctum of being and existence.

You all have been living out of fear.

Your relationships are out of fear. Fear is so overwhelming – like a dark cloud covering your life – that you say things which you don't want to say, but fear makes you say them. You do things which you do not want to do, but fear makes you do them. A little intelligence is enough to see ...

Millions of people are worshiping stones carved by themselves. They have made their gods and then they worship them. It must be out of great fear, because where can you find God? The easier way is to carve a god in beautiful marble and worship. And nobody thinks that this is sheer stupidity, because everybody else is doing it in different ways – somebody in the temple and somebody in the mosque and somebody in the synagogue; it does not make any difference. The essential thing is the same, that what you are doing is out of fear – your prayers are full of fear.

Rumi is making a revolutionary, an extraordinary statement: "Move within, but don't move the way fear makes you move." Then what is the way to move within? Why not move playfully? Why not make your religion a playfulness? Why be so serious? Why not move laughingly? – just like small children running joyously after butterflies for no special reason. Just the joy of the colors and the beauty of the flowers and the butterflies is enough – and they are so immensely happy.

In every 24 hours find a few moments which are fearless, which means in those moments you are not asking for anything. You are not asking for any reward and you are not worried about any punishment; you are simply enjoying the whirling, the going inwards.

In fact, just in the beginning it may look a little difficult. As you move a little inwards you become automatically joyful, playful, prayerful. A gratitude arises in you that you have never known before and a space opens up which is infinite, your inner sky.

Your inner sky is not less rich than the outer sky: it has its own stars and its own moon and its own planets and its own immensity; it has exactly as vast a universe as you can see outside. You are just standing in between two universes: one is outside you; one is inside you. The outside universe consists of things, and the inside universe consists of consciousness, of bliss, of joy.

Move within, but don't move the way fear makes you move, because fear cannot enter inwards. Why can fear not enter inwards? Fear cannot be alone, and inwards you have to be alone. Fear needs a crowd, fear needs companionship, friends, even foes may do.

But to be alone, to go inwards, you cannot take anybody with you; you have to be more and more alone. Not only can you not take anyone, you cannot take anything either. Your wealth, your power, your prestige – you cannot take anything. Inside you cannot take even your clothes! You will have to go nude and alone; hence fear cannot move inwards, fear moves outwards.

Fear moves towards money, fear moves towards power, fear moves towards God; fear moves in all directions except inwards. To go inwards the first requirement is fearlessness. One has not to make friends with darkness, death or fear. One has to get rid of them. One has to simply say goodbye forever. It is your attachment; friendship will make it even more deep.

Don't think that by becoming friendly with fear you will become ready to go inwards. Even the friendly fear will prevent it; in fact, it will prevent it more so. It will prevent you in a friendly way, it will advise you, "Don't do such a thing. There is nothing inwards. You will fall into a nothingness and returning from that nothingness is impossible. Beware of falling into your inwardness. Cling to things."

Fear has to be understood – you don't have to make friends – and it disappears.

What are you afraid of? When you were born you were born naked. You did not bring any bank balance either – but you were not afraid. You come into the world utterly nude, but entering like an emperor. Even an emperor cannot enter into the world the way a child enters. The same is true of entering inwards. It is a second childbirth; you again become a child – the same innocence and the same nudity and the same non-possessiveness. What do you have to be afraid of?

In life you cannot be afraid of birth. It has happened, now nothing can be done about it. You cannot be afraid of life – it is already happening. You cannot be afraid of death – whatever you do it is going to happen. So what is the fear?

I have always been asked even by very learned people, "Do you never get concerned what will happen after death?" And I have always wondered that these people are learned. And I have asked them, "One day I was not born – and there was no worry. I have never for a single moment thought that when I was not born what kind of trouble, what kind of anxiety, what kind of anguish I had to face. I was simply not! So the same will be the case: when you die, you die."

Confucius was asked by his most significant disciple, Mencius, "What will happen after death?"

Confucius said, "Don't waste time. When you are in your grave, lie down and think over it, but why bother now?"

Fear of what will happen when you die is unnecessary. Whatever will happen will happen – and anyway you cannot do anything beforehand. You don't know so there is no question of doing some homework, getting ready for the kind of questions you will be asked or what kind of people you will meet, learning their manners, their language … We don't know anything; there is no need to worry. Don't waste time.

The followers of Rumi don't have great scriptures, don't have any rituals, except whirling, and a few beautiful poems by Jalaluddin Rumi, which he used to sing after whirling and falling. He will get up and he will be so drunk – in that drunkenness he will sing a song, and those songs have been collected. That is the only literature the followers of Rumi have.

Rumi says, "We are the mirror" – that's what I have been saying again and again; that we are not the doer, we are only the mirror. Don't get identified with your doings, with your actions; remain a witness, just a watcher. But we are not taught the most essential things of life, we are taught all kinds of stupid things. The most essential is the art of watchfulness.

Rumi is right; he says, "We are the mirror, as well as the face in it."
We are the watcher and the watched. There is no separation between
us and existence. We are part of one whole, just as my two hands are
part of one organic unity. I can manage that they fight with each
other. I can manage that they are friendly, loving and warm to each
other. I can hit one hand with the other hand and wound it.

When you are seeing the tree, or the moon, or the river, or the
ocean, you are the mirror and the mirrored too. It is one existence.
This is the basic conclusion of all the mystics, that the whole of
existence is one entity, there is no duality. All duality deep down is
joined into one existence.

We are the mirror as well as the face in it.
We are tasting the taste this minute of eternity.

Just be watchful this minute. In this silence you are tasting something
which is beyond time. We are tasting the taste of this minute of
eternity. We are pain, and what cures pain, both. We are agony and
we are ecstasy. We are hell and we are heaven, because there is no contradiction in existence. They are all joined together. We are the sweet
cold water and the jar that pours it.

You can find many contradictions in life. And you can also find
that they are all complementaries. It is something very strange, that
all the mystics, whether they were born thousands of years ago, or
they are alive today, all fundamentally agree on the essential points of
spiritual growth and realization.

For example: the silence, this minute, gives you not an explanation
– but it gives you an experience. Dancing and singing, allow yourself
to be so completely overwhelmed that nothing is left behind. And you
have entered into the temple of God, where you are the mirror, and
you are the face mirrored in it; where you are the seeker and you are
the sought; where you are the devotee and you are the God at whose
feet you are offering yourself.

It happened in Ramakrishna's life ... a very strange incident. One great painter wanted to paint the picture of Ramakrishna. After great persuasion Ramakrishna agreed. When the painting was complete, the painter brought it to offer to Ramakrishna. As he gave the painting to Ramakrishna ... Ramakrishna touched the feet in the painting with his head. The painter could not believe it. He had heard that that man is mad, but now there was no question: he is certainly mad, touching his own feet with his head!

Even his disciples became embarrassed. A great silence fell. Finally one disciple asked, "It is your own painting, your own picture – and you are touching its feet with your head? You do such things ... people think you are mad, and you give them every kind of evidence. Even we become embarrassed when people ask us, 'Why do you go to Ramakrishna, can't you find anybody else who is sane?'"

Ramakrishna said, "Have I committed any wrong? I have not touched my own feet. I have touched the feet – because the painting is of somebody who is in deep silence, in samadhi, in tune with God. You are right, I must be mad, because now I recognize it is my own picture. But at that moment I only felt that the painter has done a great job. He has not only caught the body of the person, but also his spirit." And Ramakrishna kept that painting his whole life, just behind his bed. It is still there.

While his wife was alive she used to make the bed every day, even after his death. She used to bring food to his room. She used to cook all those delicious things that Ramakrishna liked.

People started saying, "One madman is dead, now this mad woman ..." Sharda was her name. Even disciples of Ramakrishna used to ask her, "When he is dead, what is the point of twice every day making food for him, every night, making his bed?"

She said, "Should I believe you, or should I believe him? Because when he was dying, I asked, 'Are you really dying?' And he said, 'Nobody dies. And you need not change your dress.'" This is the custom among the Hindus, that the widow cannot use colored clothes, she cannot use ornaments, she has to shave her head.

Ramkrishna said, "You are not to do anything, because I am not going to die, I'm simply leaving the body, but I will be here, now, always."

"So whom I am to believe?" Sharda used to say. "And if he is always here now, I cannot resist the temptation of preparing things that he used to like. I may not be able to see him, but he must be able to see me, and that is what is significant – not that I should see him, but that he is watching. And for his whole life his teaching was a simple word: watchfulness."

We are the mirror as well as the face in it.

A story is that a few people had gone hunting and they came across the camp of Jalaluddin Rumi. Just out of curiosity they looked inside the doors. It was a walled garden, and nearabout 100 disciples were whirling with Jalaluddin Rumi. Those people thought, "These are mad people. Who has ever heard that by whirling you can get truth? In what scripture, in what religion is it written? There is no record. This man is mad, and he is driving so many young people mad."

They went on. Hunting was far more significant. Obviously it was saner than to dance with Jalaluddin Rumi.

After their hunting, they went back. Just out of curiosity about what had happened to the whirlers, they again looked into the door. They were surprised: those hundred people were sitting under the trees in silence, with closed eyes, as if there was nobody – absolute silence; you could hear the wind blowing through the trees.

Those hunters said, "Poor fellows ... finished. This happens by whirling – all energy lost. Now they are sitting like the dead; perhaps a few are already dead."

Do you think they started discussing amongst themselves whether these people had achieved truth? If sitting like this with closed eyes ... "What was the need of whirling? You could have sat before." They went away.

The next month, they went again for hunting. Again, just out of curiosity – "Now what happened to those people – are they really dead, or still sitting, or gone, or what happened?" – they looked. There was nobody, only Jalaluddin Rumi was sitting there. They laughed. They said, "Everybody has escaped; they must have understood that this man is mad. He was almost killing them by dancing, whirling. He seems to be an expert, 36 hours non-stop … anybody would be dead by that time! No coffee break, no tea break, just continuous whirling …"

So they went in and asked Jalaluddin Rumi, "What happened to your disciples? We had come one month ago and there was a group of at least 100 people."

Jalaluddin said, "They danced, they found, they absorbed, and they have gone into the world to spread the message."

"And what are you doing?" they asked.

He said, "I am waiting for the second batch. My people have gone out; they will be bringing them."

Hakim Sanai

Hakim Sanai is unique, unique in the world of Sufism. No other Sufi has been able to reach to such heights of expression and such depths of penetration. Hakim Sanai has been able to do almost the impossible.

If I were to save only two books from the whole world of the mystics, then these would be the two books. One would be from the world of Zen, the path of awareness: Sosan's Hsin Hsin Ming. I have spoken on it; it contains the quintessence of Zen, of the path of awareness and meditation. The other book would be Hakim Sanai's Hadiqa tu'l Haqiqat: The Walled Garden of Truth – in short, The Hadiqa: The Garden.

The Hadiqa is the essential fragrance of the path of love. Just as Sosan has been able to catch the very soul of Zen, Hakim Sanai has been able to catch the very soul of Sufism. Such books are not written, they are born. Nobody can compose them. They are not manufactured in the mind, by the mind; they come from the beyond. They are a gift. They are born as mysteriously as a child is born, or a bird or a rose flower. They come to us, they are gifts.

The story of the mysterious birth of this great book is tremendously beautiful.

The Sultan of Ghazna, Bahramshah, was moving with his great army towards India on a journey of conquest. Hakim Sanai, his famous court-poet, was also with him, accompanying him on the journey of this conquest. They came alongside a great garden, a walled garden.

That is the meaning of *firdaus*: the walled garden. And from *firdaus* comes the English word "paradise".

They were in a hurry; with a great army the Sultan was moving to conquer India. He had no time. But something mysterious happened and he had to stop; there was no way to avoid it.

The sound of singing coming from the garden caught the Sultan's attention. He was a lover of music, but he had never heard something like this. He had great musicians in his court and great singers and dancers, but nothing to be compared with this. The sound of singing and the music and the dance – he had only heard it from outside, but he had to order the army to stop.

It was so ecstatic. The very sound of the dance and the music and the singing was psychedelic, as if wine was pouring into him: the Sultan became drunk. The phenomenon appeared not to be of this world. Something of the beyond was certainly in it: something of the sky trying to reach the earth, something from the unknown trying to commune with the known. He had to stop to listen to it.

There was ecstasy in it – so sweet and yet so painful, it was heart-rending. He wanted to move, he was in a hurry; he had to reach India soon, this was the right time to conquer the enemy. But there was no way. There was such strong, strange, irresistible magnetism in the sound that in spite of himself he had to go into the garden.

It was Lai-Khur, a great Sufi mystic, but known to the masses only as a drunkard and a madman. Lai-Khur is one of the greatest names in the whole history of the world. Not much is known about him; such people don't leave many footprints behind them. Except for this story, nothing has survived. But Lai-Khur has lived in the memories of the Sufis, down the ages. He continued haunting the world of the Sufis, because never again was such a man seen.

He was so drunk that people were not wrong in calling him a drunkard. He was drunk 24 hours, drunk with the divine. He walked like a drunkard, he lived like a drunkard, utterly oblivious of the world. And his utterances were just mad. This is the highest peak of ecstasy, when expressions of the mystic can only be understood by other mystics. For the ordinary masses they look irrelevant, they look like gibberish.

You will be surprised to know that the English word "gibberish" is based on a Sufi mystic's name, Jabbar. It is because of Jabbar's utterances that the English word "gibberish" has arisen. But even Jabbar was nothing compared to Lai-Khur.

To the ignorant, his utterances were outrageous, sacrilegious, against tradition and against all formalities, mannerisms and etiquette – against all that is known and understood as religion. But to those who knew, they were nothing but pure gold.

He was available only to the chosen few, because only very few people can rise to such a height where he lived. He lived on Everest – the Everest of consciousness, beyond the clouds. Only those who were fortunate enough and courageous enough to climb the mountain were able to understand what he was saying. To the common masses he was a madman. To the knowers he was just a vehicle of God, and all that was coming through him was pure truth: truth, and only truth.

He had made himself deliberately notorious. That was his way of becoming invisible to the masses. Sufis do that; they have a very strange method of becoming invisible. They remain visible – they remain in the world, they don't escape from it – but deliberately they create a certain milieu around them, so that people stop coming to them. Crowds, curious people, stupid people, simply stop coming to them; the Sufis don't exist for them, they forget all about them. This has been an ancient method of the Sufis so that they can work with their disciples.

Lai-Khur had made himself deliberately notorious. He was now visible only to the perceptive. A master, if he really wants to work, if he means business, has to become invisible to those who are not authentic seekers. That is what Gurdjieff used to do. Gurdjieff must have learned a few things from Lai-Khur. Gurdjieff had lived with Sufi masters for many years before he became a master in his own right. And when I have finished this story you will see many similarities between Gurdjieff and Lai-Khur.

Lai-Khur called for wine and proposed a toast "to the blindness of the Sultan Bahramshah."

Now, first the great mystic called for wine. Religious people are not supposed to drink wine. It is one of the greatest sins for a Muslim to drink wine; it is against the Koran, it is against the religious idea of how a saint should be. Lai-Khur called for wine and proposed a toast "to the blindness of the Sultan Bahramshah."

The Sultan must have got mad. He must have been furious – calling him blind? But he was under the great ecstatic impact of Lai-Khur. So although he was boiling within, he didn't say a thing. Those beautiful sounds and the music and the dance were still haunting him, they were still there in his heart. He was transported to another world. But others objected, his generals and his courtiers objected.

When objections were raised, Lai-Khur laughed madly and insisted that the Sultan deserved blindness for embarking on such a foolish journey. "What can you conquer in the world? All will be left behind. The idea of conquering is stupid, utterly stupid. Where are you going? You are blind! Because the treasure is within you," he said. "And you are going to India; wasting time, wasting other people's time. What more is needed for a man to be called blind?"

Lai-Khur insisted: "The Sultan is blind. If he is not blind then he should go back to his home and forget all about this conquest. Don't make houses of playing-cards, don't make castles of sand. Don't go after dreams, don't be mad. Go back! Look within!"

The man who has eyes looks within, the blind man looks without. The man who has eyes searches for the treasure within. The man who is blind rushes all over the world, begging, robbing people, murdering, in the hope that he will find something that he is missing. It is never found that way, because it is not outside that you have lost it. You have lost it in your own being: light has to be brought there.

Lai-Khur insisted that the Sultan was blind. "If he is not, then give me the proof: order the army to go back. Forget all about this conquest, and never again go on any other conquest. This is all nonsense!"

The Sultan was impressed, but was not capable of going back. It must have been the same situation as had happened before, when

Alexander the Great was coming to conquer India, and another mystic, Diogenes laughed at him. And he said, "Why? For what are you going on such a long journey? And what are you going to gain by conquering India, or by conquering the whole world?"

And Alexander said, "I want to conquer the whole world so that finally I can rest and relax and enjoy."

And Diogenes laughed and said, "You must be a fool – because I am resting now!" And he was resting, relaxing on the bank of a small river. It was early morning and he was taking a sunbath, naked on the sand. He said, "I am resting and relaxing NOW, and I have not conquered the world. I have not even THOUGHT of conquering the world. So if you are conquering the world and trying to become victorious just to rest and relax, it looks absolutely meaningless, because I am resting without conquering anything. And the bank of this river is big enough, it can contain us both. Rest here. Throw away your clothes and take a good sunbath and forget all about conquering!

"And look at me: I am a conqueror without conquering the world. And you are a beggar."

The same must have been the situation with the Sultan Bahramshah, and Lai-Khur must have been again the same type of man. In this world there have been only two types of people: those who know, and those who don't know. It is the same drama played again and again, the same story enacted again and again. Sometimes it is Alexander the Great who is playing the blind person and it is Diogenes who tries to wake him up. Some other time it is Lai-Khur who is trying to wake Sultan Bahramshah.

Alexander said, "I am sorry. I can understand your point, but I cannot go back. I have to conquer the world; without conquering it I cannot rest. Excuse me. And you are right, I concede it."

And the same happened with Bahramshah. He was sad, ashamed, shy. But he said, "Excuse me, I have to go, I cannot go back. India has to be conquered. I will not be able to rest or sit silently until I have conquered India."

Then a toast was called "to the blindness of Hakim Sanai" –
because he was the next most important person with Bahramshah.
He was his adviser, his counsellor, his poet. He was the wisest man in
his court, and his fame had penetrated into other lands too. He was
already an accomplished poet; a great, well-known wise man.

Then a toast was called "to the blindness of Hakim Sanai," which
must have given the great poet a considerable jolt. There were even
stronger objections to this on the grounds of Sanai's excellent
reputation, his wisdom, his character. He was a man of character, a
very virtuous man, very religious. Nobody could have found any flaw
in his life. He had lived a very, very conscious life, at least in his own
eyes. He was a man of conscience.

More objections were raised. Because maybe the Sultan was
blind, he was greedy, he had great lust, he had great desire to possess
things, but that could not be said about Hakim Sanai. He had lived
the life of a poor man, even though he had been in the court. Even
though he was the most respected man in Bahramshah's court, he had
lived like a poor man – simple, humble, and of great wisdom and
character.

But Lai-Khur countered that the toast was even more apt, since
Sanai seemed unaware of the purpose for which he had been created;
and when he was shortly brought before his maker and asked what
he had to show for himself he would only be able to produce some
stupid eulogies to foolish kings, mere mortals like himself.

Lai-Khur said that it was even more apt because much more is to
be expected from Hakim Sanai than from Sultan Bahramshah. He has
a greater potential and he is wasting it, wasting it in making eulogies
for foolish kings. He will not be able to face his God; he will be in
difficulty, he will not be able to answer for himself. All that he will be
able to produce will be this poetry, written in praise of foolish kings
like this blind man, Bahramshah.

He is more blind, utterly blind.

And listening to these words and looking into the eyes of that
madman, Lai-Khur, something incredible happened to Hakim Sanai:

a satori, a sudden enlightening experience. Something died in him immediately, instantly. And something was born, something utterly new. In a single moment, the transformation had happened. He was no longer the same man. This madman had really penetrated his soul. This madman had succeeded in awakening him.

In Sufi history, this is the only case of satori. In Zen there are many cases; I have been talking to you about those cases. But in the world of Sufism this is the only case of satori, sudden enlightenment – not methodological, not gradual; in a shock it happened.

Lai-Khur must have been a man of tremendous insight. Hakim Sanai bowed down, touched the feet of this madman and wept tears of joy that he had arrived home. He died and was reborn. That's what a satori is: dying and being reborn. It is a rebirth.

He left the Sultan and went on a pilgrimage to Mecca. The Sultan was not willing, he was not ready to allow him to go. He tried in every way to prevent him: he even offered his only sister in marriage, and half the kingdom, to Hakim Sanai. But now all was meaningless. Hakim Sanai simply laughed and he said, "I am no longer a blind person. Thank you, but I am finished. This madman has finished me in a single stroke, in a single blow." And he went on a pilgrimage to Mecca. Why? Later on, when he was asked he said, "Just to absorb, just to digest what that madman had given me so suddenly. It was too much! It was overflowing, I was overwhelmed; it had to be digested. He had given me more than I was worthy of."

So he went to Mecca on a pilgrimage, to meditate, to be silent, to be a pilgrim unknown to anybody, to be anonymous. The thing had happened, but it had to be absorbed. The light had happened, but one has to get accustomed to it. And when he became accustomed to the new gestalt, to the new vision, he came back to Lai-Khur and presented him this book, The Hadiqa. That's what he wrote on the way back from Mecca.

He poured his experience, his satori, into this book. These words are saturated with satori. This is how this great book was born, like a child is born, mysteriously; like a seed becomes a sprout, mysteriously;

like a bird comes out of the egg, mysteriously. Like a bud opens early in the morning and becomes a flower, and the fragrance is spread to the winds.

Yes, this book was not written. This book is a gift from God. This book is a gift from God, and a gratitude from Hakim Sanai to that strange madman, Lai-Khur.

❖

You cannot make a statue of a Sufi, because the statue will not express his dance, the statue will not express his song, the statue will not express his love, his prayer, his gratitude. His ecstatic madness will not be expressed by the statue. Statues can be made only of a meditator. The meditator is a statue – cold, silent, empty. Emptiness has a purity, that is true, but something is missing in it. Richness is missing in it, life is missing in it, orgasmic joy is missing in it.

And that is what happens to the people who move through the path of *via unitiva*: their path is of orgasmic unity. Just as two lovers embrace each other, penetrate each other – not only physically but spiritually too – become dissolved and a kind of unity arises … Two individuals become one. And when these two individuals become one, in fact there are three things becoming one: the lover, the beloved and the love.

Love is a very solid phenomenon to the lovers. In fact the lover and the beloved are nothing compared to the reality of love. The love is far more real than their existence separate from each other. So when lovers meet, three things meet.

To symbolize this, in India we have created a beautiful sacred place, Prayag, where three rivers are said to meet. Two are visible, the third is invisible. One is the Ganges, very visible; another is Yamuna, very visible, and the third is Saraswati – nobody can see it. It is there, but it just has to be believed in; it is invisible.

To the scientific mind it looks absurd. How can there be an invisible river? Nobody has ever seen it, but Hindus go on saying that there is a meeting of three rivers: two are of this world, and the third

225

is of the other. Two belong to the earth and the third belongs to the beyond.

This is really a metaphor of love. When two lovers meet, three things meet, three energies meet: two are of this earth, one is of the beyond. Two are visible, you can see the lover and the beloved – but you will not be able to see love, which is far more valuable than both. In fact it is because of the third that the two are meeting, it is in the third that the two are dissolving. And when the two dissolve, the third also dissolves – but again, it is a totally different phenomenon.

That's why Sanai calls his path "the path of the garden". The path of the meditator is a kind of desert. The desert has its own beauty: if you have been in the desert in the night, it has a coolness you will never find anywhere else, and it has an immense silence, a huge enormous silence, and it has infinity. It has a taste of its own. Under the starry sky, if you have been in a desert alone, you will never find that aloneness anywhere else.

No other place on the earth is as full of solitude as a desert. And there is no variety, so you cannot be distracted. It is the same for miles and miles – as far as you can see up to the horizon it is the same. There is nothing to see; if you have seen one desert you have seen all. It is the same: the same scene goes on stretching farther and farther away. There is no distraction.

That's why many meditators have moved to the desert. Down the ages, many people have moved to the desert. The attraction has been the silence and the beauty of a non-distracting situation. Nothing distracts, nothing moves, all is utterly quiet. Death can only be as quiet as the desert. It has a beauty of its own – but it lacks in richness and variety.

The garden has variety: many trees, much green foliage, many flowers, many colors, birds singing, streams flowing by, the sound of running water and the wind passing through the pines. And there are 1,001 things happening together. The garden is full, the desert is empty.

The inner being of a meditator becomes like a desert, and the inner being of a lover becomes like a garden. Hence, Sanai has called these sutras The Hadiqa: The Garden.

Still, it depends on you. One may like the desert more than the garden, then that is his path. Nothing is wrong in it, one should go on that path. One has to look within oneself and see one's potential, one's possibilities, one's leanings.

It is possible the desert may be a garden to you or the garden may be a desert to you, because one man's food is another man's poison. It is Sanai who says the lover's world is far richer – it is a lover talking about his world, remember it.

But remember one thing … Each and every master has said it, because the problem is there on both the paths. The problem is, one can be stranded on the bridge. The meditator may become so addicted to meditation that he may be stranded on the bridge. The lover may become too much addicted to love, then he will be stranded on the bridge. Love is a bridge, meditation is a bridge. And you have to go beyond the bridge.

In the ultimate state, the meditator has to drop his meditation and the lover has to forget all about his love. Otherwise you will just be close to the door but you will not be able to enter into the temple. The method has to be forgotten.

Buddha said that each method is like a raft, like a boat: use it to go to the other shore, but then leave it there and forget all about it and go on your way. There is no need to carry the raft on your head. If you carry the raft on your head you are just stupid.

But this is what is happening: millions of people become too addicted to their method. And the method CAN be addictive because it gives such beautiful experiences. The last barrier is the method, the last barrier is the bridge.

Just see the point – it is very paradoxical. The bridge takes you to the other shore: certainly it is a help, and you should be grateful to it, and you should be thankful to it. But it can become a problem. You may fall in love with the bridge and you may make your house on the bridge. And if you start living on the bridge, you are neither of this shore nor of that shore; you are in a kind of limbo. And many so-called religious practitioners live in a kind of limbo – they are neither of this world nor of that. They have become addicted to the bridge.

And the bridge IS beautiful! So every disciple has to be told in the beginning: "One day the method that has helped you so far has to be dropped. When its work is finished, don't carry it, not even for a single moment longer. When your illness is gone, you have to drop the medicine. If you continue the medicine then IT will become your illness."

ALL methods are methods, all means are means. And if you want to reach the end you will have to drop all means and all methods. That is the only way to enter into the ultimate. The lover will have to forget all about love, and the meditator will have to forget all about meditation. Yes, there comes a moment when the meditator does not meditate, because he has become meditation himself; now meditation is not a separate activity. And there comes a moment when the lover does not love, because he is love himself. There is nobody else separate from love, love has become his being – he has forgotten all about it.

Sanai is one of my love affairs. I cannot, even though I would like to, exaggerate him. It is impossible. Sanai is the very essence of Sufism.

Sufism is an English word for *tasawuf*. *Tasawuf* means "pure love". "Sufism" comes from suf, meaning wool, and a Sufi means a person wearing a woolen robe. Sanai used to wear a black cap – a white robe and a black cap. No logic, no reason, just a mad person like me. But what can you do, these people have to be accepted as they are. Either you love them or hate them. Love or hate, they don't give you any alternative. You can be for them or against them, but you cannot be indifferent to them. That's the miracle of mystics.

Socrates

Without Socrates Greece is nothing. With Socrates, it is everything. The day Athens chose to poison Socrates, it poisoned the whole Greek spirit. It has never again been to the same heights. Twenty-five centuries have passed, but not a single man has been able to reach to the same glory, to the same light, the same insight. Killing Socrates, Greece committed suicide.

And it can be seen easily. If they had listened to Socrates rather than poisoning him, and dropped their conditionings, which he was asking them to do, Greece would have been at the very top of the world today in intelligence, in consciousness, in the search for truth. But people are ignorant. They have to be forgiven, but they should not be forgotten. If you forget them, you are bound to commit the same mistake again. Forgive those people who poisoned Socrates, but don't forget, so that it never happens again.

There have been great people on the earth, but Socrates has something unique. There is Gautama the Buddha, Lao Tzu, Chuang Tzu – in Greece itself there has been Pythagoras, Heraclitus; in Persia, Zarathustra … and many others, but none of them had a certain quality which only Socrates has. That was a scientific approach about everything – and that was his crime.

You are all being benefited by science all over the world, not knowing that Socrates sacrificed himself for the same scientific enquiry. He was asking only one thing: that nothing should be believed. Everything should be experienced, experimented with, and unless there is evidence, evidence without exception, it should not be accepted. Even when you accept a thing as truth, if you are honest, accept it only as a hypothetical truth, because who knows? –

tomorrow there may be new facts known, and you will have to change the truth.

Nobody has been in the service of truth as much as Socrates. Even if you have found the truth – today it looks absolutely true, not a single flaw, no possibility that it will ever be untrue – still he says the scientific spirit will accept it only as hypothetical, for the time being … because eternity is ahead. Every day new facts will be discovered, and those facts may not go with your truth. You may have to change it, you may have to make place for those new truths. This is something absolutely unique in the whole world.

And the man was not like Jesus, proclaiming himself the only son of God, or a prophet or a messiah. That makes me tremendously respectful towards Socrates, so humble that he remained just a human being, with no claim of being special, being higher. Twenty-five centuries ago it was even more difficult, because in every country there were messiahs, prophets, messengers of God, sons of God. In that climate the man's humbleness is really surprising and makes him one of the most respected human beings who has ever walked on the earth.

Socrates does not believe in any God, but he does not say that there is no God. He is very scientific. He says, "As far as I have enquired, there seems to be no God, but who knows about the results of further enquiry? Take it as a hypothesis that there is no God, but if some day you discover God, hypotheses can be changed.

Socrates does not say that life survives after death. He says, "I will have to wait and see. When I die, only then can I see whether life survives after death or not, because nobody has come back from death and told us that life survives."

And never forget that this was 25 centuries ago. This man had such courage that when poison was given to him, he gathered all his disciples and said, "You have always been asking about whether life survives or not. This is a good chance, a great opportunity. If I had died an ordinary death then there would have been no opportunity. But now poison will be given to me" – and poison kills very slowly –

"so I will report to you to the very last moment, till my tongue also becomes numb and I cannot say anything."

And as the poison is given he starts saying with closed eyes, "My legs up to the knees are dead. I don't feel them; even by touching them I don't feel them. Life has gone out of them. But one thing is to be remembered: I am still feeling as whole as I was always. So the death of the legs has not affected my consciousness."

Then he says, "Half of my body, the lower half, is dead, but I am completely whole; half of my consciousness is not dead." Then he says, "My hands are becoming numb, my eyes are drooping, and I can feel that my tongue will stop any moment, so this is perhaps the last statement I have to make to you – that life survives after death, because I can see death happening. Parts of my body are dead and I am fully alive. Nothing is missing. So I am certain that when my tongue stops, my eyes close, and my heart stops, it is not going to matter. But don't believe me; it is just a hypothesis for you. When you die, try it." Such a scientific spirit!

I have loved Socrates for his humbleness, for his scientific enquiry, for not creating a religion, not creating a theology, not creating a following, not becoming a prophet. And Socrates was sophisticated, as cultured as you can imagine. The temptation must have been there to proclaim himself a god, and by that proclamation he might have been worshiped and not poisoned. The same people who killed him would have worshiped him; they would have made churches, and they would have still been worshiping him.

It needs immense courage when you have such consciousness, such clarity, to remain humble and just human – knowing perfectly well that this is the way to death. Sooner or later these same people are going to kill you, these people whom you are trying to make free from all fetters. Still Socrates chose to remain human. That's why you don't see any religion after Socrates, no church, no theology, no holy scripture.

But the man did a great service: he made it clear that your prophets and your messiahs are pretenders. And you are such that you get into the traps of pretenders very easily, because they strengthen your conditioning; they help you to remain in your prison. And they call your prison by good names, so you are happy.

With a man like Socrates you are not happy because he says exactly what the situation is – that you are a prisoner, and you have to come out of it. People are lazy; people want not to change. People simply want consolations. Somebody should come as if he is from somewhere higher, coming from God himself to tell them, "You are perfectly right – just go on believing in God. Go on praying to God every night for two minutes, and everything is perfectly okay with you." This you enjoy, because it saves you all the trouble of change.

People like Socrates seem to be very dangerous because they go on hitting hard on your consolations: they take away all your conditionings, they expose you to your reality. Their work is surgical. It hurts, it is painful, but that is the way a new man can be born.

Socrates remained in the very small area of Athens, not even the whole of Greece. Athens was a city state, and he remained an Athenian for his whole life.

The sentence was given that exactly at sunset Socrates should be given poison. He looks from the window and he says, "The sun has set! The man outside who is preparing the poison – tell him that he is late and he should never be late when he is on duty."

The man came in. He said, "You are a strange person! Just out of love for you I am delaying the process so that you can live a little longer. I have given poison to many people – this is my profession – but my heart is trembling, my hands are trembling. What I am doing is not right. I want to delay it as long as I can."

Socrates says, "No, that is not right. You do your duty; your personal feelings should not come into it. And moreover, I am so curious to go into death because I have lived a long life, I have known all the secrets of it, but death is such a great adventure, such an unknown. So don't delay it, just bring the poison."

People who were not afraid of death, we have killed. And these were the people who had known life; that's why they were not afraid of death. Deep down they have known that there is something that is going to continue, but they didn't have any proof, any evidence. Hence Socrates will not say it; he will say it only when the evidence is there. Such devotion to the scientific spirit!

When Socrates was poisoned, Athens was a city state, a direct democracy. Every citizen except the slaves had the right to vote and every decision had to be made by the whole city. The chief justice who was going to decide whether the majority of Athenians were in favor of poisoning Socrates or in favor of saving him, was very much puzzled. He must have been a man of some intelligence. He saw that Socrates was a simple, innocent, almost childlike person. He had not committed any crime, he had not done any harm to anybody. And that's what Socrates had appealed to the court – "Just tell me, what is my crime?"

There was no crime, there was no charge against him. The chief justice whispered in his ear that "Your crime is that you are a natural being. I cannot say it aloud, because I know if they cannot forgive you, they cannot forgive me either. But I have immense respect for your innocence and I don't want a man like you to be destroyed. You are an exception, but you prove the rule that every man can be so innocent and so sincere and so alive and so joyous. I give you three alternatives …

"First is that Athens is a city state; its laws are not applicable outside the boundary of the city. The simple thing is for you to move outside the city. You can open your school, your academy, and those who love you will be coming there. And I know for certain that the younger generation is immensely impressed by you. It is the older generation …"

But in the past, the older generation was always the majority, because out of ten children, nine used to die within two years after their birth. Now the situation has reversed: out of ten children only one child dies, nine go on living. It is for the first time that young

233

people are the majority in the world. Never in the past were the young people in the majority. They were always a minority group.

The chief justice said, "You simply move out of the city." Socrates said, "That will be cowardly. As far as death is concerned, it is going to come sooner or later. I am already old enough. But I don't want the future generations to remember that Socrates moved out of Athens because of the fear of death. Please forgive me, I cannot go out of Athens."

The chief justice said, "Then the second simple thing will be that you stop teaching. Live in Athens, but don't talk about your truth. And don't talk about people being sincere and authentic."

Socrates said, "You are asking me to do things which I cannot do. What is the purpose of my living if I cannot blossom into my absolute potential? When a tree blossoms, flowers are bound to be there and the fragrance is going to reach those who are receptive. I will continue to speak and I will continue to talk about truth and I will continue to provoke people to be natural and not to become hypocrites according to the so-called religions."

The chief justice said, "Then I am helpless. Then the third alternative is that you have to accept poison. Because the majority, although they have no evidence against you, simply say that your very presence is corruptive. Your very presence is destroying the youth; your very presence is taking the youth away from the old path trodden by the ancients. Your presence is making individuals assertive, giving them courage to be free and to stand alone even if it comes to be against the whole society."

Socrates said, "There is no problem about poison. That I can accept. I am dying for a beautiful cause. I lived in absolute glory and I am dying with a crescendo."

Socrates is reported to have said, "When I was young I thought I knew everything; when I became a little more mature I also became aware that there is much that I don't know. When I became still older I was puzzled because I used to know more when I was young – and now I know less and less every day." And finally, before he died, he said, "I know nothing."

The day he said, "I know nothing."... In Greece there was a temple in Delphi, and there was an oracle in the temple who used to predict many things in trance. The day Socrates said, "I know nothing," the same day, the same time, in Delphi, the oracle declared that Socrates was the wisest man in the world.

People who had come from Athens to listen to the oracle rushed back to inform Socrates, because such an honor had never been given to anyone by the oracle – the wisest man in the world. And when they reported it to Socrates he laughed; he said, "I used to be, when I was very young, when I was very arrogant, when I was very egoistic. Now I know nothing."

But the people said, "The oracle has never been wrong." They returned to Delphi, and they reported, "This time you are wrong, because Socrates himself denies it; he says, 'I know nothing.'"

The oracle laughed now, and said, "That is the reason why I have declared him the wisest man in the world. Only the wisest man in the world has the courage and the innocence and the humbleness to declare 'I know nothing.'"

Socrates had never done anything that you could say was done out of arrogance, or out of anger, or out of jealousy. He was not standing for any public post, he was not interested in any power politics. He was not a man of anger at all.

The story is that his wife – she must have been really a monster, but sometimes it happens that such nice people as Socrates get such monster women. It is strange, but perhaps there is some balance. Perhaps only Socrates could stand that woman; no other man I think could have lived with her for even a single day. She used to beat Socrates and he would simply sit.

If his disciples asked, Socrates would say, "It is her problem; she is angry. What can I do? It is her problem – she is suffering, and out of her suffering and anger she is throwing tantrums. I just happen to be sitting nearby so she is hitting me. But it is her problem, it is none of my concern."

One day when he was teaching his disciples, she came in angry – because that was one thing that she was very angry about, that he was always teaching truth, freedom, and never giving enough time to her. All kinds of people were coming from faraway places; and with them, strangers, he was wasting his time – strangers, who were of no interest. She was sitting there, boiling: she was his wife and he did not give that much attention to her.

This is a common complaint of all the women of the whole world: that the husband goes on playing chess with somebody, with more interest, goes on smoking a cigar with so much joy, reads his paper the first thing in the morning; and the wife is shouting, and he does not even listen to what she is saying. He says, "Okay, okay," for anything. He comes to bed and immediately starts snoring. And with strangers ...

So Socrates' wife came with boiling hot water – she was preparing for tea, but Socrates did not get up from this discussion, and the discussion was going on longer and longer, and the time for tea had already passed; it was lunchtime by then – she came in great anger and poured the whole kettle of hot water on Socrates' head. Half of his face was burned and remained always scarred. But he continued.

All the people who were there were shocked. They had completely forgotten the matter they were discussing – and Socrates continued. They asked, "Can you still remember what we were talking about?"

He said, "Yes – because this is her problem, this is not my problem." Now, this man has no anger in him, no arrogance, no desire to prove that he is a superman; there is not even a mention that he is more than an ordinary human being.

Afterword:
Beyond History

Man can live in two ways: one is in time, one is beyond time. History is the name of the life that we live in time; it leaves marks in the temporal. But there is also a life which we live beyond time – it leaves no marks anywhere. It is not just an accident that the existence of Jesus is doubtful; so is the existence of Krishna, Lao Tzu and Zarathustra. Why is their existence doubtful? They have not really left any mark in time. They lived a life of interiority, they lived in themselves. Their life had no visible, tangible impact, but they transformed human consciousness. They lived in consciousness and they impressed human consciousness. But history takes no note of them. History takes note of Adolf Hitler, Genghis Khan, Tamburlaine; history takes note of people who live in time and leave marks on the sands of time. But people like Buddha, Christ, almost pass from existence as if they have not passed at all. That's what I mean by going beyond history. Don't live in events: live in awareness.

OSHO INTERNATIONAL MEDITATION RESORT

The Osho Meditation Resort is a place where people can have a direct personal experience of a new way of living with more alertness, relaxation, and fun. Located about 100 miles south-east of Mumbai in Pune, India, the resort offers a variety of programs to thousands of people who visit each year from more than 100 countries around the world.

Originally developed as a summer retreat for maharajas and wealthy British colonialists, Pune is now a thriving modern city that is home to a number of universities and high-tech industries. The Meditation Resort spreads over 40 acres in a tree-lined suburb known as Koregaon Park. The resort campus provides accommodation for a limited number of guests, and there is a plentiful variety of nearby hotels and private apartments available for stays of a few days up to several months.

Resort programs are all based in the Osho vision of a qualitatively new kind of human being who is able both to participate creatively in everyday life and to relax into silence and meditation. Most programs take place in modern, air-conditioned facilities and include a variety of individual sessions, courses and workshops covering everything from creative arts to holistic health treatments, personal transformation and therapy, esoteric sciences, the "Zen" approach to sports and recreation, relationship issues, and significant life transitions for men and women. Individual sessions and group workshops are offered throughout the year, alongside a full daily schedule of meditations.

Outdoor cafes and restaurants within the resort grounds serve both traditional Indian fare and a choice of international dishes, all made with organically grown vegetables from the commune's own farm. The campus has its own private supply of safe, filtered water.

See <www.osho.com/resort> for more information, including travel tips, course schedules and guest house bookings.

RESOURCES

For more information about Osho and his work, see:

<www.osho.com>

a comprehensive website in several languages that includes an online
tour of the Meditation Resort and a calendar of its course offerings, a
catalog of books and tapes, a list of Osho information centers
worldwide, and selections from Osho's talks.

Or contact:

Osho International
New York
email: <oshointernational@oshointernational.com>